KNOW YOUR ENEMY

Perhaps the most intense military work we did was for Desert Storm. There was hardly a move made by Saddam Hussein and his troops that we had not predicted and passed up the chain of command the day before it happened. My major tasking throughout the war was to access Hussein and learn of his plans and intentions for the coming day.

In the daily process of accessing him, I learned one thing very quickly. He is not what I would call a "bad" man. He is absolutely what I would call a totally crazy man. His craziness, though, does not take the form of irrationality or erratic behavior.

It stems from a delusional conviction on his part that God wants him to rule the world . . .

THE SEVENTH SENSE

THE SECRETS OF
REMOTE VIEWING
AS TOLD BY A "PSYCHIC SPY"
FOR THE U.S. MILITARY

LYN BUCHANAN

PARAVIEW POCKET BOOKS
New York London Toronto Sydney

An *Original* Publication of PARAVIEW POCKET BOOKS

PARAVIEW
191 Seventh Avenue, New York, NY 10011

POCKET BOOKS, a division of Simon & Schuster, Inc.
1230 Avenue of the Americas, New York, NY 10020

ISBN: 978-0-7434-6268-6

First Paraview Pocket Books trade paperback printing February 2003

10 9 8 7 6 5 4 3 2

POCKET and colophon are registered trademarks of
Simon & Schuster, Inc.

For information regarding special discounts for bulk purchases,
please contact Simon & Schuster Special Sales at 1-800-456-6798
or business@simonandschuster.com

Printed in the U.S.A.

CONTENTS

FOREWORD

BY JIM MARRS

I n the early 1990s, I stumbled across what well might be the most profound story in human history, yet even today most Americans remain unaware of it. This story concerned remote viewing, the wondrous ability to view persons, places, and things outside the normal five senses of sight, sound, taste, smell, and touch.

When I found that the United States Army was teaching military intelligence officers how to psychically spy on the Soviets and others, my journalist hackles were raised. I knew I was onto a good story. In my skeptical mind it was an either-or situation—either remote viewing was not real, in which case this program was a giant fraud on the taxpayers and hence a good news story, or remote viewing was real, in which case it might well represent a quantum leap in the evolution of humankind and hence a great news story, perhaps one of the greatest ever.

I researched the subject for three years as carefully as I could, considering it was still a secret government program. I interviewed several members of the GRILL FLAME/STAR GATE remote viewing unit as well as members of oversight committees and the scientists who developed the technology. To my amazement I found it was all true. Not only can humans perceive apart from the usual five senses, but this perception is limited by neither time nor space.

The story of remote viewing has got to be one of the most underreported stories of the past century. What once was one of our government's most closely guarded secrets now has filtered into certain aware segments of the public where it continues to attract growing fascination and interest. Today, several experienced viewers are teaching remote viewing, or RV for short. Others have spoken about it in books, articles or public speeches. Even some dubious entrepreneurs now advertise psychic readings reportedly accomplished through RV.

Yet, despite the fact that remote viewing was developed by various tax-supported government agencies, including the CIA, the Defense Intelligence Agency, and even the U. S. Army, a majority of Americans still have never heard of this faculty. And many of those who have are not aware that scientific studies have shown that each and every person has the innate ability to remote view. Of course, people with natural ability can do it better than others. This is why learning to remote view has been compared with learning to play Beethoven on the piano. With enough practice, almost anyone can do it, but some folks will require much more practice than others. Learning to properly remote view can be a life-changing experience. It certainly changed the lives of the men and women employed in its use for the government.

But the story of remote viewing became one of the casualties in the ongoing conflict between science and ESP, military secrecy and the public's right to know, as well as the never-ending intramural competition between government agencies and power-seeking individuals. And I got caught right in the middle of it all. I experienced firsthand the difficulties faced in trying to disseminate truthful and objective information regarding remote viewing.

My encounter with this subject began in early 1992, when I learned of a speech presented by a military intelligence officer at a public conference in Atlanta. His matter-of-fact tone regarding controversial topics intrigued me, for here was no starry-eyed New Ager but a decorated military intelligence officer. Intrigued, I contacted this officer and soon learned the story of our military remote viewers.

It is now clear that this officer was no loose cannon. During his Atlanta talk, he was flanked by Col. John Alexander, a leading luminary in military nonlethal weapons research who moved freely between both military and intelligence programs, and Maj. Gen. Albert Stubblebine, former commander of the army's Intelligence and Security Command under which the remote viewing program functioned. In hindsight, it appears that his appearance was not happenstance, but the beginning of a conscious program of disinformation. The object was to allow the topic of remote viewing to slip into the public with the least amount of credibility, as the officer involved was prone to speculate on space aliens and doomsday scenarios.

The designated officer had left the military and started a remote viewing company. He became a regular guest on a popular late-night nationwide radio talk show despite a continuing loss of credibility. In a magazine interview, the man predicted a "face to face meeting" with Martians hibernating underground in New Mexico, adding, "If we don't have it by the end of August, we're getting out of the UFO game." Neither happened.

In June 1993, I contracted to publish a book through Harmony Books, a subsidiary of Random House. I spent three years working on the remote viewing story. The work was arduous, particularly so because I was dealing with a subject most people wanted no part of, not to mention that it involved a top-secret government program. Many sources refused to be interviewed and others demanded anonymity. Hard facts were difficult to come by.

By the end of 1993, a manuscript was completed under the title *Psi Spies,* which was changed by Harmony to *The Engima Files,* due to the popularity of the *X-Files* TV series. Additionally, my Harmony editor decided a "narrative" or story line was necessary to enliven my original manuscript, a lean and journalistic recitation of the facts concerning RV. Over my objections, I was required to add scenes and dialog involving others in the remote viewing unit.

In early 1995, as the book was nearing publication, the officer who had gone public in 1992 suddenly began to object to the manuscript because of the inclusion of this material. I found it most ironic that this obstruction came from the very person who had initiated the book in the first place and nothing he had contributed had been altered or deleted. Some observers saw a darker purpose behind this apparent petty jealousy. They felt someone believed the book more credible than they desired and took steps to block its publication.

This darker purpose appeared confirmed by subsequent events.

The officer, who by this time was claiming to be in contact with alien "grays," sent a letter via an attorney to Harmony disavowing the book, even though he had previously signed a release statement based on my completed manuscript. The book's editor suddenly left the project. The senior legal counsel, who had approved publication of the book following a lengthy and thorough legal review, was suddenly no longer there.

The matter was turned over to a law firm unconnected to the publisher and I was ordered not to contact or talk to the attorney there who decided the book had to be canceled because of the threats from the officer. I was told by the new editor that, while she neither understood nor agreed with the course being taken, she was powerless to prevent the cancellation.

Everyone involved with the book came to believe that the cancellation had been ordered by someone with great authority, perhaps within the government. Subsequent events only supported this belief.

The book was canceled in late July 1995, despite substantial advance orders from book sellers. On August 27, the story of RV broke in a London newspaper. The story, entitled "Tinker, Tailor, Soldier, Psi," was written by Jim Schnabel, who earlier that year had received a copy of my manuscript from the officer previously mentioned.

About that same time, the CIA, apparently about to be reassigned the RV program, ordered a study of remote viewing. Ray Hyman of the University of Oregon, an avowed psychic skeptic, and Jessica Utts from the University of California were commissioned to review the remote viewing program. Considering that Hyman, a luminary of the debunking organization Committee for the Scientific Investigation of Claims of the Paranormal (CSICOP), was biased against ESP to begin with, coupled with the fact that the review concentrated only on the weakest of the RV work and did not have access to most of the unit's work, the report's conclusion was never in doubt.

Their finished report, dated September 29, 1995, concluded that, despite the fact that a "statistically significant effect" had been observed in laboratory RV experiments, "no compelling explanation has been provided for the observed effects ... to say a phenomenon has been demonstrated we must know the reasons for its existence."

The story that the government had used psychics to spy on enemies first broke in the United States in early October in a supermarket tabloid story headlined, "How CIA's Psychic Spies Stole Russia's Star Wars Secrets." This tabloid treatment, obviously leaked by government sources, was a "kiss of death" to anyone in the mainstream media taking the subject seriously.

Remote viewing was officially acknowledged on November 28, 1995, when the story received superficial and dismissive coverage in *The New York Times* and *The Washington Post*. These articles described the psychic spies merely as "a trio of citizens with suspected paranormal powers who were located at a Maryland military base." Even with this watered-down version, the story moved no farther than the East Coast, and nowhere was there any mention that the remote viewing methodology had been simply moved to even more secret government agencies, as I suspect, and where I believe its use continues today.

Also, in all the coverage of RV in the major media, it was never pointed out that this psychic program had been funded for more than a quarter of a century under four separate administrations, Republican and Democrat, indicating that someone felt the government was getting its money's worth.

Meanwhile, the American public has been left to study only the available bits and pieces of information on remote viewing. Some of this information comes from persons with suspect motives, some from scientific and government documents, and some from former psi spies like Lyn Buchanan.

Today I am most pleased to see Lyn's story now available to the public. As he points out, the complete and factual story of remote viewing may never be known, as everyone involved in this secret program knows only what they saw, heard, and experienced. Everyone has a different perspective.

But Lyn was there during most of the program's life and not simply as a remote viewer, but as the man selected to train the army's psychic spies and to keep the data on the entire project.

No one is more qualified to tell the story of the operational use of remote viewing than Lyn Buchanan.

PREFACE

CAVEAT EMPTOR

This book is a personal account of the many changes in my life and my belief systems as I was trained and gained experience as a "psychic spy" for the U.S. military. It goes into some depth about Controlled Remote Viewing (CRV), the system used by the military to do such spying, but is not designed to teach you how to do it on your own. That takes years of training and supervision.

I have been training people in CRV for many years, and have found that there are many reasons people become interested in this field. I would therefore like to address some of those interests which you may or may not have as you stand in the bookstore, deciding whether or not to buy.

FOR THOSE LOOKING FOR THE MYSTICAL

If you think this book is about the "overmind," the "all-seeing mind of God," the "collective unconscious," etc., it is not. Granted, those things are probably terribly important, but they're just not what this book is about. In fact, they are not what CRV is about. CRV was designed for finding hostages and missing children, solving crimes, spying on people and countries, determining the plans and intentions of political, military, and business leaders. Its targets exist right here in the workaday world. So, to be honest with you right up front, if you are looking for something mystical and occult, you would be more satisfied by buying another book.

But this book will teach you a great deal about the mysteries of the human mind, and maybe something about the human spirit as it relates to real life and real people living in the harsh reality of the real world.

FOR THE PERSON SEEKING
SELF-IMPROVEMENT

If your main interest is self-improvement and self-enhancement, the exercises within the appendix can take care of that desire. Buy the book and turn directly to the appendix, where you will find the self-improvement exercises. Do the exercises and a tremendous change will take place in your life. The exercises will provide you with more self-improvement than going to some guru for a month and living on saw grass and swamp water.

But if all you do is the exercises in the appendix, you will have missed the main point of CRV. CRV was not developed for self-improvement and/or feeling good. It is an applications-oriented science. Its main uses are for police work, medical diagnostics, business, archeology, or any of a hundred other real-world fields including, of course, military and political espionage, for which it was originally designed. If you want to improve your soul and spirit and well-being, learn a way to bring home a missing child. There is nothing like it in either the real or the ethereal world. CRV deepens your character and forever changes your life for the better. And believe it or not, that is only a mere side effect.

FOR THE SCIENTIFICALLY
ORIENTED READER

Controlled Remote Viewing is a natural, psychological, and physiological process that is very tightly anchored to the real, hard-core physical world around us. It is, in fact, more of a martial art than a psychic or mental discipline. It is the process developed under the auspices of the U.S. military, and as such, it has about as much mysticism as any other hard-core science—that is, virtually none.

It does, however, make what may seem like one exception. It accepts, as a basic tenet, that mankind has an innate ability to know things beyond what can be perceived by the normal senses and/or logical thought. Once that was accepted in a scientific way, it was possible to develop inroads into a field previously inhabited only by natural psychics. You may argue that the "psychic sense" is not a scientifically accepted paradigm, but recent research—mainly that done in conjunction with the U.S. military's "psychic spying" programs—has established a well-documented and firmly founded basis of proof of the existence of mankind's "psychic" ability. If any scientist, by reason of his/her own personal belief systems, objects to the inclusion of this concept, I would suggest that he/she go study the latest findings. They are readily available.

FOR THE PERSON WHO WANTS TO LEARN ABOUT CONTROLLED REMOTE VIEWING

This is not a how-to book. It will not teach you step-by-step how to do Controlled Remote Viewing. It provides, instead, a basic familiarization with the science. It will teach you the principles, theories, and understandings on which Controlled Remote Viewing is based. It will even teach you a lot of the terminology, development exercises, and some of the most basic methods. But it will not teach you the nuts-and-bolts structure and protocols. This book will, as a bare minimum, let you learn whether or not you want to continue further in this fascinating field of mind science.

FOR THE DEBUNKER

Please understand how I feel about debunkers. There is a very real need for you to exist and for you to do the work you do. There is an astounding amount of garbage passing itself off as "psychic," and I cheer when some debunker manages to haul some of that garbage away. Even worse, much of the psychic field tries to become a substitute for religion or for good medical care or even for social acceptance. Bunk needs to be debunked.

By the same token, there is an even more astounding amount of garbage passing itself off as debunking. There is a horde of pseudo-debunkers and "wannabe debunkers" who go around loudly shooting down everything that moves, without giving anything the slightest consideration. If it looks psychic, shoot it down. The fact is that pseudodebunkers are more of an embarrassment to the debunking field than pseudopsychics are to the psychic field.

Writing this book has forced me to look back on my experiences. I realize that there are many possible alternative explanations for most of them. Therefore, I welcome all intellectual and studied criticisms of anything and everything in this book. But nonintellectual blasts from people who haven't done their homework, who have never looked into or tried CRV, will be dismissed as the amateurish garbage it is. Do your homework—then we'll talk. I think that I speak for everyone when I say, "When it comes to debunkers, we're tired of dealing with amateurs."

If you are out to debunk remote viewing as a valid field, you will no doubt enjoy this book as grist for your mill. Do or say what you will. Reinterpret everything in the book to be nothing more than my inane ramblings about what has happened in my life. I don't care. It has been my life. You didn't live it. I did. It is still my story. Nothing you can say, do, or accuse me of can change one iota of it.

IF YOU HAVE READ THIS FAR

I welcome you to the most fascinating thing which I have ever found. After more than seventeen years of being a psychic spy for the U.S. government, teaching more than 300 students, and doing studies and research on facets of the human mind which allow us to deal with things greater than ourselves, I find that very little surprises me anymore. But the wonder and fascination have never ebbed for a moment.

If, in this book, I can pass on to you some of that fascination and wonder, then I will feel that the time spent writing it has been well invested in your understanding, in your future, and in the future of mankind.

THE
SEVENTH
SENSE

ONE

APRIL FOOL'S DAY, 1984

On April Fool's, a decade hence,
A hole appears within a fence.
I will be called to patch it.
The part which leaves is very great.
Then I will learn about my fate.
I must work hard to match it.

> Predictive poem
> —Lyn Buchanan
> *April Fool's Day, 1974**

April Fool's Day seemed somehow appropriate as the day to report to my new military unit. No one had told me where it was. In spite of a very shallow and clandestine briefing at a Czech restaurant in Germany, I wasn't really sure of what the unit did, or for that matter what I would be doing in it. To top that off, I had been given two different sets of orders: one "official" set, printed on paper, and a totally different set, given verbally. The official orders said that I was to report to HHQ Co, 902 MIBn, INSCOM, Ft. Meade. Translated into human speech, that stands for Headquarters & Headquarters Company, 902nd Military Intelligence Battalion, Intelligence and Security Command, located at Fort Meade, Maryland.

But the verbal orders I had received said that I should not go any-

---

*Since youth, I have written short, predictive poems, often giving exact events, dates, and locations, but always cryptic at the time of their writing. Most have been and continue to be pretty accurate.

where near the 902nd. Upon reaching Fort Meade, Maryland, I was to check in at the military guest quarters and call a certain phone number to let a special agent know that I had arrived. Under no circumstances was I to report in to the 902nd, as my written orders stated. In effect, I had been instructed to go AWOL the first day of my new assignment.

My wife, Linda, my seven-year-old son, Lael, and I arrived at the Baltimore-Washington International Airport late in the evening of April 1, 1984. It is customary for a soldier and his family to call the unit to which he is reporting and have a staff driver pick them up. I couldn't do that, due to the verbal orders. We took a cab from the airport to the Fort Meade Guest House. The desk clerk asked for my orders and said that he would call the unit and let them know I was in. He was somewhat perplexed when I asked him not to.

In the room, I pulled out the napkin which had been given to me in the Czech restaurant in Germany. The hand-scrawled phone number on it was for a private residence in the Fort Meade area. A man's voice answered, and said that we should all wait in the parking lot in front of the guest house. He would come right by.

When we arrived in the parking lot, a dense, misty fog had rolled in, making the whole scene look like something out of a Hollywood spy movie. The guest house is far removed from the other base facilities, so the darkness was oppressive. All we could see through the swirling fog was the fuzzy, eerie glow of the guest house's neon sign at the edge of the parking lot. We stood quietly, feeling small drops of mist sweeping against our faces in the moist night breeze. With the fog, the world had gone deathly quiet, and nothing could be heard except our own breathing and the electric crackle of the neon sign's transformer. Even Lael, an active and impatient seven-year-old still on German time, was subdued by the surrounding mystery.

I looked at my wife and marveled at the courage of this woman who would accompany me anywhere in the world, on nothing more than faith that I would do the right thing. I wondered how she could keep that faith even at times like this, when she knew that I had absolutely no idea of what I was getting us into. She looked back at me and gave the slightest of smiles. The silent mist swirled and we shifted from one foot to the other and waited.

* * *

The events leading up to my new assignment at Fort Meade were, quite frankly, odd. I had been working at the U.S. Army Field Station in Augsburg, Germany, for a little over two years. I had originally been assigned there as a Russian linguist, but through some devious manipulation, had worked my way into the Computer Operations and Coordination section.

At that time, the coordination of the computers at the field station was a large task, since we had almost a hundred different computer systems with several different countries of origin. The computer systems did not "talk" to each other, and there was constant conflict among the data fields, the computers, and the people and countries who ran them.

I had been there almost a year when I received the order to design a program that would tie the field station's many computer systems together into a single reporting entity. Another sergeant—I'll call him Doug—felt that he should have gotten the job and was very hostile toward me for the selection. During the following two months, Doug repeatedly got into my programming code and placed "bombs" there, as his means of revenge. I confronted him several times, but it only fanned the flames. In frustration and as a total last resort, I reported him to his superiors, who threatened him with disciplinary action if he did it again. There were no more interruptions from Doug and in another month I had the program running and tested.

Now I had to make the necessary demonstration briefing to the commanders of the various U.S. military branches and the military commanders of more than a dozen different NATO countries that had personnel at the field station. When the day came to make the demonstration, I arrived early, checked and rechecked the program for errors or flaws. There was none. I ran it through all the testing procedures and made certain the presentation would go smoothly. Everything checked out perfectly. Right before presentation time, I went to the bathroom to make certain my hair was well combed and there were no scuffs on my spit-shined shoes or wrinkles in my uniform. At the appointed time, the commanding officers of every military unit attached to the field station began to assemble for the briefing on the new computer program.

I went through the initial song and dance about the need for such a program, what problems it would solve, what benefits would be reaped, and so on. I then turned and hit the computer's ENTER key to begin the demonstration. The computer screen went blank. Something had gone wrong. I turned back to the chuckling audience and searched for something to say when I saw Doug standing in the doorway. He grinned menacingly and pointed a finger at me. "Gotcha!" he mouthed, and turned to leave.

Something welled up in me then, which had not happened in years: an uncontrollable rage. Earlier in life, I had been one of those "poltergeist" children. I had learned in my early teens that when I allow myself to get truly angry, things around me go crazy. As Doug turned to leave, things did exactly that.

When I was about twelve years old, odd things began to happen in the form of objects around me moving or bumping, or suddenly falling for no apparent reason. It was bothersome to others, but to me, it was odd and interesting. It felt as if it was something I was doing so I began trying to learn what it could be. I learned that I could sometimes cause a few small things to happen—simple things—at will. They were not enough to really impress anyone, but they were enough to spur me on-ward. I devised some mental exercises to help me "flex my mind muscles." I developed a "little voice" that would give the orders and help keep things organized. I understood completely that it was just a device of my own making, and not a real voice. It was not an entity of any kind, a spirit, or even an alter ego. I was not really hearing things. It was just a gimmick I had devised to separate my regular thoughts from those that were supposed to make the weird things happen. I was never afraid of it, and actually thought of it as a really neat plaything. I had complete control over it.

Through this and some other exercises that I devised, I learned to make bigger things happen, and could make the smaller things happen with little effort. But as I got better at it, the things that happened "by themselves" got stronger, too. I practiced and learned more control, so these spurious incidents became less frequent, but when they did happen, they were much more noticeable. A couple of times, the little voice had done something by itself to get me out of a fight or embarrassment, but for the most part, the unbidden incidents were just funny little things. In fact, they were usually harmless pranks, at the most. They happened without my volition, and I would often see the humor in them and appreciate the unexpected cleverness behind them.

Around age fourteen, though, with hormones rising, I began competing for the attention of young girls. One day I was showing off, trying to impress the cute redheaded girl who attracted me so. I succeeded by showing her one of the tricks I had learned to do with the little voice inside my head. It did impress her, all right. In fact, she was so impressed that she went home and told her father—the Pentecostal minister. The following day, he and two of his deacons met me after school and asked for a demonstration. As soon as this demonstration succeeded, they all slammed their hands onto my head and pushed me down to the sidewalk, screaming to God to cast the Devil out of me.

I was brought up in "Deep East Texas," otherwise known as the Bible Belt. There, if the preacher said something, then God must have said it, too. They had suddenly and forcefully turned my little trick into a sin against God. They were trying to rid me of an evil which had not been there before they tried. I was scared to death and so shaken from the incident that I had nightmares for a month.

What had been nothing more than an amusing and interesting plaything now had its roots in ominous evil. It still didn't feel wrong, but what if the Devil had just been tricking me? What if he had just been preparing me for doing some great and sinfully evil deed? What if the Devil had dark and occult plans for me and I hadn't been Christian enough to know it? What a stupid and horrible Christian I had become! What a depraved sinner I had turned into! I decided that I would stop doing my neat things, and thanked God for warning me of my sins in time.

I now know that the subconscious mind, once given its freedom, doesn't give up that freedom without a fight. I didn't know that back then. At the time, to my guilt and horror, it seemed that the more I stopped doing my purposeful "neat things," the more the unbidden things increased. Of course, to my mind at the time, it was simply Satan fighting back. It had nothing to do with conscious and subconscious talents. To my fourteen-year-old mind, it meant only that God and Satan both were testing me. I was in a huge tug-of-war between them, and it required even more diligence of me, or my soul would burn forever in Hell.

I quickly learned that getting angry was almost certain to bring on an unbidden incident. These incidents were usually bad things, in hindsight, and I was always sorry for them later. Yet, at the time they happened, they seemed to save me from some bully or help someone else who was in need. The things that happened always gave me some instant satisfaction because I was suddenly able to take control of bad situations and turn them to good. But later I would see how the Devil had tricked me again and then the guilt would set in.

About two months after the incident with the minister and his deacons, the problem still weighed very heavily on me. Then, another incident happened, which was to make me spend the next thirty-one years fully dedicated to blocking these sinful abilities. I was riding my bicycle home from school one day when a kid who was always bullying everyone rode up behind me. As he sped past, he hit my handlebar, and I went spilling forward onto the ground. My face and arm went straight into some sharp gravel. The boy had nothing against me, personally. He only wanted the sport of hurting someone, and I happened to be handy. My dislike of the boy turned to instant hatred. I was hurt and my face and arm were bleeding. I looked up at him as he rode off laughing and heard the little voice in my mind say, "Die!" A sudden very heavy, tiring calmness spread over me. I watched spectator-like as he swept sideways off his bicycle, which continued a short ways down the sidewalk without him. He flew over the hood of a parked car and landed in the street. An oncoming car screeched to a stop with the boy's head already under its bumper and its front tire just inches from his face. If it had not stopped, he would have been killed. I would have been responsible. The minister had been right. Not only was my developing power evil, but now, I was evil, too. I vowed never to use this ability again.

That plan did not work, of course. Over the years, with some very notable exceptions, I controlled the uninvited occurrences by avoiding anger at all costs. Several spontaneous things did happen both with and without the anger, and of course, no one can go forever without getting upset over something. But I never again heard the voice say, "Die!"

Not for thirty-one years, anyway, until that day in Augsburg. Doug had ruined my program and made me look like an idiot before my commanders, their commanders, foreign commanders, everyone. I was instantly and uncontrollably furious. I heard the voice and quickly turned my attention back to the computer, but could not control the rage. For the second time in my life, it had said, "Die!" And for the first time since I was fourteen, I felt the very heavy, tiring calmness spread over me. Computers throughout the entire field station went dead.

During the days that followed (a length of time still classified for obvious reasons), the United States and the other NATO countries that had facilities at the field station had no electronic intelligence effort along the East German border. Field station personnel went to work on regular schedules and kept up the appearance that all was business as usual. We had to fool the Soviets' spy-in-the-sky satellites, which kept constant watch on us.

I knew inwardly that I had caused the problem, but I wasn't about to tell anyone. For one thing, everyone would have thought I was crazy and laughed at me. I quickly reasoned it all away and convinced myself that I had been wrong. After all, this kind of thing can't happen. I had believed things like that when I was a kid, but I was now an adult. Such thinking was spooky kid stuff. This was just coincidence. So I went to work like everyone else, played cards and worked crossword puzzles, caught up on my reading, and waited for the field station to get up and running again.

The software analysts checked to see whether my program had caused the computers to crash, but quickly determined that it had not. Except for the "bomb" which Doug had planted in my program, my code was squeaky clean. In fact, the final report of that investigation said that it was the computers crashing that had caused my program to fail. Further analysis showed that unattached and unassociated computer systems had been affected as well. Those systems were totally unconnected to my program. It seems that even stand-alone intelligence computers around Europe and all along the East German border had crashed at the same time. The cause had been something much bigger. The question of an act of terrorism using an electromotive pulse (EMP) arose. The analysts decided that no such EMP had been used, since nonintelligence computer systems sitting right beside the affected ones had remained intact. An EMP would have taken everything out. They checked for viruses and found none. To this day, the whole incident remains an awful one-time event without explanation.

I was later to learn that major portions of the entire NATO intelligence network had gone silent at the same time our station had. Even parts of the intelligence network that were in no way connected to us electronically had blown out. Many years later I learned that the affected area had been from the North Sea down to Italy, though intelligence computers in Australia had been affected as well.

However, our lack of electronic eavesdropping capability had not really put the Free World in danger. It seems that the Communist Bloc countries, the East Germans, Bulgarians, Czechs, and Soviets had also lost their electronic eavesdropping equipment at the same moment. Just as we had been keeping up appearances to fool their spy-in-the-sky satellites, they had been doing the same in order to fool our spy-in-the-sky satellites as they scrambled to get their intelligence networks back on line again.

I kept quiet about my suspicions that I might have, in some way, caused some part of all this. But there was one aspect of the incident that I hadn't known about. The commanding general of the U.S. Army Intelligence and Security Command (USAINSCOM) was a man named Maj. Gen. Albert N. Stubblebine. Because of the general's personal interest in mental phenomena, several of the officers in his command had been trained to spot such "human potentials." One of those officers had attended the ill-fated demonstration. He had only a passing interest in computers, but had attended mainly to see all that brass in one place at one time. He had seen the incident take place and recognized it for what it was.

About an hour after the incident occurred, General Stubblebine was called on the carpet by the commander of the U.S. Department of Defense, demanding an explanation. General Stubblebine had none to give. He vowed to get to the bottom of it. By the end of the business day, the officer who recognized the event had turned in a full report of what he had seen and suspected.

About two months after the event took place, General Stubblebine came to the field station to install a new field station commander. The necessary "GI parties" and white-glove inspections had taken place and the field station sparkled from stem to stern for the commanding general's visit and ceremony. I had no direct part in the ceremonies, so I arrived at work at my normal time. My department director met me at the door and told me to go back home, put on my class-A (dress) uniform, and report to the field station commander's office.

"Uh, sir," I said, "I'm a sergeant, now. Can't you get some private to serve doughnuts?"

"You're not serving doughnuts," he answered. "The commanding general wants to see you personally right after the installation ceremony." He added, "You must have *really* screwed up big time."

About one o'clock in the afternoon, I was still sitting in the field station commander's outer office when the general and the new commander walked in. We all snapped to attention, and the general, with the new commander following the proper number of steps behind him, proceeded past everyone. The general stopped directly in front of me, looked at my name tag, and said, "You're Sergeant Buchanan?"

"Yes, sir!" I responded automatically.

"Follow me!" he growled as he grabbed me by the arm and shoved me in front of him. I walked into the office in front of the general, aware of the breach in protocol, but helpless to do anything about it. As the new field station commander entered behind us, the general turned to him and said in a very officious tone, "I need to talk to Sergeant Buchanan. Wait outside." The new commander, forced now to end his grand entrance by standing idle in the hallway, gave me a look that very clearly said, "Whatever happens, soldier, your name is on my shit list in black, permanent ink!"

I stood at attention as the general closed the door, turned to me, got right up in my face like a drill sergeant, and with a deadly monotone voice asked, "Did you kill my field station *with your mind?*"

I knew I could lie my way out of this situation, but something within told me that he would not be asking the question if he didn't already know the answer. I knew I had better tell the truth. I was envisioning how long it would take to pay for a field station on a sergeant's salary when I heard myself answer very meekly, "Yes, sir. I did."

The general stood for what seemed like hours, staring me straight in the eyes. I tried to remain stone-faced and not to flinch in light of what I had just said. I had given them the scapegoat they needed. I was facing impending financial destruction for the rest of my life, and probably some serious jail time.

Finally, a broad grin spread across the general's face and he said, "Far fucking out!"

We talked for a few minutes about what I had felt and sensed during the incident. I have met and talked to many generals in my career, but this one was so open and friendly that I very quickly felt completely comfortable opening up to him. He asked what people called me, and I told him, "Lyn." From that point on, even through the following years, that is what he called me, and has never once called me by my rank or last name since. At the end of our conversation, he finally said, "Man, have I ever got a job for you!"

I had no idea what the job could be, and he did not tell me. I stood in silence, knowing that, having admitted such a thing, my future could never again be the same. He told me that someone would contact me soon. He then reopened the door, ushered me out, and allowed the field station's new commander to have his office back.

For the month that followed, I found myself on every "shit list" imaginable. The new commanding officer remembered my name and my face quite vividly. Everyone in my office wanted to know what had happened with the general, but I would not tell. Some accepted my silence, but my section's director was offended by it, and let me know in no uncertain terms that keeping him out of the loop was not an option. My name became indelibly printed at the top of his list, too. In time, he learned what the meeting with the general had been about, made it public within the office, and I quickly became the butt of every pointed joke and jab you can imagine.

But the whole thing seemed to just quietly blow over. I did not hear from the general again, so I figured that I was not to be selected for anything special. We all got back to work, and life returned to normal.

A month or so later, I received a call at home from a man who identified himself as "Joe." He said that he and another man, "Brian," would be coming through Augsburg and would like to meet with me. They had instructions from the general to talk to me about "something." They wanted to meet with Linda and me at a local restaurant where we could talk in a noisy, public place, away from any other military people. I gave them directions to a favorite restaurant of ours, a Czech restaurant located fairly distant from the American sectors, and not often frequented by American military.

During the meal, Brian revealed, right in front of Linda, that he was the director of a special, highly classified project that "collected intelligence by mental means." He and Joe explained the concept of "remote viewing" to us. Seeing my consternation that Linda was being exposed to secrets, Brian explained that the process of remote viewing changes people. If I became involved, I would change. The wives of his soldiers could not understand the reasons for those changes because of the security, and therefore his unit had been plagued by constant marital problems.

"I don't want another divorce in my unit," he said, "so this time, your wife gets to know what is going on. If she doesn't approve, you won't be involved." He asked Linda whether she had any problems with my doing that kind of work. To my surprise, she said that she had always known I had talents in that area and thought I would be good at it. In fact, she seemed eager for my involvement.

Joe wrote a phone number on a napkin and handed it to me. "If you ever absolutely have to get in touch with us, call this number." I tore off the number and put it into my wallet for safekeeping.

Brian and Joe said that General Stubblebine wanted me to go to a special course. He would get in touch with me when things were set up. The general's words had been, "Let's send him to that course, and then we can talk further about any possible assignment." I realized that I would have to somehow prove myself before the assignment would be granted. I had no idea how to do that.

Then, more weeks went by and I did not hear a thing. I wasn't about to fire off mail, nagging the general for information. So, I waited.

About a month after meeting with Brian and Joe, a message came into the station saying that I would be attending a special training course. The message did not say what kind of course it was, nor did it ask permission for my release from the unit or from duty to attend. It was signed by the commanding general of INSCOM, and the only questions asked by my immediate command were asked to me. I did not know what the course was about, and if I had known, I probably could not have told them. They thought I was keeping secrets from them, and there I was, back on the shit lists again.

On the appointed date, I drove to the Munich airport and waited for the plane. As I was going through the boarding gate, I heard my name being paged over the intercom. I started to go back for it, but an over-powering feeling kept me from doing so. I was afraid that I would miss the plane and wind up being AWOL at the course. I boarded, and imagined and worried all the way to the States, ran over every possible scenario in my mind. What could the call have been about? Had Linda or one of the kids been in an accident? What could have gone wrong? When I got to the States, I called home and learned that Linda knew nothing of the call. It was only after returning to Germany that I learned the answer. The field station commander had learned what the school was all about and decided not to grant me permission to go. He had tried to track me down and even had me paged at the Munich airport, to stop me from leaving.

I arrived in Washington and met one of the other people who was coming from overseas to attend the course. His name was Bob (not his real name, but close enough). He was an intelligence field office interrogator, working in one of the field offices in Europe. He would not tell me his rank, but I would later find out he was a warrant officer. He knew the D.C. area, so we rented a car and drove to Arlington Hall Station, where the INSCOM commander's office was located. We found about twenty people preparing to board a bus. We reported to the office and the general's secretary was surprised to see us.

"You're here! I thought you weren't going to make it."

We followed instructions and loaded our overnight bags onto the bus for a trip to the Monroe Institute, about a half-hour ride south of Charlottesville, Virginia. Other than Bob, myself, and one other sergeant, everyone to whom we were introduced was a major, lieutenant colonel, colonel, or of such high rank. The other nonbrass person was a female sergeant named Dawn, who was stationed in Greece, and who had also been "gleaned from the ranks" by General Stubblebine.

The general's secretary had handed me a copy of a magazine article about the Monroe Institute. This was to be an out-of-body training course. My reaction to that was one of virtual disbelief. I had read of such things years before, but to think that there was a school that taught it? No way! What would we do? Chant? Call to the spirits? Use tarot cards? Sit in a circle and cast bones?

The first day of the course, we received the orientation lecture. We would be using a sound system called "hemisync," which had been developed by Bob Monroe, the founder of the institute. The sounds played into each ear were of a slightly different frequency. As your mind tried to make sense of the two, it would have to create a "beat frequency" within itself. The main frequencies were computed in such a way that the beat frequency thus set up in the brain was the brain's normal frequency for the out-of-body experience.

They had tapes causing other beat frequencies, such things as those for concentrating very deeply, playing better golf, staying more energetic, not being hungry (so you can lose weight), and a myriad of other very practical uses. But we were to use it to go out of body? "You've got to be kidding me," I thought.

Then there was the follow-on thought: "Uh, oh! My success in this course determines whether or not I get the assignment." I had to pass a test. I was not prepared for this kind of stuff.

The first afternoon, we all went into the "chec units," which are simple enclosed cubicles the size of a bed. There were speakers on the walls and earphone jacks, so you could listen to special sounds being played as you lay there. Four or five times a day, we would lie down in darkness in the chec unit and listen to tapes of these special sounds for an hour or so. Afterwards, we met in the big room downstairs and sat in a circle, so we could discuss with the group what had transpired within our minds as we listened. Since I could not think of anything earth shattering that had transpired in my mind, I kept quiet. Keeping quiet was no way to pass a test in the military, but to open my mouth would have proven that I had failed.

That night, more tones were played to us as we slept. The following morning, we had breakfast, went to our chec units, and listened to more tones. Nothing happened again. Later, in the group, the others were making quite a fuss about their experiences. Again, I kept quiet.

That afternoon, after lunch, we returned to our chec units for more tones. I was restless and bothered and, frankly, worried that I had already failed whatever test there was. I lay in the bed, lights off, listening to the tones, and told myself to relax. I didn't relax. Nothing worked. Finally, I decided that no matter how uncomfortable I got, and no matter how nervous, I was going to just be still and listen to the sounds. Then my chin began to itch.

"I will *not* scratch," I thought, knowing that if I did, I would be in motion all over again.

It itched again.

"No!" I thought.

It itched.

Finally, in desperation, I allowed myself one single scratch. I raised my hand to scratch my chin and felt the oddest sensation: it felt as if my hand had a glove on it. The feeling was so odd that I opened my eyes and looked at my hand. My hand, right near my face, had a slight glow to it. I then looked farther down and saw in the semidarkness the same arm, still lying at my side.

"This is an out-of-body experience!" I thought. A flood of relief swept over me. Such a thing was possible, after all . . . and it was possible for me! I would have something to talk about later in the group. I might pass the general's test. I might even get the assignment.

I had heard that in the out-of-body state, you can put your hands through walls and things like that. I decided to put my hand through the bed. To my total surprise, it worked. I could even feel my hand going into the bed as it passed through. I tried putting it through the wall. It worked. I tried passing it through the earphone cord and through the volume control panel on the wall. I could actually feel the back of the volume knob mechanism.

"I've got to learn how to do this at will," I thought. "I'll put my hand back into my hand and then take it out again over and over. That'll teach me how to get out of body any time I want." I put my glowing, ethereal hand back into my real, dull, boring, lying-there-in-the-darkness hand. The tape ended at that moment, and I have not been able to get out of body again since that day. I have tried and tried, but can't seem to make it happen.

In the discussion group that followed, I related the incident. At one point, I said something about my physical hand, which had been lying at my side, and "my real hand," which was passing through walls and the bed. As I related the experience, a startling realization welled up within me. All the stuff I had learned in Sunday school about having a spirit within me suddenly became real. For the first time ever, I honestly realized that the "body me" was not the "real me."

I returned to Augsburg and waited for news of a new assignment to arrive. The wait was long. My direct command wanted to know what was going on. I didn't know, but they did not believe that.

Two months went by. Finally, I got a call from the Military Personnel Center (MILPERCEN). A colonel told me he had orders from somewhere that he was not able to determine, assigning me to a clandestine organization. He strongly advised against it. It would be bad for my career progression.

"So, I'm going to transcend these orders," he said. " We're assigning you to Fort Riley, Kansas, to a tactical battalion. I see you haven't had any tactical time so far. That's what you need."

I protested, but the colonel very forcibly told me that he knew what was best for me, and that I would be assigned to Fort Riley.

I realized that if I did nothing, the whole assignment would fall apart. I phoned the number on the napkin and told the unidentified man on the other end what had transpired. He said he would take care of it.

The next evening, the colonel from MILPERCEN called again. He told me that he had had a personal visit from the commanding general of INSCOM, who had come into his office and "chewed him out." He told me that I would be assigned to the clandestine unit. "And from now on, Sergeant, don't you *ever* send another general to our office. Please."

The orders came through about three weeks later. They gave me two months to transfer out of the old unit, set up transportation of household goods, and get all the other logistics taken care of for a permanent change of station.

Just as a way of saying, "You don't do that to me," two days before my final workday at Augsburg, I arrived about six A.M., and was greeted at my desk by a military policeman.

"Are you Sergeant Buchanan? Leonard Buchanan?" he asked.

"Yes."

"Well, I have a warrant for your arrest. It says here that you're AWOL."

I was caught off guard by that one. "Uh, Sergeant," I replied, "I don't know how to explain this, but people don't go AWOL by getting into uniform and reporting for military duty at six A.M."

"No," he answered, looking at his instructions. "It says here that you didn't show up for your duty assignment at Fort Riley. The commander there put out the order to have you arrested."

The Augsburg Field Station commander delighted in toying with me before finally sending a message that those orders had been rescinded and that I was not AWOL. He gave me a stern scowl and said, "I could have let you go to jail, you know."

So Linda and I stood in the guest house parking lot, watching the fog and mist swirl around the neon sign, waiting for a mysterious someone to appear. A large car drove in, drove past us, and pulled into a parking slot. Since it had passed us by, we ignored it, and were somewhat surprised when a very tall, slender man walked up from behind us and stuck out his hand in greeting.

"Hi," he said, and grinned. "My name's Bill."

Bill had planned to take us to dinner, but since it was very late and we were tired from the trip, he postponed it for another evening. He took a copy of my printed orders and said that they would be taken care of. He checked again to be certain that I hadn't notified the 902nd of my arrival and cautioned me not to do so. "As of tomorrow," he said, "you will completely disappear from the U.S. military system. Pack your uniforms away and don't go anywhere near your assigned unit."

I asked what I should do next. "Well, you've met Joe. He's probably our best remote viewer, and runs the computers, too. He's retiring from service, and it's going to leave a big hole in the unit. You're going to be filling it. You've got a real job cut out for you. But we'll worry about that tomorrow." He pointed in a direction away from the guest house. "If you walk across that field, the first pair of buildings you come to is where we work. They look like they're abandoned, but knock on the door, anyway, and we'll let you in. Come there in the morning and we'll talk about what you do next."

As Bill drove off into the fog, Linda and I looked at each other. We then quietly turned and went into the guest house for a night of uneasy sleep.

TWO

THE FIRST THING
I LEARNED

*"I don't care who or what you blame it on! I don't care
whether you choose to admit it or not, or accept it or not, or
even to know it or not. The fact is that you are who you are
and you are what you are, and ultimately, that's what you've
got to work with and live with, so just shut up and do it!"*
—Cormira to John in
Gravity Can Be Your Friend[1]

It was a short walk from the guest house across the large, open field
and past two dilapidated, abandoned-looking old World War II
buildings, surrounded by tall weeds. There were other buildings with
military crests and insignias farther on across the next street. Surely
those were the buildings Bill had meant. Not these. As I continued between the old derelict buildings, Bill's voice came from a group of trees
nearby. "Good morning!" I was surprised to see him standing amid the
trees. He was just taking a walk in the woods as he smoked a cigarette.

"Come on in," he said, and walked toward the derelict building to my
right. He opened the door with his key and motioned for me to enter.

Inside, I could hear the sounds of people behind partitions, smell the
coffee brewing, and see a giant mural of stars in space painted on the far
wall. A cheerful woman rose from behind the only desk I could see and
came over to greet me. "You must be Lyn!" she said. "Welcome to the
unit." Before I could answer, she introduced herself as Jeanie and started
ushering me toward the partitions and introducing me to everyone in

the office. As I listened to her steady stream of chatter about Brian, the director, and Joe, and everyone else, I knew immediately that even if the next few years of duty here proved to be miserable, this woman would provide at least a small island of cheerfulness. With Jeanie around, this assignment couldn't be all bad. In fact, all the people I met that day and in the days to follow surprised me with their down-to-earth demeanors, cheerfulness, and I guess you would have to say, their normality. This was not a coven of weird people—it was a military unit dedicated to the mission and filled with great people

I was to need Jeanie's cheerfulness only a few minutes after first meeting her, when Brian actually "read me on"[2] to Project CENTER LANE, the official name of the project at that time. After all the papers were signed and filed away, Brian briefed me on the actual day-to-day operations of the unit.

"I have good news and I have bad news," he began. "The good news is that we finally managed to get you here. The bad news is that we can't train you or even use you. We lost our funding two days ago and we're closing the project down."

The unit, he explained, was funded from year to year, one year at a time. Every year it had to jump through hoops to prove to congressional subcommittees that it could be effective. The very nature of a unit of "psychic spies" was an anathema to the military. It was also suspected to be an anathema to the American public. The politicians who funded the project were always fearful that they might be found out and have to explain their actions to their constituents. The unit had already lasted almost fourteen years in this manner, but each year, they faced the renewed annual potential of closure. The unit had gone through the same "We're closing down" scenario every year, but each time, almost at the last minute, some miracle had happened to let it continue for yet one more year. This time, however, there was a difference. No miracle had happened, and it looked as if Project CENTER LANE actually would close down.

A few days later, Brian was called "downtown"[3] for a meeting. On the way into D.C., he encountered road construction and a sign that read, CENTER LANE CLOSED. He took it as an omen. It was.

Joe was leaving the unit, and I had been assigned to take over his position as computer operations manager, database manager, property book holder, and a few other positions. Everyone in the unit wore dozens of hats, since the unit was so small. Within a couple of weeks, I had settled into the positions, but with the knowledge that I wouldn't be there long. We were given a month or so to clean up all the paperwork, pack up the office and files, and get ready to close our doors forever. I saw very little of Joe during those weeks, as he hurried to complete his retirement paperwork and get properly processed out of the army. I asked to be trained in remote viewing during the little time remaining, but the pressure of getting paperwork completed did not allow for it.

I would not, however, get this close to such a momentous thing and not learn it. There is an old saying in the military that there are a thousand reasons why you can't do what you want, but always a way that you can. I spent every spare moment talking to the people who were already trained, reading old session transcripts and project reports. I made and kept a personal copy of the unfinished *CRV Manual*, which was the first and only written attempt at a how-to book at that time. For the next month, my duties consisted of office work, programming little routines for the Wang computer, cleaning and closing up the database with final reports and summaries. There was also one especially horrible task that was given to me, more to keep me out of everyone's hair than anything else. I was to read an unpublished book by Drs. Robert Jahn and Brenda J. Dunn of the Princeton Engineering Anomalies Research (PEAR) Laboratory, entitled *The Quantum Mechanics of Consciousness*. It was about three hundred pages of little more than quantum physics formulas. I was told to translate it into language humans could understand. If possible, I was to provide a one-page executive summary so the brass could act as if they had read the work and speak coherently about it.

After a month or so, I managed to produce a condensed eighteen-page summary. Actually, it was very well received. It made the rounds within the intelligence community and, from what I hear, brought many of the doubters among the top brass and financial overlords around to the concept that such things as psychic functioning might actually be possible and, further, scientifically achievable. It at least gave them the seed for such a belief.

Then, the miracle happened. Suddenly, the threat of project closure eased. Several hostages had been taken by the Arabs, and someone needed us. More funding became available. Although CENTER LANE was still to be closed as a project, we would continue remote viewing under a new project name: DRAGOON ABSORB. Project DRAGOON ABSORB actually turned out to be a temporary stopgap. It lasted about two weeks and then was replaced by other funding and another project name: Project SUN STREAK.

The new funding, however, did not include a contract slot for the person who had been training the remote viewers, a man named Ingo Swann. Ingo Swann is the person who developed the scientific process called Coordinate Remote Viewing (CRV), which he later changed to Controlled Remote Viewing. It is the main remote viewing process that I was ultimately to learn, and the most used method the entire time I was in the military unit.

The unit would be in existence for another year, and I would be in it, but I would have to be taught remote viewing by the people whom Ingo had already trained. At the time, that meant little to me, but in the weeks that followed, I met and became friends with Ingo, and realized how unfortunate for me that really was.

Now that the project was back on track, the decision was made for early implementation of "in-house training by already-trained personnel." That had always been a goal of the original contract, but now it became a reality. I was to be the guinea pig, to see if these people who had learned remote viewing from Ingo could now also teach it. The other members of the unit would begin formally training me to become a military remote viewer. My outlook on the future brightened considerably.

On the day my formal training began, I was taken across the driveway to the Operations Building. It was as ramshackle and dilapidated as the Admin Building in every respect. Skip, our operations officer, had prepared a small beginning lecture. We sat in the front room of the Operations Building.

"Look at the room around you," he said. "Now, look at the floor molding along the walls and follow it with your eyes all around the room."

I did.

"Now," he continued, "look at the molding around the ceiling and follow it all around the room."

I did.

"Now, realize this . . ." he finally continued, "no matter how things have been in all your life, and no matter how things are in the entire world . . ."

He paused again for effect and it worked. "In this room," he continued, "it's OK to be psychic."

I don't know if it was the way he said it, the tone in his voice, or what, but the impact was astounding. A lifetime of trying to hide the abilities that I had always felt the need to release—trying never to allow the small voice ever to say anything again—trying *not* to be psychic—all melted away.

I learned a lot of things those first few months in the unit. I learned that there were actually people out there doing this stuff. I learned that, with proper training and practice, it could be done extremely well. I learned that the army wasn't as cut and dried as I had always thought, that there were people in the military who were open to using esoteric means for intelligence collection. But in the end, I will always count the thing Skip taught me as the first thing I learned about CRV. It is the one lesson that has stayed with me more than any other, and it paved the way for the work I was to do for the U.S. government. To this day, I remain in total gratitude to Ingo Swann for developing the methodology with which I would do my work in the coming years, but when I think back to give credit where credit is due, I credit Skip for that one insight. Without it, I would probably have never become a remote viewer.

It is rare that a person can point to one moment in his life and say, "The change took place here." But at that moment I accepted my ability. I think this may be one of the most important lessons I ever learned: *It really is OK to be who you are. It really is OK to be psychic.*

Ingo Swann's training contract had expired, and was not renewed. But the unit had some property in Manhattan that Ingo had been using for training, and we needed to retrieve that property. Brian selected me to go with him to New York to retrieve it. I only received one instruction from the other people in the unit: to be sure not to leave New York without going to Ingo's favorite deli and getting a cheese Danish. Other than that, a trip to Ingo's was nothing to the others. For me, it was a trip to Mecca.

We rented a truck to carry the property back in and arrived in New York during what seemed like the worst traffic jam in human history. I was later to learn that it was just normal downtown New York traffic. We finally made our way to the building where Ingo trained the military viewers and began loading tables, chairs, track lighting, etc., into the truck. Afterwards, we went to Ingo's home—what appeared to be an old warehouse in the Bowery, which had been renovated into a home.

Ingo met and greeted us very cordially. I had heard from the others how strict and rigid a teacher Ingo was, but the man who met us was anything but. I have rarely, even in the South, met anyone so cordial and friendly. Ingo is very soft spoken, smiles a lot, jokes a lot, and feels immediately like an old friend.

I was surprised at what I saw in Ingo's basement, where he does most of his personal work. Back in the unit, everyone worked in a very sterile environment. Everything in the session rooms was painted battleship gray, with battleship gray carpeting. The windows were painted over with battleship gray paint. The other viewers had told me that it was that way because Ingo had preached to them the necessity of having an environment with absolutely no distractions. In fact, Ingo's New York training room, from which we had taken the tables and chairs, had been battleship gray and sterile. But where Ingo actually did his own work was a different matter completely. There were finished and half-finished paintings everywhere. There were things lying around in unorganized piles everywhere.

How someone could concentrate in such an environment was not totally beyond me—I'm pretty much the same way with my work areas at home. But how someone could do a remote viewing session with all those distractions was astounding. Then it dawned on me that the person who could do that would have to be a really good remote viewer. Ingo Swann was one of those rare people.

NOTES

1. From an unpublished science fiction novel by Lyn Buchanan.

2. To "read you on" is a phrase used in the intelligence community which means that you are about to be exposed to classified information, and that there are legal ramifications involved. First, you have to read and sign a security warning. It basically says that

if you divulge any of the information you are about to see, you will face strong penalties—a minimum of ten years in jail and $10,000 fine, and even a death sentence in the most severe cases. Then, after you have signed your life away, you get to read the papers that tell what the project is all about, and other classified information about the unit and its work and mission.

3. "To go downtown" to most of the military and intelligence units around the Washington, D.C., area means that you will be going into Washington to one of the major command units, to the Pentagon, to one of the federal agencies, "on the hill," or to the White House.

THREE

THE MILITARY UNIT

"History repeats itself," John said.
"What?" asked Cormira.
"I said, history repeats itself."
                    —*Gravity Can Be Your Friend[1]*

O ur unit was quite different from most military units in many ways, beginning with the fact that our unit's life span was always one year long. It was not one of those black projects that get set up, forgotten about, and then keep functioning for reasons unknown to everyone. We had to prove ourselves every year or our charter was up and we would all get reassigned to some other military unit. We overcame this problem each and every year, often at the last moment, and often through what seemed like a miracle.

We were different from other military units in other ways as well. Most military units work as a well-oiled team. In our unit, none of the people in the unit could know what anyone else was doing. That was necessary. A remote viewer's worst enemy is his/her own imagination, and seeing each other's work was guaranteed to ratchet the imagination into overdrive. This has some far-reaching implications which will be discussed in the next chapter. So, although we were together in the same office, talk was limited, interests and hobbies were not shared. When it was time to go home, we all went our own ways and rarely ever had anything to do with each other off duty. During the occasional social function, there was absolutely no shop talk of any kind.

In fact, many of the things that "normal" people take for granted were off-limits to us by necessity. For example, if I were listening to the morning news on the way to work, I might hear that some terrorist group had committed some frightful act in one distant country or another. When I arrived at work, I expected to be tasked with a CRV session on that event. The actual session I worked that day might have nothing to do with the event, but my imagination would be kicking and screaming at me throughout the entire session to find the hostage. Whether it was a newscast or one of the unit members talking about his/her session to someone else, the result was a torturous battle with the imagination and, usually, lower accuracy as an end product. So, even the daily newscast and newspaper were considered off-limits by most of us, through our own volition, simply to save us the pain of the internal struggles while we worked.

Most of the time, we were not even allowed to know what our own targets were about, even after the sessions were complete, because we might be called on to do further work on that same target. If we knew what it was, our imaginations would get in the way.

But we all had our imaginations intact, and we all had hunches about what project we were working. The projects that many of the unit's viewers think they worked and now claim to have taken part in are merely what they assume they worked. While several people in the office were working one problem, a single person might be working a totally different task. Viewers would piece together tidbits from one or more of their sessions with items in the daily news and comments heard over partitions and would conclude, "I worked on this or that." In many cases, they were right. In other cases, they were wrong. In fact, most of them worked on targets that were much more exciting and historic than they realize, even today. But the end result was the same: almost everyone who was in the unit was, in a very real way, in it alone.

One problem stems from that situation. Nowadays, everyone tells a different history of the unit and their time in it. Sometimes an ex-military man will relate in a lecture or interview about a task he worked on, and another ex-military viewer will contradict the first, saying that no one ever worked that problem. The second viewer doesn't remember it, so it can't have happened. Each tells the unit's history as he or she saw it, interpreted it, and believed it to be. Consequently the history now being presented to the public is fractured and disjointed, contradictory and confusing.

I know because my secondary job within the unit as database manager allowed me to see the data from all the taskings. There are several ex-military who are presently contradicting each other's accounts, with some telling of targets worked, and the others saying there was never any such target. Let me put something to rest, as much as possible, even though I know full well that it will not stop the controversy: I have not seen any account of projects worked by any of the ex-military viewers, either in their lectures or in their writings, which I find to be false. I remember entering data into the database for each of the accounts I have read in print. If one of the other viewers does not remember working on any one project, that does not mean that the project did not exist—it only means that he/she either does not remember it, was not aware of what the tasking was, or simply was not involved. That is not to say that some accounts have not "grown considerably with the retelling," as they say.

But having said that, let me also admit that, being human, I suspect that my memories may have grown with the retelling, too. They are as I remember them, having been directly involved. However, the same projects which I remember as extremely important may seem unimportant to another viewer. They may remember the whole project going a different way simply because they were given different feedback or worked a different aspect of the project. It is sad that the very history that we all lived is now so contradictory. Some of it is faulty memory, but for the most part, it is an artifact of the way our office was organized and the amount of secrecy and separation we had one from another.

In like manner, there were many targets with which I was never involved. Although some of them might be extremely important and historic, I don't remember them as well as those with which I was involved. I remember them only as database entries. Therefore, I would caution the reader of this book to realize that my stories, just like the stories of the other group members, are to be taken as personal accounts and as singular viewpoints of personal participation in historic events.

There is also admittedly a great deal of misinformation, disinformation, and misdirection involved in almost everything you will read about the unit and its work. This was, after all, an intelligence unit for the government. Your grandchildren may someday learn the whole, real truth about it, but you never will. There are basically three facts of life you must understand when dealing with the world of governmental and military intelligence:

1. You must remember that in the intelligence world, every truth is part lie and every lie is based on some truth. If you try to separate the two, you will only wind up confused and frustrated. If you are an outsider, you will slowly learn that there *is* no separation of the two—the lies and the truth are just two of the many sides of the same ever-flipping coin. If you are an insider, you will slowly and often painfully learn that sometimes the coin lands by chance, sometimes the way it lands is rigged and you'll never know by whom, and sometimes there is not even a coin at all.

2. If you are lucky and work hard, you will find some of the truth. If you are lucky and work really hard, you might find the *whole* truth—as someone wants you to know it. If you are phenomenally lucky and really work your tail off, you might even go on to find the *real* truth. But no outsiders, and in fact very few insiders, ever—*ever*—learn the *whole, real* truth.

3. All assumptions are wrong.

Some of the "factual impurities" (I always loved that euphemism) exist for the express purpose of hiding facts. Some just work around issues that are still highly classified. Many are the result of people trying their best to make sense of what happened. Most of the unit's recorded history is either classified, forgotten, anecdotal, or just plain imagined. Therefore, in many ways, my brief overview may be more accurate than the detailed accounts you will read elsewhere.

BACKGROUND

In Russia, in the late '60s, a man named Pinkowski approached one of our diplomats with some classified papers. The KGB arrested Pinkowski, but not before the contents of the papers became known to U.S.

intelligence. The content dealt with Soviet attempts to use psychics as passive intelligence collectors. Even further, it disclosed, the Soviets were using them in an active mode to gain mental control over foreign leaders.

The whole thing seemed ridiculous to the U.S. intelligence community and was laughed off by most U.S. intelligence services. However, there is always that little paranoid group that has sense enough to say, "What if . . ." And so it was that a very small and clandestine investigation was started within the U.S. intelligence community. It was nothing serious, but it was a beginning.

Not long afterwards, a young lieutenant named Fred (Skip) Atwater finished Command Staff College. One of the research papers he wrote at the college led him to information about the subject, and he took the information seriously. When he returned to his unit, his commander asked him what he wanted to do next. He brought up the subject of psychic spying. He told his commander that it was something that everyone had evidently ignored, but that it had the potential to be a serious threat. On the outside chance that it was possible, there would be no defense against it. On that basis, Skip argued, it should be looked into.

As fate would have it, Skip's commander knew about just such an investigation already under way and assigned him to work with the people who were already interested in the problem. Skip was put in charge of a project to test whether or not psychic spying could actually reveal our secrets to the enemy. Since the Russians would not be willing to give us feedback on what their psychics found, he would be forced to have some of our own psychics spy on our secret projects to see whether or not psychics posed a threat against our classified missions.

Skip's mission, then, was threefold. He had to first find people with whom to work. Because of the secrecy of the assigned targets, he wouldn't be able to work with just any psychic or palm reader off the street. He had to test military people for psychic abilities, and do so in such a way that they would not know what they were being tested for.

Step two was to gather them together into a group. Reassigning people within the military is a very difficult task, since the very structure of the military chain of command requires that people work within their assigned skills. Those skills have to be declared and personnel slots authorized. Arranging for the clandestine creation of slots that, for all purposes, would not really exist was a monumental undertaking.

The third step would be to finally see whether or not this eclectic group could effectively use their talents to spy on the U.S. military's most closely held secrets. This project would be called Project SCANATE, which, instead of being a code word, was simply short for "Scan by Coordinates."

Through a long series of sometimes deceptive testing, Skip identified six potential candidates. He brought them in and briefed them. Their initial target was received through the chain of command and dealt with the government's most highly classified project of the time—the highly computerized Abrams tank. It was so secret that even Skip, who headed the project, was not allowed to know what the target was. Skip tasked one of his candidates named Joe, and Joe not only described the tank but drew a highly accurate sketch of its interior, down to the image on the targeting computer's display screen.

Skip gathered all the session summaries and sent them off. Were they successful? They would have to wait for feedback to find out. The feedback came quickly enough. The CIA raided the place, carried off all their paperwork, and tried to arrest Joe for spying. They refused to believe that such detailed information could be obtained by mental means. It was an unchallenged success.

A new unit was formed as a result of the SCANATE sessions against U.S. military targets. This new unit consisted mainly of the six viewers, Skip Atwater, and a commander, Scotty Watt. The group became a formal unit. Their mission, now called Project GRILL FLAME, was originally to complete a risk assessment on any "psychic threat" against the U.S., but also to determine whether or not this psychic spying could be useful to us, if we used it against foreign military and governmental targets.

During this time, those people in the government who knew about the project had been receiving more intelligence information about the Russian psychic effort, through normal channels. The overall feeling became, "If the Russians have it, then we must have it, too." However, the people who would fund and support this effort were naturally very cautious. They didn't want a bunch of seances and chicken-guttings going on under government supervision. They wanted a scientific process. Further, some of the supporters wanted a process that would not depend on the widely varying talents and abilities of natural psychics. What they really wanted was an understanding of the talent, so they could develop a standardized teaching method. They wanted a method that could be taught to anyone. They wanted something that could be taught to the dumbest grunt soldier on the battlefield in five minutes, so he could tell his commander what was over the hill and where to point the guns.

Psychics everywhere will readily tell you that such a thing is not possible—that the part of mankind that does this work will not buckle to the rules and regulations of the scientific world. But there was another factor involved which made the attempt to gain scientific approval worth the effort. In Washington, D.C., everything is run by money and politics. The money for the project was easy to come by. The politics was something different. For any politician to be caught funding a psychic program would mean the end of his career. The project had to be scientific, even if only on the surface, before any funding could take place. The government began looking for a responsible laboratory to do the research work.

It so happened that at the time, Dr. Harold Puthoff, a laser physicist at Stanford Research Institute (SRI), had been doing some impressive work along these lines on his own time. It was a private interest, but he had published a few papers, and those papers had attracted the attention of the right people. He was approached and in 1972 the CIA gave him $50,000 to conduct a formalized study of the phenomenon.

Puthoff, along with another laser physicist, Russell Targ, began by taking people off the Stanford campus, off the streets, people passing through the hallways, etc. This was not the standard testing normally given the general public. He selected and tested those people who were reported to be highly talented natural psychics. Two of them proved to be of exceedingly high talent. Pat Price, a retired police chief, and Ingo Swann, an artist who, at that time, was working at the United Nations. These two performed outstandingly. Puthoff developed new methodologies for testing them, and they even began to develop new methodologies of their own.

During this time, the operational unit back in Fort Meade, Maryland, was working with natural psychics to collect intelligence information on enemy targets. Each psychic worked using his/her own method to gain whatever information could be gleaned. It was a haphazard and nonuniform group, but the job was being done with great success.

There was not a lot of communication between the researchers on the West Coast and the operational psychics on the East Coast. But on occasion, the psychics of the unit would be tested at Stanford, and in the process they would gain new ideas for new things to try back at the unit.

Ingo Swann got caught up in the idea that the process could be scientifically formulated and began working to develop his own understanding of what happens during a psychic event. One thing led to another, and he and Hal Puthoff developed a methodology that could actually be taught to the average person. The methodology does not "teach someone to be psychic," but instead teaches them to get rid of all those blocks that prevent them from using the natural and hidden talents they already have. For most people, that is a surprising amount.

So Ingo moved from research to operations and began teaching the members of the unit at Fort Meade how to work his methodology. He lived in Manhattan, so the members of the unit began traveling there for training in 1980. From that point on, the methods used within the military unit became standardized and uniform. Analysis and reporting became more dependable. A database became possible. The whole project did not just take on a politically acceptable scientific air, it actually became scientific in truth.

By this time, the project name for the unit had become CENTER LANE. It had also been moved over into the U.S. Army's chain of command, under the direction of the U.S. Army Intelligence and Security Command (USAINSCOM, or INSCOM, for short). The project was to undergo further name changes in the following years, but CENTER LANE was the unit's designation when I arrived there on April Fool's Day 1984.

I was in a unique position within the unit. While I was one of the remote viewers, and was supposed to be kept blind to the detailed viewing information, I was also the database manager and had to keep all the records on each of the projects. While the other viewers were working "blind"[2] to the targets, I rarely ever had that luxury. I therefore had to work with some background knowledge of the target. The customers would always provide our unit with enough information to know what and how to task the viewers. Usually, they told us more than we needed to know. I almost always had access to that information before I worked the sessions. In a way, it made the viewing work much harder for me, since I had background knowledge and my imagination could run full speed.

In a way, though, it also made me a better viewer. I fully understood that the customer would not have tasked us with the target if logic, simple intuition, or reason could have solved the problem. I quickly developed the personal policy to "always go for the unknown." Whatever snap conclusions my logical mind gave me had to be ignored. Maybe these conclusions were right, but probably not, since the customer would surely have thought of them, too.

I was also the property book officer, which meant that I signed for and was responsible for all the equipment, the computers, every pen and sheet of paper, the company car, and even the facility itself. As the computer operations manager, I was also responsible for quality control of the software, purity of the data, and all of the specialty programming. At one point, I was also the training officer, an administrative job that entails record keeping, room assignments, etc. I gladly gave up that position to another person who was newly arrived in the unit. After about a year and a half, I became one of the unit's trainers, then later, the unit's only trainer until my retirement.

All that sort of makes me sound as if I were pulling "Superman" duty, but in fact, everyone in the unit wore multiple hats. The small number of personnel in our unit (almost always fewer than eight people) did not change the fact that we were a fully functioning military unit, complete with all the responsibilities and duties of one.

As I said earlier, one of the unit's jobs was to prove ourselves and get re-funded every year. At one point, a senator visited our unit for a "dog and pony show." He was on the committee deciding whether or not to fund our unit the following year. He wanted to see what he would be voting on. He brought a target with him which had been picked by one of his own staff members and hidden in an envelope so that even he did not know what the target was. The thinking was that his ignorance of the target would ensure that we could not "pull information out of him" and thereby cheat. He watched a remote viewing session, expecting to see something spectacular, with heads twisting in full circle, trumpets floating in the air, tables rising from the floor, or something of the kind. None of that happens with Controlled Remote Viewing. When the demonstration was over, he had a meeting with our director.

"To tell the truth," he said flatly, "I'm totally underwhelmed. I came here wanting to see what you people really do, and who you really are. All I saw was two soldiers sitting at a table, smoking and joking, and every now and then one of them wrote something down."

The director, who by then had received the final report on the senator's target, handed it to the senator and said, "Well, here's what they wrote. Open your target envelope and read the summary and judge our work for yourself. That will tell you what we really do and who we really are." The director later told us that it was probably the bravest thing he had ever done. If the session had been a bad one, we would have all been out on the street within a week.

The senator took the still-sealed envelope out of his briefcase and opened it. He studied the target picture and accompanying text for a moment, then turned to the viewer's final report. As he read, he kept glancing back and forth between the target and the report. "Damn!" he kept saying. "Damn! Damn!"

The project was funded for another year and would eventually be called SUN STREAK. This was our project's name until a couple of years after I retired from the unit, at which time the unit was moved back to the Central Intelligence Agency.

The CIA took charge of the project in 1993 and renamed it Project STAR GATE. At this time, the Cold War was essentially over, and the intelligence community was suffering severe financial and personnel cutbacks. The unit was cut back to one remote viewer, a tarot card reader, and an automatic writer. The CIA decided to disband the project.

To make the unit's dissolution appear to be for good reason, a committee of two, a statistician and a psychic debunker, were given the task of evaluating the project's usefulness. They studied the work the unit had done from 1990 to 1992, when the unit only had a single Controlled Remote Viewer, and had virtually no tasking because of the end of the Cold War. Still the statistician determined that there was sufficient statistical evidence to continue the project, but recommended that it continue on a purely experimental basis.

The debunker declared that there was, indeed, statistical significance and reported that the science of statistics was therefore as flawed as the science of parapsychology. He suggested that the unit be disbanded until the science of statistics could become accurate enough to prove how useless and false parapsychology was. So, as the CIA intended, the unit was disbanded in 1994.

NOTES

1. From an unpublished science fiction novel by Lyn Buchanan.

2. This is an important footnote and should be read carefully for understanding many things in the rest of the book. There continues to be a lot of confusion and controversy over this one aspect of remote viewing. If a person is allowed to have any information, the imagination is driven and pollution occurs. Yet, within the operations of the military unit, it was a very regular occurrence for the viewer to be told ahead of time what the target was, and what unknown aspect of the target was being sought. For example, it was not at all unusual to be told that we would be looking for the (unknown) location and condition of, say, one of the Lebanese hostages. The viewer, with knowledge of current events, would begin the session with a map of Lebanon open at his/her workplace.

People do not see how this could be considered a "blind" viewing condition. The truth is that it was anything but "blind." Yet, the viewer was still considered to be "blind" to the specifically targeted questions. Every viewer was fully aware of the fact that if logic, surveillance, satellite photography, or any other means of gaining intelligence information could have provided the answer to the specific questions, the viewer would not have been tasked. Therefore, the definition of "working blind" was somewhat changed from what a person would normally expect. People within the unit often knew, from their individual participation, what projects they were working on. However, if they even mentioned the project to another viewer, it might drive that viewer's imagination to think that he/she was working the same project. Therefore, viewers within the unit were often aware of the project on which they worked, but were not aware of the projects on which others were working. Above all, they were not allowed to discuss among themselves either the nature of the projects or the details of their findings. "Working blind," for us, had a modified definition. In our situation, it rarely meant "totally blind" to the nature of the project, but always blind to the unknown.

FOUR

A MILITARY INTELLIGENCE TOOL

S ince Controlled Remote Viewing was basically developed as an intelligence gathering tool for the military, some of the best and most interesting work we did involved hostages, terrorism, drug running, and other events of worldwide interest.

PADUA, ITALY

The most widely known story of the work done by the military's remote viewers concerns General Dozier, a senior military officer at NATO headquarters in Italy. In 1981, when General Dozier was taken hostage by Red Brigade terrorists, a massive manhunt was undertaken to locate and rescue him.

The remote viewing unit was tasked with the problem of locating the general. Remote viewer Joe McMoneagle came up with information that directed the police to Padua, Italy, and eventually to the exact building where the general was being held. The official story is that General Dozier had already been rescued before Joe's information got to the right people, but I have never personally been certain that this was the case.

Not widely known is the fact that throughout the hostage crisis daily and sometimes hourly reports of the general's health and well-being were forwarded up the chain of command. This episode set the stage for the remote viewing unit's involvement in almost every hostage crisis that followed.

TEHRAN, IRAN

In 1979, the ousted shah of Iran, who had earlier escaped Iran in fear for his life, entered the United States for cancer treatment. In Tehran, Iranian students poured into the streets to protest, demanding that the United States return the shah and his multimillion-dollar fortune to Iran. These protests seemed innocuous until the morning of November 4, 1979, exactly one year before the United States presidential election, when a mob of around three thousand students stormed the embassy's gate, overran the guards, and took the sixty-six people inside hostage, in the name of Khomeini. Every U.S. intelligence unit was on the alert for possible repercussions and ramifications throughout the world. The remote viewing unit was immediately tasked with tracking the health and welfare of the hostages, determining the political plans and intentions of the students and Khomeini, locating weaknesses (potential collaborators) within the ranks of the students and government, and finding methods and avenues for either settling the problem or rescuing the hostages.

With information about the mental state of those holding the hostages and the political plans and intentions of the government—some of which was provided by the remote viewing unit—President Carter realized that there was no diplomatic end in sight, and severed diplomatic relations with Iran on April 7, 1980.

Shortly thereafter, on April 24, a top secret operation called Operation Eagle Claw was executed. The mission called for eight Marine helicopters to fly into Iran, land, storm the embassy, and rescue the hostages. The helicopters were launched from the U.S. aircraft carrier *Nimitz* for a six-hundred-mile trip into Iran. At the same time, six transport planes were dispatched to meet the helicopters in the Iranian desert at a location called Desert One, several hundred miles southeast of Tehran, where the helicopters would pick up additional troops. From Desert One, the combined rescue team would fly to Desert Two, where the rescuers would board trucks for a fifty-mile trip into Tehran. Once in Tehran, the raiders were to hide briefly near the U.S. embassy where they were to be aided by several Iranians who had been identified as potential collaborators. They would then storm the American embassy and free the hostages. From there, they would fight their way back out of Tehran, with orders to kill anyone who got in their way. Surviving hostages would board the helicopters at Desert Two to be carried back to Desert One. At Desert One, the freed hostages would be flown out of the country aboard the aerial transports.

The actual storming of the embassy and freeing the prisoners was estimated to take only about two hours. Unfortunately, Operation Eagle Claw ran into massive and unforeseen problems. Shortly after the helicopters took off from the *Nimitz,* one of them was forced down by rotor blade trouble and a second one returned to the *Nimitz,* its pilot blinded by a sandstorm. Only six helicopters reached their rendezvous point with the transports. However, one of them had to be scrapped because of partial hydraulic failure caused by the sand from the high desert winds. Planners had not taken a sandstorm into consideration when planning the operation. Because the plan called for six operating helicopters, the mission was aborted.

During refueling for the return flight, the sandstorm continued, and three additional helicopters became inoperable. One of these accidentally collided with a transport. Both vehicles exploded, killing eight American servicemen. The survivors abandoned the scene, leaving the four remaining helicopters, weapons, maps, several highly classified documents regarding the operation, and the dead bodies behind in the flaming wreckage.

At the moment when the helicopter crashed into the transport plane, one of the unit's remote viewers at Fort Meade, who was in session at the time, stood up in horror. "They've crashed," she said. The information was immediately sent up the chain of command to President Carter, and actually reached him a full ten minutes before the news came to him through normal channels.

WILLIAM BUCKLEY

Shortly before I reported for duty in the remote viewing unit in April 1984, the CIA's station chief in Beirut, William Buckley, was kidnapped by Shiite guerrillas. The CIA and the Reagan administration believed that Iran had some control over the Lebanese groups. The Iranians took advantage of this by offering to negotiate the release of Buckley and other hostages in exchange for weapons and weapons components. This was, of course, the beginning of the Iran-Contra affair.

Another in the long series of hostage crises began. I was not yet fully trained in formal Controlled Remote Viewing (then called Coordinate Remote Viewing), but the government needed information, and they were desperate enough to use me in spite of my lack of training. Any results I came up with would, of course, be taken with a large grain of salt, but I got the opportunity to pitch in and work real-world operations, nonetheless.

The tasking was in the form of the latest photograph of Buckley. His condition had deteriorated to the point where he was gaunt and thin. When I first saw the photo, he reminded me of Pat Paulsen, a gaunt comedian who was popular on the Smothers Brothers television show at the time. In fact, he looked so much like the comedian that all the viewers were calling the project "the Pat Paulsen project."

We worked for several months on this case, among other hostage cases, such as that of the priest Terry Waite and the many other people being taken hostage during those very tumultuous years. But it was during the early Pat Paulsen case that the database began showing a surprising statistic. It revealed that one of my main strengths was to access people mentally. Most of the session tasks I received from that point on for hostage situations would center around this strength.

COL. RICH HIGGINS

One of the last hostage crises we dealt with was the abduction of Col. Rich Higgins,[1] who was yanked from his United Nations jeep and kidnapped in 1988 by Iranian-backed Hezbollah terrorists in Lebanon. As a unit, we tracked his condition and situation for months.

One day, I was in the middle of a session when I was startled by an extremely strong impression: "RASAIN." "Where did that come from?" I asked myself. Knowing that you write down every impression that you get in session, I dutifully scribbled, and continued my session.

S7: "RAS AIN!"

Not thinking about the sudden impression, I wrote up my report on the colonel's condition and a description of his immediate surroundings. I turned the session in and went home for the day.

The next day, I got a congratulatory note from the project director. He said, "You were right on location with yesterday's session. They investigated and found that, sure enough, that's where the colonel was being held yesterday. Unfortunately, he was moved overnight, so we don't know where he is, again. Good work, anyway."

"I located him?" I asked.

"Right." The director smiled. "He was being held in the town of Ras Ain."

I felt good, but success can also be a mixed blessing. A few days later, given the same task, I found Colonel Higgins standing in an outdoor location. He was on the slight slope of a sandy embankment. Then, suddenly, he was on the ground, head downwards on the slope, face down in the sand, dead. Some men with guns were walking away from the body, laughing and joking with one another. I reported my findings, and three other viewers were immediately tasked with his condition and situation, in order to confirm or disprove my findings. The other three viewers found him to be quite alive. But I was certain of what I had found. The next day, we got the report that the Hezbollah had sent pictures of the colonel's dead body to the CIA overnight. During that session, I had evidently witnessed his execution. There was no joy in being right, this time.

CHERNOBYL

On Thursday, April 25, 1986, a new member of our unit, Gene, reported for duty. He was going to be trained as our new monitor and project officer, but would not become a viewer. The director called the unit's viewers together and told us that we would take this opportunity to show the new man what we could do. Each one of us would work a predictive session. Predictive sessions were some of our least successful sessions. One reason for the low scores was that the people for whom we did our work often took steps to change the predicted events. Although we got feedback that what we had predicted would certainly have happened, we always scored our sessions on what actually happened. As a result, our own predictions, passed to someone who could act upon them, made our predictions incorrect. The project in this story, however, was not to be information to be turned in and acted upon by anyone.

Our task, the director said, was to predict any major event that would be reported in local newspapers over the weekend. We would do our work at home that evening and bring the results in for our Friday office meeting.

When I did my CRV session, I found a man in a white lab coat walking away from a huge wall of dials and gauges. The wall was painted a light green, reminiscent of a power plant of some kind. I gave myself a command to move to a piece of equipment which would identify his job. I saw a round mechanism with a window in its top. The window was only an inch or two across. Small hairlike trails were being made back and forth within the area under the window. Each trail formed quickly and then faded away, only to be crisscrossed by other trails of the same kind. I recognized it as a Wilson cloud chamber, used in nuclear research and teaching. So, I concluded that the man in the lab coat had something to do with nuclear science.

I then moved back to the man and began accessing him mentally. He was thinking of two Arabic-looking men who had driven up outside his home in a late model sedan. The driver was standing outside the car with the door open and talking to him. The other man remained in the car on the passenger side. The Arabic-looking man was making promises to the lab-coated man. He promised new possessions, a new car, and a new place to live far from the lab-coated man's present home. The lab-coated man was to do something that would attract everyone's attention so the Arabic-looking man could get something accomplished without being seen.

I next moved back to the lab-coated man's workplace. He was doing something to a piece of equipment, then turned and walked casually out of the room. The session ended at that point.

The next day, each viewer announced the results of his/her session and put his/her credibility on the line. Would the things predicted actually happen over the weekend? One by one, we gave our predictions, each one duly noted by the new project manager. When it came my turn, I concluded that there would be a nuclear plant disaster that weekend. Everyone pointed out that I had jumped to that conclusion and that it would not, therefore, be accepted. We finally decided that I should predict that there would be something in the news over the weekend about a nuclear power plant, but that a prediction of a disaster was not warranted from the information that I had. We then went home for the weekend.

When the weekend was over, the new project manager brought in every local newspaper he had been able to get his hands on that weekend. Everyone went through the newspapers and found their stories. I searched through them all and did not find anything anywhere about a nuclear power plant. I had failed.

It was two days later that Jeanie, our secretary, entered with the news that sensors in Iceland had picked up elevated radiation levels in the atmosphere. They had investigated and found out that on April 26 (the previous Friday), the nuclear power plant in Chernobyl had had a massive meltdown. I went around the office bragging that I had predicted it, until the new project manager pointed out that I would still not get credit for the session. The task had been to predict what would be *in the newspapers that weekend*. The Chernobyl event was not in the papers.

"Well, it will be in the newspapers next weekend," I waffled. "I just got the wrong weekend, but I got the right prediction."

"Are you trying to teach me to accept excuses?" he asked.

Thinking about it, I agreed with him completely. I had predicted the Chernobyl disaster, but had not met the assigned task.

As for the two Arabic-looking men and the information that the whole disaster was planned and executed by someone, that part of it seemed to be a total miss. The Chernobyl disaster has always been listed as a mere accident.

But years later, while searching for information on the Internet, I learned that almost fifty tons of the original fuel at Chernobyl was missing. The following information comes from Russia's official Chernobyl Web page on the Internet.

MISSING FUEL MYSTERY

Scientists have been able to estimate the amounts of radioactive fuel blown into the atmosphere and into the remains of the Unit No. 4, but they leave about 10 to 50 tons of reactor fuel unaccounted for.

"Finding the missing fuel is an extremely important question for us—the nuclear safety of the [reactor] depends on it," says Edward Pazukhin, head of the ISTC's department of nuclear safety. Pazukhin says this because a growing pool of water in the bowels of the reactor may cause the remaining fuel to go critical.

It is thought that much of the missing fuel will be found in one of those rooms under the reactor. Scientists have drilled holes into the west wall of room number 307/2 through which probes measured heavy gamma radiation and a high neutron flux. They believe some of the missing fuel may be in that room.

So, this missing fuel mystery raises the question, for me at least, of whether the Chernobyl disaster was purely an accident. What if, I wonder, the world's worst nuclear meltdown were actually a diversion tactic that got out of hand?

LOCKERBIE, SCOTLAND

David Morehouse, in his book *Psychic Warrior,*[2] wrote about our involvement with Pan Am flight 103, which crashed into Lockerbie, Scotland, at 7:02 P.M. on December 21, 1988. The plane was on its way from Frankfurt via London toward New York at 31,000 feet, when it suddenly and violently blew up. The plane, or rather pieces of it, were scattered on the ground around the Scottish city of Lockerbie, but one large part of the plane crashed directly onto residential buildings in the city. Most people are not aware of just how extensive the damage to that airplane was. News coverage in the U.S. was extensive, but far from complete.

From the very beginning, investigators knew that the explosion could not have been caused by a simple malfunction. They suspected a terrorist attack of some kind; there had to be a bomb placed somewhere in the luggage compartment. The problem was to find and investigate every piece of luggage that had been loaded onto the plane. Beyond that, perhaps someone who loaded the plane had placed an unauthorized piece of luggage aboard. If so, the investigation of authorized luggage would lead them nowhere. The task the investigators faced was all but insurmountable.

Our remote viewing unit was asked, through proper channels, to assist. We were enlisted to help find the exact location of the bomb within the plane, and try to identify how it had been placed on board. Later we were asked to help find the perpetrator(s) involved.

What this amounted to for the remote viewers was basically to be on board the plane at the moment of the explosion, freeze time, and identify the location of the bomb within the plane. It was a very trying experience for all of us. As with many, if not most, of the operational targets within the session, we were given target information instead of proper frontloading. We went into session knowing that we would be viewing a site where, at the targeted moment, hundreds of people were to die violently.

Just as a car wreck can attract a lot of attention, so any extreme event at a target site, pleasant or horrible, will attract a remote viewer's attention away from a less emotion-laden aspect of the target. Here, we were tasked with finding and identifying a suitcase that was directly adjacent in time and space to one of the century's most horrible disasters. It is as though you were tasked to listen to a whisper at a rock concert. It makes for very difficult viewing.

More than once, during this series of viewings, viewers' attentions were drawn off target to the disaster and horror at hand. Because accessing people mentally comes easily for me, I was especially prone to being drawn off task. Within seconds of the explosion, there were spirits of people walking the aisles, wondering what had happened. The burning tongues of fire mixed with the blasts of icy cold wind coming from all sides to cause every sense organ to be in a state of total confusion and panic. For me, the pull of the people in need was too great, and it was virtually impossible to stay on task. Yet, I did manage to identify a pink "something" before getting pulled away.

I only worked a couple of sessions on this target. Other viewers in the unit worked many more. In the end, the unit as a group identified the proper baggage, described the perpetrators, and moved on to other assignments. But, for many, the lasting effects of the experience took many months to get over.

KEY WEST, FLORIDA

In the early 1990s, our unit was approached to work drug interdiction cases. We were to work with the very effective Joint Task Force Four out of Key West, Florida. This case was special, though. Instead of working in the ops building at Fort Meade, we would actually get to go to Key West for on-site work. We went in two shifts. In the first shift, Paul Smith, Angela Delany, and I went as guinea pigs, just to see whether or not a bunch of crazy psychics could handle the real-world demands of the drug interdiction business.

We reported to Joint Task Force Four headquarters at the U.S. Naval Air Station. We were given a very quick in-briefing and taken to meet the station's commanding officer. He had many questions to ask us about remote viewing, and what it could and could not do. Among those questions, he asked me, "Can you do evil with it?"

"Yes, sir," I answered. "But it's more likely that evil is a matter of interpretation than a definite value."

"Explain," he said.

"If we use it to save an American soldier's life, that is good. But if in doing so, we are responsible for the taking of an enemy's life, the question has to be whether it was evil or not. It would not be evil for us, but for the dead enemy's family and for his country, it would be seen as evil. In the long run, we have to be responsible to use this ability the best we can, and let good and evil sort themselves out."

The commander was not happy with this answer. He had wanted someone to tell him that it could definitely not be used for evil. But I had laid out the truth, and he decided to work with it.

He then asked for a demonstration. He had been briefed that Angela works differently from the way Paul and I do. She was not trained in CRV, so he requested that Paul and I do one session, and then have Angela do another. For these sessions, he had one of his staff officers choose targets.

Paul and I flipped a coin to see who would be the viewer. I lost the toss, so Paul viewed and I monitored him. We were given absolutely no information, not even coordinates. Paul began his session and found a location that was underground. He began describing the entrance to this location, and noticed a cleverly concealed portion of that entranceway that led to another underground location. Paul commented that this entrance was so cleverly hidden that it would not be visible to the people actually at the location. As monitor, I cued Paul with, "Describe the entranceway." He did. I then cued him with, "Now, move into the hidden location. Something should be visible." At that point, the officer who had made the target selection interrupted. "We can't go on with this."

The commander asked why not.

"The location he is describing is one that no one here has the clearance to know about," he answered. "I can't give any feedback without revealing above-top-secret information. I'll just say that Captain Smith not only found the targeted underground installation I had selected, but also quite a bit of material that he should not have found. We can't go on with this session."

The session ended with everyone who had attended the demonstration duly impressed.

Angela then worked a session where the target was a person. I was not privy to the feedback, but from what I understand from a later report, she did an excellent job, as well.

During that initial trip, Paul, Angela, and I had the opportunity to go out on a P3 Orion flight, which Joint Task Force Four uses for its surveillance missions. We were tasked to look out the windows as the plane flew over the ships in the Caribbean and tell the pilots whether or not a ship had drugs on it. The crew was a Naval Guard unit from New Jersey, consisting mainly of young boys. They were there for their two-week obligation during the summer.

The P3 Orion is equipped with several highly sensitive radars. Normally, for their flights, they fly at a fair height and use scopes to locate ships. They may then go to a lower altitude for a closer investigation, but only for identification purposes.

Once we left U.S. waters, the Joint Task Force Four officer who had accompanied us gave special orders to the pilot. Basically, he was to buzz the ships at extremely low altitudes so Paul, Angela, and I could "read" them for drugs.

Over the next few hours, the pilot buzzed one ship after another, barely skimming the masts, superstructures, and antennas. The young guardsmen hung on for dear life, and at one point, I looked over and saw one of them so wide-eyed he looked as though he had two pie plates on his face.

Ship by ship, we gave our feelings and they were recorded. I was surprised to find so many that had drugs of some kind, but on second look, almost all of them seemed to be more in the form of "private stashes" of crew members than the type of shipments that would interest Joint Task Force Four. Before the flight, I had suspected that our imaginations would run away with us, and we would find drugs everywhere. In fact, very few of the ships we buzzed gave us any impressions of such cargoes. I do not know how many of the leads we turned in were followed up on, but I do know that some busts were made because of our flight.

In fact, the first trip proved to be very successful overall. Angela, Paul, and I worked hard to make a good showing for the application of remote viewing toward this task, and the commanders and personnel of Joint Task Force Four were satisfied and impressed enough to authorize and fund another, more completely staffed mission.

The second trip to Key West included the other viewers from the unit. Linda, Robin, Greg Sloan, Paul, and I worked with the Joint Task Force Four people for the following month. There was also a brief mission with Joint Task Force Five in California. According to the final report of the overall project, we were directly responsible for the intercept and seizure of more than $82 million in drugs. The report also gave the estimate that our efforts, as good as they were, had not even made a dent in the amount of drug traffic that existed. The final evaluation was that we had proven the value of remote viewing for the problem, but that if we could not be stationed there as a permanent force, we were not of sufficient use. Joint Task Force Four wanted us down there as permanent personnel. But the Pentagon was unwilling to release us from our other duties.

MANUEL NORIEGA

In 1983, Panamanian general Manuel Noriega inherited the position of commander of the Panamanian Defense Forces from Gen. Omar Torrijos Herrera. In acquiring this position, Noriega became the de facto leader of Panama. A one-time operative for the U.S. Central Intelligence Agency, he was implicated in drug trafficking, the sale of U.S. secrets to Cuba, and other illegal activities. In January 1988, U.S. officials urged him to step down, but he refused.

Following the murder of a U.S. Marine on the streets of Panama City in December 1989, President George Bush ordered troops to Panama. A long and very involved stand-off ensued, with Noriega holed up in his home compound. Throughout this time, the remote viewing unit was tasked with tracking his movements throughout the compound, as well as the movements and activities of his troops around the country. We were also tasked with securing his plans and intentions so our intelligence effort could predict his actions and activities.

Finally, Noriega was captured and brought to the United States to stand trial. In April 1992, he was convicted on charges of racketeering, money laundering, and drug trafficking, and sentenced to forty years in prison. We were never apprised of how effective our intelligence was or of how much it influenced the decisions and activities of our decision makers. We only knew that, day after day, they retasked us for more information throughout the entire episode.

THE ROGUE U.S. DRUG AGENT

In 1989, the customs service was looking for Charles Jordan, one of its agents, who had been discovered engaging in drug trafficking. Jordan was on the run and everyone suspected that he was either in Mexico or was headed for South or Central America. When the tasking came in, the project officer at the time briefed us with the whole story. This was a severe breach of protocol, but was not unusual in real-world operational projects. We were to find Jordon's location. Two of the CRVers found him in Florida and two others found him in the Caribbean area. One of our non-CRV viewers predicted a location in northern Canada, and another non-CRV viewer, Angela, found him in Wyoming. Angela also said that there appeared to be an old Indian site nearby and that the phrase "Little America" was of great importance to locating and catching him.

The project manager for that project largely ignored her results and even mentioned them to some of the other viewers, so everyone could have a good laugh. This, too, was strictly against protocol. But even though he discounted the information she gave, he was still required to turn it over to the customer.

A couple of days later he would eat his own words. Customs officers arrested Charles Jordan in an RV park in Wyoming, near a historic Indian burial site. Jordan was about to pack up and leave the RV park and head for a rest stop/tourist trap named "Little America," about ten miles down the road.

Some years later, a debunker, working for the CIA to prove that the STAR GATE project should be disbanded, would insist that there was no evidence that anything either psychic or useful had taken place during this project.

THE DRUG TUNNEL

During the late 1980s, there were several murders of U.S. drug agents in Mexico. During this time, we were enlisted to gain information on these murders, on the murderers, and on the locations of the bodies, which were usually missing. In one case the project manager did not give us a heavy burden of information up front. We were only told that there was a building that the DEA was interested in. They wanted us to find out what was inside.

I went over to the operations building and did my session. I found a one-story building which, at one end, had a strange entryway into a lower area. I made a sketch of where the entrance was located within the building and how to find it. I could not find anything I would call a basement, yet I could clearly see that the entryway led downward. I followed through the entryway and found that it led to a long, low, and narrow room which was in darkness. Since there was no furniture or other accoutrements, I dismissed the room as unimportant and returned to the upper level, which seemed like a warehouse of some kind.

I was still bothered by the long, narrow room located underground. I noted that it led away from the building rather than being under the building, and that it seemed to be more of a passageway than a room. After reinvestigating it, I again could find nothing interesting in it, so again dismissed it. Near the end of the session, I realized that there was another building that should be looked at. It was also a one-story warehouse type structure, but the people working in it were speaking Spanish. I noted that it had an entrance to an underground area exactly like the other, but that it stretched out in the opposite direction.

David Morehouse, another viewer at the time, found the same underground room in the targeted building and had followed it to its far end. He had made sketches of a long tunnel with light fixtures evenly spaced along its length. He identified it as a means of getting people and goods from one place to another in secrecy. Other viewers also worked the target, but like myself, focused on the more active area in the building above. That was the tasking, so that is what we viewed. None of the other viewers located the underground entrance or the long, dark passageway.

In reality, the Drug Enforcement Agency was not interested in what was going on in the building they had tasked. Although they knew about the second building, they had not bothered to task us with it. Of all the information turned in, they were only interested in that portion of my session that located the entranceway to the tunnel and David's description of it.

As it turned out, the tunnel was a means of smuggling drugs and people between Mexico and the U.S. They had already identified and located the buildings. They suspected that there was a tunnel, but could not confirm it without getting agents onto the scene. What they needed was information that would allow them to raid the place quickly enough to prevent the destruction of the tunnel and any other evidence.

The information that the viewers had provided about the normal activities within the building served to let the DEA know that we were viewing the same building they had staked out. Acting on our information in conjunction with their other means of intelligence collection, they raided the place and stopped a major entry port of drugs and illegal immigrants into the U.S.

The following day, the *Washington Post* carried a picture of the tunnel and on seeing it, David grabbed his session, turned to the sketch he had made, and held it up to the photo on the front page. The match was uncanny.

We never got feedback from the DEA on the exact location of the entranceway within the structure, so our feedback came in the form of a newspaper article. Either way, the bust was a good one and one more avenue of drug trafficking had been closed.

COLOMBIAN DRUG LORDS

One after another, we were tasked with keeping track of the locations and activities of the Colombian drug lords. We were also tasked with locating and evaluating the operating efficiencies of their drug-production facilities. While we were able to gain a great deal of intelligence in these matters, we were rarely ever able to provide map coordinates to help the drug agents locate the facilities. The DEA would find the facilities on their own and then ask us for information on production amounts, types of drugs being manufactured, protection, number of personnel, and how the drugs were taken out to market. We were not as effective as we would like to have been in these operations, but we were used continually throughout the "war on drugs."

DESERT STORM

As a military intelligence unit, the bulk of our activities consisted of collecting intelligence on foreign military leaders, plans, and activities. Often we had to find out what types of activities went on within facilities photographed by aerial surveillance or "spy in the sky" satellites. "Walk-in" intelligence—that which comes from people who walk into intelligence offices around the globe and provide information voluntarily—would bring about investigations. Those investigations would often create more questions than answers. Many of those questions were brought to us.

Our unit was also tasked on many of the "minor" military events. When U.S. troops went into Grenada, we provided predictive maps, delineating where actions should be taken, and what series of events would unfold.

On several occasions, we were tasked to keep track of Khadafi's activities and locations. His dealings with terrorist organizations and with wanted international terrorists was a major concern of our customers, as were Libyan air and sea activities.

Perhaps the most intense military work we did was for Desert Storm. There was hardly a move made by Saddam Hussein and his troops that we had not predicted and passed up the chain of command the day before it happened. My major tasking throughout the war was to access Hussein and learn of his plans and intentions for the coming day.

In the daily process of accessing him, I learned one thing very quickly. He is not what I would call a "bad" man. He is absolutely what I would call a totally crazy man. His craziness, though, does not take the form of irrationality or erratic behavior. It stems from a delusional conviction on his part that God wants him to rule the world. He looks at the people and events that prevent him from doing that and is honestly confused that other people cannot understand what God wants. If God wants him to rule the world, then it simply must be, and it is his burden in life to make it so.

MEN IN BLACK

We had a mole in our unit. It took us years to find out who he was, but we did learn his name in the end. However, he was not a mole for a foreign power, but for another unit within our government with whom he was currying favor. They did not care so much about our day-to-day activities as about our individual strengths and weaknesses. To my knowledge, no one else in the unit had ever been approached by these people to provide that information, but evidently, he had, and he did.

One day I went to the Post Golf Course cafeteria for lunch. I noticed that some men in black suits came in right after me, and that they sat across the cafeteria from me as I ate. After working in the intelligence arena for years, you learn to spot the "men in black" (MIBs) from a great distance. Do you know how Jehovah's Witness missionaries are always spotlessly dressed and never have a hair out of place? The rule is often jokingly stated that if you see two men who look like Jehovah's Witness missionaries, and they are not carrying any literature, you are probably looking at two MIBs.

A word of explanation is due here. Most people think that the MIBs are aliens from the planet Zurkie, or something. They are not. They are specially trained agents who do both interrogation and investigation in a highly clandestine mode for many branches of the government. I have met them on several occasions, and even worked with them once. They are people like you and me, who have a job to do. Of course, if you are on the receiving end of that job, dealing with MIBs is not at all pleasant, but neither is it dangerous or threatening. They are there to ask questions. Just answer the questions and they will go away.

Anyway, I wondered what these two were doing there in the cafeteria, but I know enough to never ask or even appear curious about it. So, I kept my eyes on the TV program playing in the cafeteria and ignored them. When I finished my lunch and rose to leave, they rose, as well. I pretended not to notice, and went to dump my paper plate and trash. Without looking at them, I proceeded out the door and to the parking lot.

A moment later, as I approached my car, I heard one of them behind me. He said, "Sergeant Buchanan?" and opened the rear door of his black sedan, which just happened to be parked right beside mine. He stood there with the door open, not even motioning for me to get in. I got in. He went around the car and got in beside me. The other man then got into the driver's seat and drove us out of the parking lot. We cruised slowly around Fort Meade for a few minutes. Finally, the man beside me said, "We know that you have been developing Controlled Remote Influencing."

I did not answer immediately. Active mental work had been strictly outlawed in the unit, and I knew that I could lose my job, rank, and possibly even go to jail for having done any active mental work. Finally, I said, "Well, on my own time, but not in the unit."

"Your work has been progressing well," he stated, more than asked.

"Extremely well," I answered, "but I am doing it on my own time at home. It has nothing to do with the office." I acted somewhat indignant and challenged him: "So, how do you know about it?"

The MIBs are not known for their subtlety. He ignored my question and said, "We want you to kill Mikhail Gorbachev."

"No," I answered flatly without hesitation.

He sat and stared at me, waiting for me to qualify my statement. I sat and stared back at him, unflinching. There would be no argument or concession of any kind. He finally motioned to the driver, who took us back to the parking lot.

When we arrived, the man beside me got out. I reached to open my door and found that the inside door handle did not work. He came around the car and opened the door for me. I got out and stood there, waiting for some other instruction or comment. None was given. The man walked back to the front passenger side of the black sedan and opened the door.

"I'll tell you what I will do," I called to him. "I'll try to get Gorbachev to get rid of communism." He looked at me blankly, then got into the car beside the driver and they were quickly gone.

I was joking, of course. It was a stupid thing to say, but it did relieve the tension. However, throughout the afternoon, I got to thinking of how great an experiment that would be. I dismissed the idea, but over the next couple of weeks, it kept coming back to me. Finally, I decided to at least try it.

Over the next two and a half months, I worked repeatedly to instill the idea into Gorbachev's mind that communism was not working on many financial, social, military, and political levels. I used specific phrases that I had designed to access his subconscious mind, where they would have the most effect. But, after two and a half months of work, nothing happened, so I gave up and began working on other things.

I think that I was probably the most surprised person in the U.S. when Gorbachev made his famous speech that effectively ended Communist rule in Soviet Russia. Had I had some influence on his decision? I did not know. It took me another month, but I finally got a transcript of his speech and within it were all of the subliminal phrases I had been trying to pump into his subconscious during my sessions.

I have no grandiose illusions that I brought about the end of communism in Russia. Ending communism was a logical and intelligent thing to do at the time, and I truly believe that it would have happened, had I not been involved. But I still wonder: Did I just pave some subconscious pathways that allowed the thoughts to occur more easily? Just as I do not have the ability to say honestly that I did play a role in the process, I also cannot honestly say that I did not. I will always be left to wonder.

GET HUSSEIN

Some years later, I was again approached by the MIBs. Not the same two men, but obviously peas from the same pod. They approached me in much the same way as the first time, asking how my research was going, and then abruptly announcing that they wanted me to kill Saddam Hussein.

This time, I said, "No. I don't kill people. You guys tried to get me to do something like that to Gorbachev, and I refused then. Nothing has changed. I won't use what I am learning to kill anyone."

Again, I got a silent stare, as they waited for me to get uncomfortable and start talking. That is the beginning of compromise, as far as they are concerned. I thought of Saddam Hussein and the many evil things he was doing, and I realized that he really did need to be taken out by someone. But I was not that someone. I would not do it.

"I will tell you what I will do." I continued my line of thinking out loud. "I will make him sick to the point where it takes him out of leadership for a while. Other than that, I won't do anything for you."

They still sat in silence, staring at me. When I would not add anything further to what I had said, one of them asked, "When?"

"When do you want?" I threw the ball back into his court.

"In two weeks," he answered, after some hesitation.

"Will do," I said. The interview was over and within minutes, they were gone.

Two weeks from that day, I began working on making Hussein sick. Over the next nine or ten days, the press speculated that Hussein might be dead or injured, because he had not made any public appearances or given any orders that were traceable to him. Over that same period of time, I was also extremely sick, because of the work I was doing. Finally, after watching the news and seeing that nothing was apparently going to come of it, I decided to put an end to my work. I did not hear from the MIBs again after that, and have not heard from them to this day.

Once again, there is no proof or feedback that anything I did may have caused Saddam Hussein to be missing during those days. There are no reports to say whether he was sick or not, and if so, how sick he might have been. Therefore, I cannot with all honesty say that there was any connection between my work and his disappearance.

I only point up that such work could be a possible military mental intelligence tool. A very scary one. I would stress that I am adamantly against the use of mental control by any branch of the government, by any business, or by any individual person. I abhor it, and find it one of the most distasteful and freedom-robbing activities one person could do to another. But I would be remiss not to mention it because I personally feel that it is real.

The scientific techniques, methodology, and protocols of CRV are not toys. They were not developed to teach people how to do parlor tricks or "dog and pony shows." They are the real thing. Like any real, professional tool, they can become extremely dangerous and even destructive in the hands of amateurs. As the common admonition goes, "Don't try this at home."

"YOU'RE NOT GOING TO BELIEVE WHAT COMES NEXT!"

During one of the days when I was tasked to do a simple "plans and intentions" session on Saddam Hussein, I was working alone in the viewing room, without a monitor, when I thought I heard someone behind me say, "You're not going to believe what comes next!" I turned around quickly to find that, just as I had suspected, I was alone in the room. Though odd, I decided that it had been my own mind telling me something. In fact, its warning was to come true as soon as I resumed the session.

I viewed that Saddam Hussein had somehow gotten an American missile and had plans to fire into the high holy ceremonies during the feast of Ramadan, destroying the al Haram mosque in Mecca, as well as all the other leaders of the Arab world, who had come there to worship. That would leave him as the only Arab leader alive to lead a holy jihad against the evil Americans.

I could not believe that, so I started to scratch it all out and redo the session. No Arab leader would do such a thing. Yet, there was the information, just as the warning had said. I decided that, just in case it were true, I had to write it up.

When I turned in the summary of my session findings, the director's response was no surprise: "I can't believe that!" But he, too, sent it forward, just in case. The same thing happened a dozen times or more up the chain of command.

It was not until several years later that someone in an office I cannot disclose mentioned a ridiculous report they had once received from my unit, and began to relate the report I had turned in to the director. Not knowing that I had been the viewer, he said that this one report had sold him on our usefulness. "I couldn't believe it was true," he said, "there was no way it could have been true, but like all reports, it had to be checked out."

"So," I asked, "was it true?"

He looked at me very sharply, as though I had breached etiquette by asking. I could not resist. Since the day of that session, I had always wanted to know.

"Well, that single report averted a world war," he answered in a very guarded tone, and our conversation moved on to other things.

THE BURNING OIL FIELDS

Near the end of the Gulf War, we had predicted that Hussein would withdraw troops. A tasking came down asking which way the withdrawal should be funneled in order to be most effective. During my session, I sketched two maps and found that if the withdrawal were funneled in one direction, the oil fields would be set on fire, causing a horrible ecological disaster which would last for years to come. If, on the other hand, they funneled the withdrawal in the other direction, no such disaster would occur. Sure enough, over the next week or so, the withdrawing troops were funneled from the northeastern direction, and the oil fields were set ablaze. Unfortunately, this had been one of those hundreds of times when the customer looked at our work and decided not to listen to that crazy bunch of psychics.

NOTES

1. A complete record of the abduction and murder of Col. Rich Higgins is recounted in the book *Patriot Dreams: The Murder of Colonel Rich Higgins* by Robin Higgins, Hellgate Press, ISBN 1-55571-527-3.

2. *Psychic Warrior* by David Morehouse, St. Martin's Press, NY, ISBN: 0-312-14708-2.

FIVE

THE CIVILIAN
WORLD

One bad apple don't always spoil the whole barrel,
but it can sure make it smell like it.
                    —My grandfather, from whom I
                    learned much of my personal
                    philosophy

A number of people in this field are advertising to the civilian world that they teach the U.S. military's "highly classified" methodology of remote viewing. What they are really saying is that they do not know what they are talking about. Even more, they are showing that they don't even know that they are showing their ignorance and lack of homework. In reality, not a single one of the methodologies or protocols for remote viewing was ever classified. Only the governmental and military ties to those remote viewing methods were classified.

Because of other, non-CRV-related work I did, mainly centering around computers, the highest level of clearance I held, personally, was TOP SECRET/SIOP (ESI). ESI, or Extremely Sensitive Information, is information and material related to the Single Integrated Operational Plan (SIOP) for the conduct of nuclear war fighting operations. The other members of the remote viewing unit at Fort Meade held SECRET (SCI) clearances. The unit itself was a Special Access Program which was classified SECRET or SCI for Sensitive

Compartmented Information. SCI material requires special controls for restricted handling within compartmented intelligence systems for which code word compartmentation is established. Code words are selected in such a manner that the word used does not suggest the nature of its meaning.

The remote viewing unit at Fort Meade went under what were called project code names, but were actually nicknames, a combination of two separate unclassified words assigned an unclassified meaning employed only for unclassified administrative, morale, or public information purposes. These were SCANATE (one word, but it stood for Scan by Coordinates), GRILL FLAME, CENTER LANE, DRAGOON ABSORB (for a period of about two weeks), SUN STREAK, and STAR GATE. There were two other special project code names while I was there, but they have not been declassified, and are not to be included in this list. How many other special project names came before I arrived in the unit or after I left, I do not know.

In our particular unit, the Special Access Project access levels were:

Level 1: That the government was funding research into remote viewing science on the West Coast, at Stanford Research Institute, and was using it for actual operations on the East Coast, at Fort Meade, Maryland.

Level 2: The existence, location, purpose, personnel strength, assets, etc., of the unit.

Level 3: Names of its personnel, chain of command, code names, and other particulars that might allow anyone to zero in on any knowledgeable or participating individual. This is the information for which spies will bite the poison pill and die before releasing it to their enemies. Above all, you never tell the names of your fellow agents.

Level 4: The customers for whom the unit was working, the information the unit gathered for them, routes for handling that tasking and information, and any other intelligence items that might reveal information about the customers. Considered even more important than the lives of the individual agents, you always protect the customer, its name, and information about it, no matter what the cost. In many Special Access Projects, this information is considered to be so highly sensitive that it gets classification ratings over and above the project itself.

I hope this background information will help you understand the severity of incidents that followed one person's release from the unit under less than desirable circumstances. Let's call him Ted. Ted had been sent to Ingo Swann for CRV training by another military unit, and had only received partial training, dropping out of training after completing Stage 2 (the training we received included the first six CRV stages). Years later, he volunteered for an assignment to our unit and was accepted. When he arrived, as a captain, he was within a year of being eligible for promotion to major. To help him get the promotion, he needed to work in a personnel slot that required a major. One of the many positions I had been working at the time, training officer, was a major's position and suited the need perfectly, so he became the unit's training officer. I kept my position as the unit's trainer, but gave up the major's slot to him.

This man had a great personal interest in flying saucers, ETs, aliens, etc. During the early parts of his stay there, any time there was a lag in operations, he would begin giving us ET targets, supposed crash sites, and so forth. No one really objected as they were interesting targets, and certainly a relief from the *National Geographic* pictures we normally practiced with. We had no way of knowing when we got an ET site until after the sessions were over, because all we were given were coordinates. The problem was that our efficiency reports needed to reflect our success rates, and as long as we were doing targets that had no feedback, we could not score the outcomes, so we could not show that we were doing anything.

When we asked to have the ET targets stopped, he continued to give them to us. At one point, we approached the director about the problem and the director gave him the direct order to stop using such targets. He complied for a few weeks, and then instituted what he called "advanced training." His advanced training was nothing more than more UFO crashes, ET colonies on other worlds, Galactic Council meetings, and so forth. When the viewers finally rose up in anger and gave an ultimatum, that kind of targeting finally stopped. This had lasted about two or three months, but today, that man is out in the civilian world telling everyone how he ran the unit and had "his viewers" do advanced training on "esoteric targets."

I was at his house one day shortly after his release from our unit, helping him move, when he swore to me that he would kill the unit and everyone in it, if it was the last thing he ever did. I remarked that he had many friends in the unit, and that maybe he should consider a little leeway in that statement. He assured me that he meant what he said.

On leaving the service, Ted formed a remote viewing company. Many people have formed companies based on the fact that psychic information is helpful to business and individuals and there was nothing at all wrong with Ted doing that. But he started advertising his very classified ties to the military remote viewing unit in order to further his company's growth. In doing so, he revealed to the world at large that the unit existed. That, in and of itself, was a breach of security and was illegal. In his declarations to the press, he also provided Level 3 and Level 4 information, giving viewer names and customer names, as well. Many of these things are still classified today.

When I challenged him a year or so later on his actions, he simply laughed and said that if the government did anything about it, it would be the equivalent of an admission that they had a psychic spying unit, and it would only prove him right. He knew that the government would never admit to such a thing, so he felt very secure in what he was doing.

Before Ted began committing these breaches of security, he had called on many military remote viewers for help for his company. I was one of these people. However, we had agreed to work for him in total secrecy. The very day he began revealing classified information, most of us severed ties with him. A couple of the unit's remote viewers continued with him for a time, but within a year, they had turned their backs on him as well.

Ted called me one day after I had retired from service and asked me to come to work for him. He wanted to hire me to be the training director of his company. I refused. Over the next few months, he continued to call me, urging me to quit my job in the D.C. area and come to Albuquerque to work for him.

I repeatedly told him that I would not work for him. After months of such calls, he told me that his company would fold if he did not have me as his training officer. "I'm sorry," I answered. "I might work *with* you, where I will have the right to refuse any work that might violate security problems, but I will never work *for* you." He hung up the phone. Ever since then he has treated me as his mortal enemy.

Ted then turned to the few students he had managed to train. One of his students, in whom he had great hopes, also turned away from him. After a nine-day course with Ted, this same student wrote a book and started a remote viewing institute of his own. I happened to meet this student when I gave a lecture in his home town. He invited me to his office to see the draft of the book he was about to publish. The first chapter of that book was little more than a list of all the viewers of the unit, their names and where they lived, and a list of the customers for whom the military unit had worked. You must understand that, at the time, everything about the military unit was still totally classified. You should understand, too, that there were units in other countries, Russia especially, that did not practice psychic spying as much as psychic influencing and control. Had this information fallen into their hands, every member of the unit would have become a target for them. In other words, this was the equivalent of an attempt on his part to actually "kill the unit and everyone in it."

"Where did you get this information?" I asked in astonishment.

"Ted gave it to me and told me to put it in the book," he answered.

"But this is all highly classified information!" I challenged.

He thought it would help sell the book. I told him it would probably get the book confiscated.

He understood and spent the rest of the afternoon shredding and destroying every hard copy and electronic copy of the first chapter.

Within the unit, there had been a great amount of turmoil about Ted's actions, yet there was nothing to do. Ted had been right that if the government acted on it, it would give his statements legitimacy. If the government denied it, it would convince people that he had been telling the truth. The government took the best solution to the problem and just kept quiet.

On September 6, 1995, the CIA issued a public letter alerting the public to the existence of our remote viewing unit. It drew the attention of newspaper reporters across the nation. The press had a field day with it. It was the CIA's first official admission that it had been involved in parapsychological work.

6 September 1995

As Mandated by Congress, CIA is reviewing available information and past research programs concerning parapsychological phenomena, mainly "remote viewing," to determine whether they might have any utility for intelligence collection.

- CIA sponsored research on this subject in the 1970s.

- At that time, the program—always considered speculative and controversial—was determined to be unpromising.

- CIA is also in the process of declassifying the program's history.

We expect to complete the current review this autumn and to make a recommendation regarding any future work by the U.S. intelligence community in this area.

A decade before the 1995 AIR (American Institute of Research) investigation of STAR GATE, in 1984, the CIA had requested the National Academy of Sciences' National Research Council to evaluate the remote viewing program for the Army Research Institute. The results were unfavorable. This study, called the "NRC Report," was basically a whitewash to quell the public notion that such a subject could be used by the government for any real purpose. Project CENTER LANE was, at that time, closed down for all to see. In reality, the name had simply changed to SUN STREAK and the project proceeded normally in continued secrecy, with everyone thinking that it had gone away.

I strongly believe that the CIA's public statement in 1995 was not a planned end product of the AIR report, but was, instead, a direct reaction to the public inquiries generated by Ted's persistent public revelations. Oddly enough, in spite of the treason and treachery this man committed, we owe the present public awareness of both the military history and the technology of remote viewing to him. That does not excuse what he did, but it was because of Ted, alone, that the public at large became aware of CRV.

SIX

REACTIONS

*There are two sorts of curiosity—the
momentary and the permanent. The momentary
is concerned with the odd appearance on the
surface of things. The permanent is attracted by
the amazing and consecutive life that flows on
beneath the surface of things.*

—Robert Lynd,
Solomon in All His Glory

The people involved in the military's remote viewing project were real people and the job they had was pretty much filled with the same stresses other jobs have. Political and financial problems and all the other aspects of the modern workplace were just as much a part of our daily lives as any other worker in any other office. It was a workplace strongly influenced by the government and military, but it was a human workplace nonetheless.

The human side of the story probably has more anecdotes and tales—often much spicier—than the mission-oriented side. Some of these stories originated in secret meetings in dark corners and dimly lit rooms and corridors, but many originated from simple everyday interaction with military and government employees around whom we served. The most amusing and interesting personal stories, though, generally came from our own personal reactions to CRV, as we grew into more proficient viewers, and the reactions of people outside our group, if and when they ever found out about us.

And find out they did, as I learned at the farewell luncheon from my old unit in Augsburg, Germany. I had been very careful to keep secret any details of where I was being assigned and what I would be doing. For one thing, I wasn't sure I was being told the truth, myself. I was fairly certain that General Stubblebine had not said anything to anyone, after all the secrecy that had gone toward getting me into the project. At the luncheon, friends rose to roast me one by one. They made fun of computer programs that had not worked properly, of the days when I had come to work without my security badge and had borrowed a bicycle to ride the ten miles back home to get it. They laughed about how the really stupid things I had done had made them all want to be members of Mensa, as I was, so they could do really stupid things, too.

As the last person finished speaking, he said something to the effect of how I would now need to turn in my computer, and finally start using my brain, instead. "Or should I say, your psychic abilities?" The room suddenly went quiet. I could feel the blood rush into my face and then the room erupted in laughter. I should have known that in the intelligence field, there are no secrets.

Even when we were standing in the parking lot of the guest house, waiting for our new assignment, I still had suspicions in the back of my mind that this was possibly not real. Perhaps I had only been given a cover story and would really be doing something else. Or all this had to be some sort of huge and elaborate joke, and Alan Funt would step out any minute to announce that we should "Smile! You're on *Candid Camera!*" My personal reaction when I actually got into the unit and learned that it was for real was one of relief. I hadn't dragged my family halfway around the world for nothing.

When I arrived at Fort Meade in 1984, the unit really had no provision for enlisted personnel. Everyone else in the unit was an officer. They were assigned to a classified military personnel system that deals with specially assigned intelligence officers. It keeps the personnel records of those in "black" projects out of the normal reporting channels. For all intents and purposes, these people stop existing.

That was not the case for the enlisted. For me, the system was much more ill equipped and chaotic. I was assigned to a local military unit which would be responsible for me in name only, would carry me on its records, would give me great personnel efficiency ratings, and otherwise would never see me or even know who or where I was. That way, whenever I came out of the black project, I would have great reports in my personnel file, a ready-made fake history, and proof of my time in grade for promotions and awards. The fact that I could only get the promotions and awards under very unusual circumstances while in the black project would at least not affect my ability to get them after I left it.

Military units hate carrying these kinds of records, because they have only so many slots for personnel, and when a slot is taken up for some intelligence agent, it means one fewer worker for them. When we come out of the black projects, we may have the records and the qualifications to catch up on promotions, awards, etc., but the unit has had several years of being short staffed, and has nothing to show for it.

I was officially assigned to the 902nd Military Intelligence Battalion. For all general purposes, the 902nd was stuck with me. They kept my personnel records in their files, counted me against their personnel strength, but never had the benefit of using me for any actual work. I never went there, never stood formations or inspections, never pulled KP or guard duty or shared the responsibility on any other duty rosters. The 902nd, being an intelligence unit, often gets stuck with such people, so they were accustomed to handling and dealing with such records. In this respect, they were a sort of a catchall for those personnel whose job titles might euphemistically be labeled "miscellaneous."

After I reported to the CRV unit, my personnel records were then sent over to the 902nd by interoffice mail. I figured that once they had filed my folder away, they had quickly forgotten that I was even there. But I was to find out one day that I was wrong.

Not long after I entered the CRV unit, I needed to set up an allotment from my monthly paycheck. All personnel matters were normally done through Jeanie, our secretary, but she was on vacation for several weeks. No problem, I thought, I'll just go over to the 902nd and take care of the paperwork myself.

I entered the orderly room wearing civilian clothes instead of a military uniform; we always wore "civvies" in the CRV unit. I stood for a moment, waiting to catch a clerk's eye, and finally one of the women asked if she could help. I told her that I needed to change my allotments, and that I would need a blank allotment form. She looked at me and decided against it.

It gave me an almost comfortable, nostalgic feeling to know that the army had not changed its first rule of Personnel Actions: If it is something the soldier wants, the answer is always "No."

"I'm sorry, sir," she said, "but you'll need to go to your own unit to get one."

"This is my unit," I replied.

She gave me a look that had a tinge of pity for all imbeciles everywhere, and said, "No, sir. This is Headquarters, 902nd. These buildings all look alike. It's easy to get lost." She pulled a telephone book from a top drawer. "What is your unit, sir? I can call them for you."

"The 902nd. This is my unit," I repeated.

Somewhat agitated now, she said, "Well . . . sir, I know everyone in this unit." She looked at my business suit with a bit of contempt and continued, "Both uniformed and plainclothes. Are you sure you want the 902nd?"

"Yes. This is my unit."

"Are you just reporting in?" she asked.

"No, I've been in the unit for several months."

"Sir, I don't know you. What's your name?"

"Buchanan. SFC Leonard Buchanan."

"Well, Sergeant Buchanan, I don't think—" She was interrupted by the clerk in the next cubicle whose eyes had suddenly appeared over the partition.

"Buchanan!" the other clerk said. Her hand appeared over the partition and pointed toward one of the closed and locked safes.

The clerk with whom I had been speaking looked over at the safe in question, then snapped back toward me, wide-eyed. She sat frozen for a moment. Then, as though spring-loaded, she jumped out of her chair and actually ran over to the rack of blank forms. She returned, however, as though wading upstream, and finally, from full arm's length, holding the paper between her thumb and one finger by only the smallest grip on one corner, handed me the blank allotment request form. Her eyes were focused on her desktop, as though to keep from looking into my voodoo eyes and getting some kind of double whammy.

"Thank you," I said, and took the paper. She stood there keeping her eyes averted and would not answer, so I left without further talk. As I closed the door behind me, I quickly glanced back into the office to see ten or twelve pairs of eyes peering furtively over partitions, watching me leave. When I quickly looked into the office, the eyes all disappeared back behind partitions and she was left standing alone at her desk like a deer caught in the headlights, the look on her face saying that she had just had the narrowest escape of her life.

I returned to our office and asked what the people at the 902nd thought we did. I was told that they were not supposed to know, but that all kinds of rumors had gone around up there. Nothing was confirmed or denied, so it was pretty well left to the wildest things they could imagine. "They know that we do things with our minds," Bill answered. Then, with a grin, he added: "They think we do things with other people's minds, too."

THE PRESS

A year or so prior to the CIA's revelation in late 1995, Ted, the man referred to earlier, had been eagerly seeking out media people to tell his story. He had not been one of the unit's viewers. In fact, he had been one of the lower administrative officers in the unit. But, somehow, in his mind, his importance to the unit had grown drastically with the retelling. In his version, he was the leader of the unit, briefed the president about psychic intelligence information on a regular basis, trained all the viewers, and virtually did everything important that was ever done in the unit.

At one point, he hired a book written about his grandiose exploits, and in its original version, it even said that he often corrected Ingo Swann on finer points of remote viewing, and that Ingo thanked him profusely and humbly for the wisdom he provided. In the end, the writer he had hired began learning the truth, and scrapped the story. The book was a pure flight of fantasy, and never made it into print. If it had, the public's view of the remote viewing project would have been one of disdain and ridicule.

TELEVISION

Not too long after I retired, and while the project was still classified, I was contacted by the *20/20* television show. The interviewer wanted to know whether or not I was a remote viewer. I confirmed that I was, in fact, a remote viewer. She then wanted to know whether I had done any remote viewing while I was in the army.

"I won't fall for a question like that," I answered. "You ask whether or not I did any remote viewing *while I was in* the army, and if I were to say yes, you would twist that and say that I did remote viewing *for* the army. Then you'll twist it further and tell people that I said the army was into remote viewing. Well, I worked on my car on weekends *while in* the army. Are you going to tell everyone that the army is into clandestine auto repair?"

After a long bout of verbal fencing, she realized that she would get nowhere along those lines, so she then promised that *20/20* really did not care about that anyway. They only wanted to know more about remote viewing. She proposed that I work with some other remote viewers on a "dead case" project for the Baltimore County Police Department.

I made certain she understood that people with security clearances are very leery of the press. I warned her that if she attacked and tried to pull any hard-nosed investigative reporting tricks on me, it would be the end of the interview, and that we had ways of screwing up an interview so it would be unusable.

She agreed and once again assured me that they were not interested in the military aspect of remote viewing, but only what it could do for the police. Under those circumstances, and those circumstances alone, I agreed to help with the police case, and to appear on the show.

When the day came to meet in Baltimore, Dave Morehouse, Mel Riley, and I showed up for the police project. She had done her homework well. We went through our individual sessions dealing with different aspects of a murder case. Afterwards, we compared the results with the investigating officer. He was extremely satisfied and even excited at the information we provided. Dave had given a detailed series of events about the murder, complete with maps, with areas marked that were new to the investigation. Mel and I were tasked with finding the missing person's car and any weapon that was used. After the sessions, Mel and I laid our maps on the table, and realized that one edge of the map I had drawn matched lines exactly with the edges of the map he and Dave had drawn. Together, we had generated three parts of a single map of the location.

Then, the woman from *20/20* interviewed us individually, not allowing any of us to witness the other's interview. She said that it was for purity of content. When she came to me, I sat down in front of the camera. She logged in my name as it would appear on the show, and let me know that she would be asking the questions, but that on the final version, it would appear that Lynn Sherer was conducting the interview.

"How long have you been remote viewing?" was her first question.

"About eight years," I answered.

She continued, "Where did you learn to do remote viewing?"

First of all, it was a dumb question. If she wanted to establish the military connection, all she had to ask was, "How long have you been out of the army?" and the answer of "About a year" would have conveyed the proper information.

"I learned it from friends," I said. It was true. The other people in the unit were my friends.

That answer made her angry. The next question out of her mouth was flaming and direct. "Did you remote view the inside of Noriega's home on direct orders of the U.S. government?"

The question and its abruptness took me aback. "No," I lied. Actually, I had done extensive work on that case. I then realized that the stock answer for all such questions would have been best. I should have answered, "I am not an authorized spokesman for the U.S. government. If you want to know about governmental orders, you will have to ask a spokesman for the government." But, it was too late. I had lied. I tried not to show any facial expressions, knowing that such things are often used by the show to get across what they want to say. I sat and smiled blandly at her, as though waiting for another question.

Like I said, she had done her homework, and the answer I gave made her furious. She very quickly ended the interview. Later, off camera, she approached me in a huff and accused me of lying. "Like you lied to me, you mean?" I answered, and walked away.

The week that segment was to air on *20/20*, Christopher Reeve had a horseback riding accident, paralyzing him, and the entire show was dedicated to that. I had reported the *20/20* interview up the chain of command, and the segment we did never aired.

When the story about the "CIA-sponsored project" finally surfaced in the popular press in late 1995, the official policy remained "Leave it to their imaginations." The problem was, of course, the press. The press had a field day, splashing headlines around that had no relationship at all to any real facts. Probably the most flagrant violator of any rules about "truth in print" or "check your facts first" was the *Washington Post*, the newspaper closest to the information. They, like many other newspapers around the nation, immediately went out and got interviews with any local psychics they could dredge up. These people knew nothing about the project, but many of them claimed to be working for the government secretly. Some claimed that remote viewing is a natural talent, so no scientific method would ever work within the field of parapsychology. Some suggested that the whole thing was a giant hoax to hide something more evil the CIA was surely doing. Not a single story was accurate.

As a side note along this line, there was a columnist for the *Washington Post* named Jack Anderson. He was nationally syndicated. He had, for several years, beaten the bushes around Washington to find just this story. He knew that the military had such a project, but had not been able to find out anything about it. It was one of his major goals to crack this case. It is a tribute to the security practices we had that his lead writer was married to one of the members of our team—and did not even know that the answer to the story Jack Anderson was so eager to get was right there in her own home.

Once the CIA revealed the project's existence, Ted, the rogue agent who had tried to blow our cover, now had an audience. He began making even more noise, in hopes of making more news, but the press quickly grew bored with the story and was only interested for a short period of time.

Ted appeared repeatedly on Art Bell, who reminds his audience that the show is for entertainment purposes only. Nonetheless, this man's claims have been such an embarrassment to the other project members that many people now believe that the CIA hired him to make a shambles of the story, just so no one would ever take the project or any of us seriously.

When all the hoopla finally died down, some serious news investigators began to delve more deeply into the real story. They found some ex-military viewers who were willing to talk, and began connecting the dots and piecing together valid information.

A couple of ex-military viewers wanted to tell their personal stories. Those project people have "come out" and revealed their parts in the project's history, as they remember it. They do so in small lectures, short interviews, and articles and books much like this one. Today, the interesting stories lie not with the viewers, but with the public's reaction to them.

The public's reaction, upon hearing the stories of the military's CRV unit, have ranged from totally unconcerned to enthusiastic to violently antagonistic.

I have a huge file of letters, E-mail, and phone notes from people who have been overwhelmingly enthusiastic and supportive of the military's effort, and of the efforts of all the military-trained CRVers who are now working in the civilian arena. I also have a huge file of very serious death threats against me, my family, my dog, and my cat. There is an alarming number of people in the world who honestly believe that "the government" (whom they can now identify as me, since they finally have a name to stick the blame to) has been invading their minds, destroying their lives through psychic means, spying on them psychically, etc. I have received calls and letters from people demanding to know why I destroyed their children's minds by "boring into their psyche and eating out all the good brains." Callers have blamed me for causing cancer, herpes, crooked feet, and ruined marital relationships. I have been accused of doing these things as a "minion for the government overlords," as a "turncoat against Humanity." I have been blamed as a "Human deserter to the Alien cause," as one who did these horrible things out of service to the "Betazoids from Zeta Reticuli."

I do not know these accusers from Adam, but they somehow feel that I have been in their minds, causing every ill they have ever had in their lives, and they want it stopped. They want me stopped. In the beginning, I got two or three death threats a week. Now, I only get about one a month. I have learned to file them away; in case something ever does happen to me, there will be a list of suspects to investigate. I feel very sorry for these people, but I have learned the hard way that any attempt to reason with them or deal with their mental situations only makes things worse. For the most part, I ignore them and get on with my life.

The religious reaction has been just as single-minded. I have received calls, E-mail, and letters from concerned people who want to help save my soul from Satan and "return me to the Straight Way." Early on, I tried to explain to these people that there was nothing in CRV that is against God or anything in the Bible. I tried explaining that I am a Christian, attend church, and even help teach Sunday school. But my words repeatedly fell on deaf ears and closed minds. At one time, after all this became declassified, a Jehovah's Witness missionary was at the door and asked me what I did for a living. I decided to tell him, just to see his reaction. Big mistake. From that point on, I got visits every couple of weeks. Each time, he would bring another new missionary with him. One day, I was in a grocery store, and one of the new missionaries asked to speak to me in private about the remote viewing. She was actually interested, and honestly wanted to know more about it. She had had psychic events in her life, and had felt that they were not evil, but her church said that they were, and she wanted to have an honest, unbiased opinion on the matter. In our conversation, she revealed that the missionary who came by every few weeks always brought a new missionary with him to show them that Satan can seem like a nice person— one you would not suspect of being evil from talking to him. He was bringing each new missionary by my house to show them the face of the Devil incarnate.

But the largest public reaction, by far, has been virtually no reaction at all. The average Joe is generally unconcerned with anything the government does. He expects the government to waste money on stupid pursuits. He also knows that there is not a damned thing he can do about it. The story of how "The CIA Spent 20 Million Dollars Using Psychics" was just another in a long series of news items about how the government squanders our hard earned tax dollars. It is like the story of the large grants used for saving an endangered toad, the $20 million toilet for the NASA space shuttle, or the $600 wrench for the Pentagon. The reaction was a disgruntled "Typical!" followed by the person getting on with his/her life.

But some reactions made it all worthwhile. Some people are curious about psychic phenomena, are neither believers nor disbelievers, and honestly want to know more about it. Surprisingly, though, there has been an entire range of reactions even within this group.

A few react with, "That's good! It's about time." They feel a sense of relief that the phenomenon has finally gotten its just recognition.

Just as many react with, "That's not good! Mankind isn't ready for this yet." Or they have some other fear or sense of danger that we are getting into something we aren't mentally ready for. This is the "messing with God" syndrome.

Naturally, a good number of people have reacted from their suspicions of the government. "So, now the government's even taking over our minds!" This stems from a vague and often justified feeling that anything the government is involved in can't be all good. There is always a sense of helplessness and hopelessness in the voices of people who have this reaction.

The suspicion shows up in other ways, as well. "It must work! No wonder they tried to hide it all these years." These people have a negative sense of having been cheated out of valuable knowledge which should have been made available to the public.

The same reaction can show up in a slightly different way, as well. "It must not work at all. No wonder they tried to hide it all these years." This reaction seems to always carry with it a positive sense of satisfaction that the government has finally been exposed for hiding its mistakes. Many of these people are also satisfied that with the government's hiding of the project, the ridiculous belief in psychic phenomena has finally been exposed for the sham it is.

Some have faith that where there is smoke, there just may be some fire. "With all that money put into it, something must have been learned." These people react with interest in the hope that the expenditure of so large an amount of money must surely have proven either the value or nonvalue of psychic applications.

Others have just the opposite reaction when they learn about the expenditures. "With all that money put into it, they probably still don't know anything because they're the stupid government!" These people see the project and expenditures on it from the viewpoint of unshakable pessimism. For them, any expenditure, if done by the government, is simply pouring good money after bad.

Some people add their frustration at the waste and stupidity they have seen in government, as well as what they perceive as an inability to do anything about it. "With all that money they wasted, they probably still don't know any more than I could have told them long ago." This group includes those people who feel that they know everything there is to know about "being psychic." They feel any such study should have included their expertise. Anything else is a waste of time, money, and effort. Over these years, I have learned that the egos of these people are insurmountable, and believe it or not, these believers in psychic phenomena have usually proven to be the most stubbornly antagonistic group of people in the public sector. They are even harder to deal with than flagrant and belligerent "debunkers."

Fortunately, though, this coin also has another side. I have also met a large number of nonegotistical, nonviolent, nonpushy "practicing psychics." This category includes people who are quietly working for police departments, stock brokers, or other corporate customers. Honesty and accuracy are the yardsticks by which their work is measured. Bravado and posturing are not a part of their lives or practice. I have a very strong respect for these people.

One evening, near the end of a radio talk show where some of us were being interviewed, a caller identified herself as Bevy Jaegers, and claimed to have been one of the CIA's original psychics. "Oh, no!" I thought. "Another crank." But subsequent conversations proved to me that she is one of these very valid and honest people. She was the daughter of a policeman and has had a long history of psychic events in her life. She decided to use her talents to help police departments, so she organized and ran a group of psychics, many of whom she trained herself. They work for police departments, never asking for or accepting payment, publicity, or credit. Her group is called the U.S. Psi Squad. Its record of successes is quite impressive, but it remains virtually unknown as it works quietly behind the scenes to do good in the world. Very few people have impressed me as much as Bevy and her group.[1]

On the other end of the spectrum are the more vociferous groups which include the people who wear robes and beads and will tell your fortune in the front parlor of their home "for a paltry fee." These people have been very strongly affected by the public revelation that psychic phenomena can be reduced to a science and learned by anyone. I have not met a single one of them who has not felt that his or her livelihood is very threatened, or who has not begun making all manner of false claims. Some have lied that they were a part of the project. Some make claims that the whole science revolved around their vast knowledge and talent. One and all, they have either condemned the scientific work or tried in vain to align themselves with it.

The worst of these are the 1-900 number "psychic hot lines," and gurus who are willing to take over your lives (and your money). The extremes of this group are the equivalent of the Crazy Harry's Used Cars of the automotive world. They live on the principles of the old poem:

> *He who has a thing to sell*
> *And goes and whispers in a well*
> *Is not as apt to get the dollars*
> *As he who climbs a tree and hollers.*
>
> —Author unknown, found on
a sugar packet in a restaurant

Some of these people claimed to be members of the military's remote viewing project. Others claimed that they were "consulted." And still others said they were asked to join the project but refused.

Not long after Bevy Jaegers's death, someone wrote to the U.S. Psi Squad and volunteered to come in and be a guiding authority with the work they do. In his letter, he said that he had been a member of STAR GATE at Fort Meade, and that he had been the trainer for the unit, as well. Not a single item of what he said in his letter had even the smallest amount of truth to it. Yet, he was more than willing to pass himself off as the expert, in the wake of their loss.

There was another outstanding example of the same type. While still in the unit, I learned that there was a Psychic SIG (Special Interest Group) within Mensa in the local Baltimore area. I decided to attend a meeting just to see what it was like. Most Mensa meetings are of the very highest quality, very friendly and outgoing, and there was no reason to suspect that this meeting would be any different. I arrived a little late at the home of the person who regularly held the Psychic SIG meetings, to find a single man positioned in a chair of authority in a semicircle of about ten women. One of the women was sitting on the floor at the man's feet. This woman was a slightly retarded person who waited on the man hand and foot during the meeting, jumping and getting him drinks whenever he wanted, but serving no one else. The man was espousing *his* mastery of psychic powers and claimed several times how the government had asked him to work for them. But, he said, he had been so good that he had scared the politicians witless, and they were afraid of his astounding personal powers. The women were listening attentively to his every word. I took a place among the semicircle of women and listened for a bit to his cryptic, self-serving explanations.

"Everything which is unknowable is known to us all," he told us. "It is our ignorance which is our knowledge." At another point he told us that "access to the infinite is what limits us." And so it continued with such contradictory platitudes and psychobabble for over half an hour. No one else in the group was allowed to speak.

I finally asked a question about what the group did in order to make use of this talent, and his answer was a very smug, "They come to hear me discuss it."

As the "meeting" went on, I asked a few more questions, each causing more irritation and hostility on his part, until I finally said that I had a long drive home and had to be going. He said, very dismissively, "Do be sure to come back some time."

"I doubt I will be able to," I replied. "It is a long drive for me, and besides, I thought you might actually do something here."

With a dismissive wave of the back of his hand toward me, he turned his attention back to the women and continued espousing his personal glory. He continued to amaze the all-attentive women except for one, who accompanied me to the door. She was both embarrassed and apologetic and asked whether she could speak to me some time about psychic phenomenon, as this was the only place she had found so far to discuss it, and she was not at all pleased with the situation. Being still in the unit, I did not want further contact with anyone in the public, so I told her that I would enjoy that, and then left without giving her any contact information. This was my first experience with the "psychics" of the civilian world. To be honest, it both scared and disappointed me. I have been glad to learn since that not everyone out here in the civilian world is that way.

Backing off from those unpleasant extremes, another reaction to news that such a unit existed has been that of mild to strong envy, both of the desirous and sour grapes kind. Some have gotten almost starry eyes at the prospect of doing such work and said, "It's a shame I wasn't a member of the project. I would have loved it." I assure them that they would have. They always ask whether or not there is still such a project, and if so, how they can get to be members of it. They are also interested in what it takes to be a member. "How did they decide who to pick for that project? I wonder if I could qualify."

Others react very defensively. "I'm glad I wasn't involved with any-thing like that. The controls and restrictions [or misuse, lack of under-standing, etc.] would have been intolerable for my free spirit." I assure them that they are right, as well.

There is also a deep-seated belief that nothing of this nature can be used for evil, and the military is one thing they perceive as such. "I pity the people who were involved there. You just can't use the talent for things like that!" The phrase "things like that" is, of course, undefined and left to the imagination, but generally implies the murder of troops, war in general, espionage, and all the myriad other sins of the military-industrial complex.

Then, there are the more practical types who say, "I wonder if they learned anything that can help me become better at what I do." I always love to meet this type of person. They are open to discussions, willing to learn, and I have found that many times, I have learned a lot from them as well. As contradictory as it may sound, you can find within the New Age community some of the most closed-minded people in the world. Somewhere between being open to all kinds of new experiences and ideas and becoming set in their own personal cosmologies—complete with a need to make everyone else believe the same—something hap-pens.

Not surprisingly, there is another parallel group of people who have almost the same exact range of reactions as psychics do. Yet, these peo-ple are not usually related to the field of parapsychology at all. These are scientists and researchers. The majority of them have their own scien-tific goals and interests, and simply do not care. Those who do take no-tice fall into roughly the same categories as above. One would not think that the strict and "left-brained" scientists and the free-thinking "right-brainers" would be so much alike. In reality, they are.

That is especially true when interested researchers learn that more than 75 percent of that $20 million funding went for research and not for operations. That is correct. Of the $20 million spent on the project, almost $15 million went to the West Coast for research. The military unit existed for more than twenty-four years on a budget of around $5 million dollars. In Washington, that is barely coffee-fund money.

Reactions from interested scientists to the funding information ranges widely as well. Resentment and frustration cause some to say, "Why do they give money for that and not for my study of toads?" I have heard very few have a reaction that does not have an eye for government money. Many come right out and ask, "How do I get my reputation linked with that? I want grant money, too."

A large number of scientists, though, cut right to the heart of science and ask the more practical question, "How do I get the data from those studies?" I cannot tell you how much respect I have for a scientist or researcher when this is their first reaction.

Some people in the public sector, though, have reacted violently. As I said above, much of this violence is directed not at the government, but at the members of the project, whose names are now becoming known.

By far, the most interesting reactions have come neither from the scientists nor from the two sides of the war camp of believers vs. nonbelievers. The most interesting reactions have come from those who live their lives on a constant diet of conspiracy theories. This type of person generally holds one or more of three major beliefs:

"The people who are 'coming out' are telling the truth, finally, and the government, being embarrassed about it, has started a campaign of lies as a cover-up." They feel that the CIA's announcement that the psychics were virtually useless was obviously a ploy to denigrate the value of the project. This much, by the way, I will vouch for as being true. But because of this belief, many of these same conspiracy people feel that the project personnel who are "coming out" are heroes, to be worried about and protected from the inevitable destruction the evil government will surely bring down upon them in its revenge. I will speak of this elsewhere in this book, but the bottom line is that such a belief has not been totally unwarranted.

"The project people who are 'coming out' are good guys who actually believe they are doing the public a service, but . . ." They believe that, in re-

ality, these project people are unwitting pawns and agents of an evil government which is trying to hoodwink the public with yet another labyrinthine scheme—and none of the populace will ever know why until it is too late. The project people are, therefore, unwitting agents of the Great Evil. Innocent, but connected to evil nonetheless, and therefore should be dealt with warily or shunned completely.

"The project's people who are 'coming out' are more than willing puppets of evil and are actually major players in the government's supposed grand scheme against the common man." The project people are therefore seen as dangerous liars—mindless minions of the government's mind control programs. The conspiracy people who hold this opinion see the project people—especially those who are "coming out"—as being the visible spokesmen for the evil regime. They are to be at the very least shunned, and as a best precaution, should probably have their mutilated carcasses strapped to ant hills.

It is the people who hold these beliefs who, by their very threat, rob the project people of their freedom, and have caused most of the project people to vow they will never "come out."

Whatever the individual's reaction, the general feeling among the conspiracy populace is that the project people who are coming out are, either in ignorance or by intent, still lying to the public. They believe that we are telling only the good parts and hiding any facts about "mind control" and "spying on Americans" that we project personnel must surely have done. In actual fact, we did not, but there will never be a way to get that truth across to these people.

Those who are simply and purely interested in parapsychology as a field of learning and endeavor reacted in several ways. The person who has been a practicing psychic might be glad the government has looked into the area of psychic applications and may or may not want to get in on it. Many look into CRV and feel that the rigid protocols were good for military applications, but have no use in the civilian world. They actively discourage technology transfer. Others want to investigate the rigid protocols to see whether or not they can use some of them to add structure and control to their own work. Most feel that they already have the answers, anyway, so why even bother to see what the military did? Many go below the surface aspects of CRV and begin to ask the deeper questions. They look into the benefits of CRV's strengths and the drawbacks of CRV's weaknesses. The discussion, for them, is not limited to governmental, industrial, or private espionage, or the potential for healing, finding missing children, working archeological digs, winning the lottery, and making a killing in the stock market. They want to "get under the hood" and see what makes this thing called the human mind work. These are the people I enjoy working with the most. I am that kind of person myself.

As the years have gone by, the subject of remote viewing has moved further and further away from the sensationalism about covert psychic spies. The mood lately has been much healthier. It has largely changed to the attitude of, "So, let's see what we can do with this stuff." Disbelief has turned to acceptance and remote viewing has become a part of our new paradigm as a modern nation and world. I, for one, could not be happier. I have always viewed the world of espionage and secrecy as a fairly pointless game. I have always joked that if we want to kill our enemies, just drop all our classified documents on them. Those who weren't killed by the massive weight of it all would be left to read it, and would die from sheer boredom. When people these days ask about the military's use of remote viewing, I generally just want to tell them, "That was a part of my old life. I'm starting a new life now."

NOTE

1. Very sadly, Bevy died of a severe infection soon after I wrote that paragraph in present tense. It has been very painful for me to go back and change the verbs into the past tense. I have met very few people of the caliber of Bevy, either among the psychic community or anywhere else in my life. I became very good friends with Bevy and her husband, Ray, and the loss to him, to me, and to the world at large has been very severe.

SEVEN

WHAT DO WE DO WITH IT NOW?

Psychic functioning has been a part of our culture since the dawn of man. Just because it is looked on with suspicion in the United States does not mean that it is not used around the world to satisfy many daily human needs. Almost every country in the world has a psychic spying unit, and believe it or not, the fact that we had one, too, is actually not all that noteworthy.

In the process of having that unit and developing the techniques of using mental abilities for hard, real-world espionage, we learned a lot. And now, the time has come to ask, "What do we do with it now?"

The answer begins with the question, "What *can* we do with it now?" What are its capabilities, and how can those capabilities be used in our daily lives? CRV has both strengths and weaknesses. There are things it can do and things that it cannot. A firm understanding of those strengths and weaknesses will go far in preventing a lot of mistakes in trying to use CRV in civilian applications.

CRV's biggest weakness—in fact, its biggest embarrassment—is its almost total inability to get information in the form of numbers and/or letters—alphanumeric information—at the lower levels of training and experience. During a CRV session, alphanumeric information comes to the viewer in much the same way as do dreams. If you have ever had a dream of reading a newspaper and remember how the type on the page floated, changed, and warped, you understand how it works in CRV. With a great deal of training and experience, a viewer can work around this problem to get the alphanumerics, but it may take years to reach that level of proficiency.

How, then, you may wonder, could we "read documents locked in safes"? In the higher stages of training and experience, Ingo provided for what he calls "analytics." This is normally called "Phase 8 functioning," and is not presently taught to the public. The process is long and difficult, and consists sometimes of viewing the document a single letter at a time, divining the shape of each serif and stroke until the letter has formed on your viewing page. But even for the most experienced viewer, when the viewed line consists of, say, a curved line that arches around in a circle and into a closed loop, it is very difficult for the viewer not to jump to the conclusion that it is an *o*. It could be a lower-case *a* or the beginning of a lower-case *g, p, q,* the bottom part of an 8, 6, etc. So, when we say that an advanced CRVer can read a document in a safe, we do not mean that he can just put the tasking envelope to his forehead and say, "The answer is . . ." It can sometimes take months to reproduce a multipage document. Except for the most sensitive intelligence, it is usually not worth the time or effort. Why, then, even care about this capability? Because sometimes it is worth it, especially when that intelligence information cannot be found any other way, and when lives or future plans depend on having the knowledge.

Fortunately, the reading of alphanumerics is not always necessary. A few years back, I was hired to view a multibillion-dollar contract and look for loopholes in it. The contract contained extremely sensitive business information, and my employer was worried that I would be a security risk for his company's project plans. He was very relieved when I told him that I did not need to see the contract, but only wanted to know how many pages long it was.

"Sixteen," he answered with a good deal of surprise. "That's it?"

"That's it," I answered.

I began working on the document that evening and, by feeling for the physical locations on sixteen blank pages, I was able to find places where they should advise the company's lawyers to reconsider the wording. Four days later, I returned the locations of the potential loopholes I had found. One was a very large loophole, indeed. My customer sent the contract back to his company's lawyers with instructions to reconsider the sentences and paragraphs at those points on the pages. Within a week, he called me again and gushed that I had saved his company from almost certain ruin. To this day, I still do not know the wording of those loopholes or what changes needed to be made.

Today, the company enjoys prosperity and success in its business. But perhaps I should have been just a touch more psychic. The man took credit for discovering the loopholes and to this day has not sent me a single penny of the agreed-on. Lesson learned: While successful business people tend to make good psychics, good psychics are not always successful business people.

Many people feel that another of CRV's major weaknesses is the need for so much extensive training and practice. It would be nice to take a weekend course and come out a major psychic. Many "schools" try to sell that idea to the public, but the end result is always disappointment. CRV is very up-front about the fact that this is a long and difficult process and will take a lot of dedication and discipline.

One example of this requirement is called "CRV dowsing." In a way, remote viewing is a bit like dropping a spy behind enemy lines under cover of darkness. When daylight arrives, he can describe everything around him and pick out items of special interest. But he does not know where he is. He cannot point to a spot on a map and say, "I am here." He can only radio descriptions back to someone familiar with the area in the hope that the other person can determine the exact location.

But with an extensive degree of advanced training and after possibly years of experience, a remote viewer can do such work, and can even do it with a very high degree of accuracy. It is called, for lack of a more scientific term, CRV dowsing. It is not a simple task. Like CRV training, CRV dowser training involves a lot of practice, data collection, databasing, and analysis.

Once the CRV methodology became public knowledge, and people began to find out how much work it really is, a number of quite unscientific "remote viewing" methods began springing up. Most of these claim to be improvements on the original CRV. In reality, they are simplifications of CRV, for the purpose of making training easier and quicker and therefore more appealing to would-be students. Unfortunately, they sacrifice depth and advanced capabilities in the process.

The real thing is very much a martial art, and requires the same diligence, time, and effort as any other martial art. Anyone can go in, sign up, and get their white belt the first week. But it may take years for a person to earn their black belt status, and then only through continued practice, training, further instruction from more experienced experts.

Similarly, you can't get your black belt in a martial art by watching a how-to video or reading a book. The CRV discipline is not a toy. It is the real thing. Ask yourself why you have not taken up a martial art. For almost everyone, the answer is not that they are afraid of getting hurt. The answer is usually that they don't want to put in the time and work required.

One of CRV's strengths is that, when performed properly, it can find information that cannot be gained through any other means. An often overlooked strength is that it is also capable of finding information that *can* be gained by other means, thereby giving you confirmatory information. A CRVer will often pick up on some aspect of a target that is, say, debated by two or more eyewitnesses.

Another strength is CRV's reliable and often amazing accuracy. To everyone's surprise (mine included), the military's CRV unit had the highest accuracy rating of any of the intelligence community's vast array of intelligence gathering tools. That includes such awesome tools as "spy in the sky" satellites, aerial photography, and even ground agents on site. The CRV method can produce information about a target site that is about 90 percent correct. We have had many police departments and other agencies who are overjoyed when a process produces information that is only 10 percent correct. They are ecstatic about CRV.

Perhaps the most important strength of CRV is that it gives the viewer total control over his/her session. Previously, psychics have been at the mercy of their talents and have, at the very best, taken years to gain even the slightest amount of control over them. CRV provides control from the very start. What is more, it gives the viewers complete control over their positions and movements in both time and space.

The U.S. Army Intelligence and Security Command has as its motto "Knowledge is power." The computer generation has moved us firmly into the information age, and in these times, the person who can get and control information with a high degree of accuracy has power. That power can be personal power, but it can also be power within the business, financial, political, military, scientific, and other realms of human activities and relationships.

The stock investor who can see into the future can get rich. Although seeing into the future and acting on what you see will ultimately change the future, the person who has information about that vague and amorphous aspect of life can make decisions and perform actions that are beyond the scope of the humans with which he competes every day. In like manner, the businessman who has greater knowledge of the marketplace in which he works has an advantage over his fellow businessmen, which will make him quickly rise above his competition.

There are many people who realize right away that CRV is the perfect tool for industrial espionage. That is true, but industrial espionage is illegal. I do not engage in it, and when some business approaches me about doing some CRV work for them, I am very careful to make certain that I am not going to be engaged in such activities. Unfortunately, sometimes after all the correct assurances, I find that I have been lied to. So, a forewarning is in order: My company, Problems Solutions Innovations, does not get involved in industrial espionage, and will report any and all such attempts to the proper authorities.

Another strength of CRV is that it cannot be detected. It has often been said that, because of CRV, there are no more secrets. But believe it or not, even while it robs the target of its information, it provides secrecy to the operation itself. The military used CRV as its main viewing method for many reasons, but the main one was that we could go in, get the information, get out, and leave absolutely no trace behind. People at the targeted site would never know that their security had been breached and would therefore never feel the need to change their plans.

With other methods, targeted people sometimes feel a "psychic presence" or a "feeling of being watched." Animals are sometimes alerted, which in turn alerts humans there. Not so with CRV.

The reason is that in CRV you simply interview your subconscious mind and report what it knows. No actual mental or psychic presence at the target site is necessary. You will hear CRVers say such things as "when I got to the site" and "while I was there." They say such things because CRV can produce such strong impressions that the viewer will sometimes feel that he is actually there. But in truth, he is only building a "mini-virtual reality" in his mind during the interview process.

This brings up another of CRV's strengths. Because no part of the viewer actually "goes to the site," there has never been any danger that a viewer will experience what many psychics call "walk-ins" or "spirit invasions." When CRV is done properly, there is no way a viewer can get mentally, emotionally, or spiritually trapped or waylaid "at a site," because the viewer is not at the site.

That brings up a danger, however, which some consider to be another of CRV's drawbacks. As viewers build this virtual reality, they will often buy into it. This is a phenomenon very well known to people who deal with electronic and computerized forms of virtual reality. When you buy into a virtual reality, you tend to forget that it is virtual, and start believing it is completely real. Then, just as a hypnotist can convince you that you have been burned, and a burn will appear on your skin, things that happen in the virtual reality begin to have real-world results. These results can be physical, mental, or emotional. Viewer safety is always a problem. The monitor must watch for emotional reactions and get the viewer doing something else, should any strong emotions arise.

When accessing a target person, the viewer may also get mentally "sucked in" to that person's thought systems, beliefs, emotions, etc. The viewer may begin to identify with that person so strongly that the viewer loses all sense of self. The monitor must be very watchful for such a condition. CRV has a provision for bringing the viewer back to his or her own natural state. The process is called detoxification, and absolutely *must* be learned before a viewer is allowed to access a person mentally. When a viewer trainee goes into this phase of training, he is constantly warned that CRV is the real thing—not a toy—so be careful.

By far, one of CRV's strongest points is its spin-offs. The whole CRV process is aimed at setting up a line of clear communications between a person's conscious and subconscious minds. When such communications are established, everything in the subconscious mind becomes available to you. What was your phone number when you were three years old? Where did you leave your car keys? What is Great Aunt Maude's birthday? Many people learning this process come to realize that CRV used for psychic spying is almost a waste of its greatest potential. It can actually help you to "know thyself."

Psychotherapists, psychoanalysts, and the entire gamut of mental therapy people make their livings off the fact that you can't communicate with your own subconscious mind. Now you can. And CRV training teaches you to do so in an ordered, logical fashion without emotional turmoil or discord. You have control over the process. People learning CRV often come to make peace with themselves and grow spiritually.

When you learn CRV, your life changes. As you change internally, your life will also reflect those changes outwardly. This is, of course, one of CRV's benefits.

But there is a hidden drawback included in the benefit. Even if the changes are for the better, those around you may not like the new you. For example, let us say that you are an alcoholic who, after getting in touch with yourself, no longer needs the alcohol. But your alcoholic partner may decide to seek out another drinking buddy as a result. CRV will have changed *you* for the better, but that change may cause untold readjustments in your life—not all of which may be pleasant.

With these strengths and weaknesses in mind, it's obvious that remote viewing can be used in the business world, much as it has been used by the government. As long as you keep the dangers and drawbacks in mind, the benefits and strengths of CRV can be astounding in business applications.

Decision making is probably the most obvious. Starting in the mid-1990s, I began a project called "Influencing the Past." The purpose of this project was to see whether or not decisions can be influenced from a future time by passing hindsight back to the moment of decision. During this time, I kept meticulous records. My decision-making accuracy (correct decisions vs. incorrect decisions) jumped more than 30 percent. During that time, my wife and I came out of a deep debt into which we had earlier been cast by a very poor business decision. For the first time that we could remember, we were in the black financially, and in fact, became a bit prosperous. Our lives became more comfortable and happier. For a company or corporation, that would translate into money and power in the marketplace. Decisions are what make or break a company.

If, as the army's military intelligence services' motto states, "knowledge is power," then foreknowledge is power in reserve. The company or business that can foresee coming events can prepare for them, design new products to meet the coming trends, and capitalize on information to which no one else has access.

Many companies survive, but few prosper. More often than not, the product is good, but the company just cannot entice the public to it.

Customers complain that companies don't care about them. Sensitizing the personnel who will be the company's people interface is crucial to a company's competitive placement in the world of business. As a person learns to connect with his/her inner self, he/she also learns to become sensitive to even the most subtle cues coming from others. In a business setting, this skill is of the utmost importance, from the salesman dealing with the customer to the board member sitting at the negotiating table. The ability to read people is often the difference between financial success and failure.

The amount of personal growth that takes place when a person learns to open his whole mind, at all levels, to the world about him, is phenomenal. When lines of communication are set up between those levels so nothing is hidden from the person, a person becomes truly alive and awake.

But beyond that, there is a strength and benefit to CRV that in my opinion outweighs all the others. As one person becomes more self-aware, it raises—at least a little—the level of awareness within mankind. The implications of this basic fact are enormous. It was made clear to me one day with a very unexpected comment from Skip Atwater.

We had been working a hostage crisis for several months. We had had a few successes, and many failures. Many times, the failures were not because we got bad information, but because no one acted on it. It seemed at times that no one even cared about the information we were sending up the chain of command. There were several times when the situation got the best of each of us.

One day, Skip Atwater and I were walking over to the Operations Building when the discouragement welled up in me and I asked, "Why are we doing this? Nobody is paying any attention to what we are saying. What contribution is our viewing making?"

Skip looked at me calmly, his expression saying that everything was OK. He answered, "The contribution isn't just in the information we come up with. That's good enough. But the real contribution is in the simple fact that there is someone here doing all this. Even if they ignore everything we say, you six guys are breaking ground for building a better mankind. That can't be all bad."

EIGHT

THE SEVENTH
SENSE

Look at the room around you. Look at it with your eyes, listen with your ears, and feel it with your hands, smell it with your nose. Sense the ambient temperature. Capture the patterns of light and dark. See the shapes and sizes of the things in the room. Then take a pen and paper and thoroughly and completely describe the room around you in writing. Describe it so completely that if you hand your written description to someone, they will not be able to say, "Oh, here's something you missed."

You will find that this is not as easy an exercise as you thought it would be. There will be hundreds of things you glossed over and thousands of details you missed. I once asked a class to tell me the color of the training room walls. The paint color is actually called "desert white." It is white with the slightest tinge of beige. One student answered, "White." The next student said, "A little off-white." The third said, "Slight beige." The fourth student, who is a very famous and extremely talented artist, answered, "It is about a thousand different colors." He then pointed out to us that it had a greenish tinge where the light reflected from the center courtyard touched the ceiling. It had a bluish tinge where the light from the swimming pool did the same. It had a different tinge of blue where the light came to it from the clear desert sky. There was a touch of purple where the light reflected off a nearby bowl of amethyst crystals by one window, and a touch of bright greenish blue where the light reflected off a large bowl filled with turquoise stones next to another window. "In fact," he continued, "there isn't a single place I can find where there is pure white, off-white, or beige."

Look again at your written description of the color of the walls of your room and then at your walls. Did you gloss over your description by writing down what the overall color was, and miss the myriad colors from wall to wall? More than likely, you did.

That little exercise is thousands of times simpler than what someone does in a remote viewing session, which involves describing a location in the greatest of detail. One of the most basic tenets of CRV is that if you can't describe the room around you, using your senses, then you can't be trusted to describe a location halfway around the world, using only your mind.

I've titled this book *The Seventh Sense,* not *The Sixth Sense,* because your psychic sense is not the sixth sense. It is the seventh. People attend the CRV training hope to develop their psychic sense. But perhaps the most surprising and life-changing side effect of taking a CRV course is that it develops not one but two brand-new senses.

We have been raised in a culture that values the physical sciences, almost to the exclusion of our humanity. We have been taught that we have only five senses: sight, hearing, touch, taste, and smell. Each of those senses has a physical body part to which it can be associated. The scientific culture in which we grew up did not believe that there could be a sense without an associated body part or sense organ, so the total of our senses must be five.

Yet, if you take a hundred people, one at a time, and put them, let's say, into a huge cathedral, they will each get a sense of reverent hush. If you put each one on the edge of a tall cliff, they will each get a feeling of "Whoa!!!" and instinctively back off, much the same as if they had touched a hot iron or smelled garbage. If you put each into a lion's den, they will very dependably get a sense of panic and dread.

In like manner, if you walk into a place where there is grave danger, you will tend to tense up and become much more aware. If you enter a party that is a real flop, you will immediately feel the ambience of the place and want to leave. If there is a situation where your involvement would go against your own self-preservation, morals, fears, or dislikes, you will be repelled. If there is a situation where your involvement would enhance your self-preservation, morals, desires, and likes, you will be attracted. In short, you will react to what you sense in your environment and will do so in a fairly predictable, dependable, and repeatable manner. What you are feeling is the ambience of the place.

Science says that something has been proven when it can be shown to have predictable, dependable repeatability. The sense of ambience is predictable, dependable, and repeatable. But, since there is no body part associated with it, it is ignored as a human sense by the scientific world.

It is also ignored in education, child development, and personal training. It is therefore drastically underdeveloped in most people. Yet it can be developed. Actors and comedians learn to "read the room" as they perform. Police learn to "read the scene" of a crime. The rarer and more esoteric occupations of spy and ninja learn that this awareness may well mean the difference between imminent life and death.

A training course in Controlled Remote Viewing deals with honing all the senses, and ambience is one on which we focus most, since it is the least developed in almost everyone. For most people attending the course, this is a totally new aspect of awareness, and the experiences they receive as they develop it are often astounding. (See the Ambience Exercise in Appendix 4.)

The end result of this ambience training creates a wonderful side effect. People have called and written to me after the course, saying that they now realize they had been walking around mostly asleep for years, and now they are finally awake. They begin seeing the world in such completeness and beauty that they pick up the paintbrush or pen and begin creating works of art. They go at their jobs with a new and more complete understanding and begin to excel easily, where before they only got along, at best. In fact, this side effect of CRV training is probably more beneficial in the workaday world than the CRV training itself.

The sense of ambience is not psychic, but as people learn it, they develop a keen ability to perceive things to which other people are virtually blind. People who develop this sense often report that friends and acquaintances have started asking them, "What are you? Psychic or something?"

Over the years of working with both trained and natural psychics, I have become convinced that probably more than 90 percent of everything that passes for psychic is nothing more than a person's innate ability to read the ambience of the person in front of them, the situation, or the extremely subtle tones and nuances of people present.

I first felt the stirrings of this new sense in response to my military CRV training back in 1984. One day, I was headed home at the end of the day, driving the seventy miles from office to home. I normally took a different route each day to break the monotony. I was on 301 heading south and decided to take the route through the small town of Croom, just off the major highway. It was autumn and the leaves were turning glowing reds and golden yellows, with a brilliance I have only seen in the northeastern U.S. The drive through the beautiful woods would be a lot more inspiring than the bland and unchanging freeway, I thought. I turned left into the crossover and waited for a break in the oncoming traffic. I watched to my right as the traffic heading north toward Baltimore sped by. It was particularly heavy that day, so I sat and sat, waiting for an opening.

Suddenly, my right foot, completely on its own, popped off the brake and down onto the gas pedal. I heard my tires screech as I darted out into the heavy oncoming traffic. Then, other tires squealing, horns honking, people cursing, and a sudden "whump" on the back of my pickup truck. The whole incident is still somewhat blurred, but I remember vividly seeing the driver of an oncoming car, his eyes big as pie plates and knuckles white on his steering wheel, not able to accept what was surely his own impending doom.

Somehow, I made it alive to the other side of the road and pulled forward around a small hill where there was a parking pull-off. But I knew from the "whump" that I had caused a wreck. I stopped the truck and got out to see what damage had been done. There was no damage to my truck, but in the truck bed was a stop sign, with its post snapped off and splintered to shreds. The oddity of that sight was lost in the panic of the moment. I decided that I had better go back around the hill to the highway and see what damage I had caused to others. As I rounded the hill, I looked to my right, thinking that whoever had hit me would be stopped by the road. There was no one there, and the traffic had almost resumed its hell-bent-for-leather pace as though nothing had happened. I looked to my left and saw a sixteen-wheeler in the median about five hundred yards down in the direction I had originally been going. The median was plowed up in a line between the crossover and the truck, and the truck's front was buried a foot or two into the ground. The truck's entire front axle and front wheels had come to rest high up in some trees on the other side of the freeway.

While I had been sitting in the median, waiting for a break in the northbound traffic, I had no idea that a sixteen-wheeler, traveling south behind me, had lost its front axle and was hurtling directly for the place in the median where my car was sitting. I was watching the traffic in the other direction, so I had no way to see the truck coming directly toward me like a twenty-ton bullet. But something within me had sensed the immediate danger and taken over my body. At that point, my conscious mind was a mere passenger and nothing more. It was a mere observer of a situation that it could not comprehend. My subconscious mind had taken over my body and moved me from there, through heavy oncoming traffic, to a place of safety—all without my understanding or awareness. The "whump" I had heard as I darted across the lanes of heavy traffic was the stop sign being clipped off and thrown to one side by the fully loaded sixteen-wheeler as it plowed right through the spot where I had been sitting only a microsecond before.

Sometimes your sensitivity to the world around you can be even keener than your conscious awareness of it. None of my "normal" five senses would have saved me in that situation. I could not have seen it coming, as I was looking the other way. I could not have heard it coming, as the radio was playing loudly to keep me awake. Even if I had been able to hear it, there would have been no time to react. It was the ambience of immediate and impending danger that caused the reaction and saved my life. From that moment on, and from many other incidents in which the sense of ambience has come to my aid, I have been convinced of the importance of its development.

SYNAESTHESIA

About a month or so into my initial training, the practice target was a church service in a very ornate cathedral. At the front of the dais was a table set up for a communion service. The table was draped with a purple tablecloth on which sat the gold utensils for the bread and wine. At one point in the session, I zeroed in on this table as the most important part of the target site. I had identified it as something that was:

Wide (side to side)
Narrow (front to back)

Rectangular
Flat on top
Wooden
Draped
Has some things sitting on it

As soon as I began to stall, the monitor cued me with, "Move to your perception of 'has some things sitting on it' and describe." I wrote his cue into the transcript and began describing the "things." My perceptions were:

(Move to "has some things sitting on it" and describe.)
Gold colored
Round
Pointed on top

Sketch:

Metallic
Gold (color)
Not real gold
Contains something

The monitor then cued with, "Move to 'contains something' and describe."
I continued:

(Move to "contains something" and describe.)
Liquid
Dark color
Bitter taste   AOL: like wine

The monitor then cued, "Move to 'draped' and describe."
I wrote:

(Move to "draped" and describe.)
Clothy texture
Long
Wide

Overhanging
Tastes purple
Soft
Clean
Cloth-like

When I stalled again, the monitor suggested, "OK. Let's take a break and discuss something. Did you say, 'Tastes purple'?"

"Yes," I answered. "It tastes purple."

"What does purple taste like?" he asked. "Do you mean, like wine?"

"No," I answered, not really understanding his question, "It tastes purple."

"And what does purple taste like?" he continued.

I thought for a moment, still not understanding why he would ask such a simple and obvious question. "Well . . . you know . . . purple tastes purple." I spoke somewhat slowly, in order to say it as simply and clearly as I could. I still could not understand why he was asking me a question about such a simple thing. Maybe he had not really understood me. I thought I had been clear enough about it, but evidently I had not.

After the session, we returned to the other building where I wrote and turned in my summary. About a half an hour later, my monitor came by my desk and asked if I had a minute.

"Could you tell me again what purple tastes like?" he asked again.

I thought for a minute, now realizing how absurd the question was, but clearly remembering the taste I had experienced. I looked up at him with a grin and said, "Hey! I just tasted a color."

He smiled again and said, "We have some interesting sessions coming up."

Over the next week or so, the monitor selected targets that would have strong sensories—smells, tastes, colors, temperatures, and so forth. During that week, I had several such new experiences. In one session, I saw the sound of the wind in the trees, and could even see as different colored dots where the individual leaves were making sounds of their own. The sounds were as separately spaced as the image of leaves in a photograph, and I could perceive their separation as though I were looking at the leaves, and not at the sound they were making.

During that week, I also began sensing the real world around me in a totally different way. I would touch a piece of wood and smell its texture. I would look at a bird flying over and actually hear its path across the sky. It was like being a child again. I was learning to sense the entire world in ways I had never been able to before.

In one practice session, I mentally touched my tongue to a lemon and *heard* its rich and overpowering flavor. But I didn't just hear the lemon's sourness. I actually heard the harmony and interplay of tastes among the lemon's seeds, juice, and rind. It had never before dawned on me that the parts of simple things had contained the harmonic "chords" of nature. And the chord was so amazingly pure. Over the next few weeks, the abilities of each sense were used to understand the perceptions of the other senses in wonderfully new ways. It was one of those "golden" times in my life.

But as the weeks progressed, the experiences, both in session and out, began to dwindle. By the end of that month, they no longer happened, and have not happened again. I somehow "dumbed back down." It was somewhat like the story of the retarded boy who was given superior intelligence, then slowly began to lose it. It is like the average Joe who suddenly gets caught up in an exciting case of international intrigue, then returns back to his everyday home and job. He spends the rest of his life forever knowing that there is another, more exciting world out there, and forever unable to enter it again.

Things are back to normal now, but I'm left with the knowledge that there are wondrous understandings just beyond the limits of my ability to perceive them. Normal life truly is retarded in many ways. For the rest of my life, I will remember—and never be able to experience again, or even explain to anyone—how a lemon sounds, how purple tastes, and the colors of the wind in the trees.

The explanation of what happened to me is very simple, however. My conscious mind, which had always obtained all its information from the various sense organs, was not accustomed to getting information directly from the subconscious. This was a new source of information, and simply put, the mind did not know how the information should be routed. As my mind experimented with new routing paths, it inadvertently sent a perception or two to the wrong place. Within a couple of weeks, my mind had learned the proper routing and the mistakes went away. Now, here I am again, living as a mundane creature, no longer able to experience such wondrous errors. Years later I learned that psychiatrists have a name for this phenomenon. It is called "synaesthesia." It is evidently very rare, and has been the subject of years of clinical studies.

Synaesthesia does not happen to everyone, but when it does, it is one of the many training milestones in learning CRV. It is an indicator that the proper mental growth is taking place. It clearly shows that new paths of communication are being set up between the conscious and subconscious minds that the basics of Controlled Remote Viewing are being integrated into the student's internal system.

Just the week before final editing of this book, a student, Dominique, was working a training session and said, "Tastes green." I did not interrupt the session, but simply smiled to myself, and felt envy for the golden time she is about to enter.

HYPERSENSITIVITY

One of the sometimes less pleasant side effects of properly learning CRV is that of hypersensitivity. To do well at CRV, you need to hone your sensitivity to the things in both your immediate environment and at far distant sites. In a way, that is wonderful. It opens you to the world about you, to the people around you, and to the wonders and complexities of life. But on the other hand, there are times when we don't want to be sensitive. There is sometimes a very fine line between great sensitivity and "raw nerves."

One day, as these sensitivities were developing within me, I went to one of the Post Exchange cafeterias for a coffee break. Just a moment before I entered the door, the person working the counter had pulled the plastic wrap off a huge package of Styrofoam cups and placed the cups beside the coffee urn. As I entered the door, I felt as if I had walked into a thicket of spider webs. I grabbed at my face, trying to clear the imaginary strands away. Several people looked up at me as though I were going crazy, and a few even laughed. It took me totally by surprise. The coffee urn was on the far side of the cafeteria, about forty feet from me. I finally realized that there was nothing on my face and forced myself to enter and walk to the cafeteria line. The closer I got to the coffee urn, the more the feeling spread to my hands and neck. It was then that I realized that the feeling was coming from nothing more than the static electricity on the Styrofoam cups. You can normally feel the effects of this static electricity from a distance of a few inches. But I had somehow become so sensitive to it that it felt like a full-blown assault from around forty feet away.

This hypersensitivity extends to other senses as well. Trying to carry on a conversation in a restaurant can be very distracting when you are also aware of what is being said in all the conversations going on around you. It can be very unpleasant.

One thing that became painfully clear to me is that 60-cycle current is probably one of the most debilitating and pervasive of all the inventions we live with. A modern digital clock is probably the most blatant emitter of 60-cycle radiation we have in our homes, and where do we keep it? Right at the head of our beds, facing us, where it can bombard us with radiation as we sleep. No wonder we've been likened to a nation of zombies.

But there is also a positive aspect of this hypersensitivity. I have heard it said that one of the worst things a wife can say to a husband is, "I'll tell you what's wrong! You don't know what's wrong! That's what's wrong!" There is no defense the man can ever have for such a statement. The man is left totally stripped of any way to defend himself. For one thing, it is true. He has no idea what is wrong. Not understanding the problem, he cannot rectify it, prevent it from happening again, or even apologize for it with any grace. But, as your sensitivity grows, you begin to know "what's wrong" long before it ever goes wrong. You become aware of the world—and the people—around you, sometimes even before you know it yourself.

PREREACTION

Prereaction is related to precognition, but on a different level. When my body suddenly took my foot off the gas and my car darted out into traffic, it was an example of prereaction. Prereaction happens to Controlled

Remote Viewers because of a very intricate set of physical exercises a student must go through that allows the subconscious mind direct access to the body. In fact, these physical exercises are so important to the process that people quickly understand remote viewing as a physical discipline, not a psychic one. It really is a martial art.

CRV training begins with teaching the student a particular set of physical movements. Students first draw the most minimal graphic representation possible for the concept of "land." They usually draw a straight horizontal line. Then, we have them draw the most minimal graphic representation possible for the concept of "water." They usually draw a horizontal wavy line. We continue for the concepts of "manmade," "natural," "space," "motion/energy," and "living/biological/organic." The graphical representations they make are called ideograms because they are graphic representations of basic concepts, or gestalts, not of specific things.

"Gestalt" is a new word to most people, so I usually explain a gestalt as the major aspect or "—iness" of any specific thing. For example, at a particular location, "water-iness" may be important, and so can "land-iness," and it may also have something that has a "manmade-iness" to it.

Students then practice ideogram drills. (See the Ideogram Exercise in Appendix 4.) To be honest about it, the ideogram drill is designed to be one of life's most boring activities. A computer program calls out the various words and as it does, the student draws the ideogram he has devised for that word. The action is repeated until it becomes so ingrained that it gets turned over to the subconscious mind. In fact, that is one reason the exercise is designed to be so boring. After you have been working the drill for a minute or so, your conscious mind wanders to other things. During that time, the ideograms are being drawn by your subconscious mind.

As the ideograms become more ingrained, you get to the point where you can hear a set of coordinates and your hand will draw an ideogram, much like a knee-jerk reaction. In session, the ideogram is drawn and you can look at it and say, "I don't know what the target is, but it has something manmade, some water, and some land." Your first contact with the target site has been achieved and the session has begun.

Sometimes, you may even physically react to a situation as soon as your subconscious mind perceives it, without waiting for your conscious mind to even begin knowing what is going on. For example, you may suddenly answer someone's question as soon as they think of the question, but before they verbally ask it. You may suddenly reach for the telephone before it rings. You may suddenly dodge just as something that would have hit you goes flying by. This phenomenon cannot be called precognition, because the cognition part just isn't there. It is a direct result of the fact that CRV training is as much physical as mental. CRV involves the whole person, not just the mind alone.

The opening of new sensory pathways and the resultant new experiences are like some kind of wonderland. How any particular student reacts to these new experiences is largely determined by what the student brings to the training in the form of his own inner fears, motivations, upbringing, and expectations. What students get from it is always a new understanding of the world around them of the mind within them, and of the wonderful creation of which they are a part.

But the underlying result is that they open so many new, totally nonpsychic avenues of sensing the world around them that their peers begin to suspect they are psychic. Adding to those new pathways a learning of the true sixth sense, ambience, many students realize that psychic functioning, the "seventh sense," is neither as spectacular nor as necessary as they once thought it to be.

NINE

NEW EMOTIONS

A human being is part of a whole, called by us the
Universe, a part limited in time and space.
He experiences himself, his thoughts and feelings,
as something separated from the rest—a kind of
optical delusion of his consciousness.
                              —Albert Einstein

Training in Controlled Remote Viewing begins by setting up a clear line of communication between your conscious and subconscious minds. The opening of that line of communication generally follows a fairly set pattern.

The first phase is marked by shyness, distrust, and fear. During your whole life, these two minds—the conscious and the subconscious—have been like neighbors on each side of a high fence. One often throws its trash over into the other's yard and petty wars begin, leaving the two with a quiet but seething resentment for each other. Each lives as though the other is not there, and as though the wants, desires, and needs of the other are of little importance, or simply do not exist.

Remote viewing breaks down the wall between them. Suddenly, the conscious and the subconscious have to face each other. What was once ranting and raving at each other in private, with an occasional fist shaken over the fence, must now become dialogue. Now, they are neighbors who can see into each other's lives and windows, who can borrow and lend what the other needs, and who must, for the sake of both, learn to be friends.

In the second phase of this process, the two minds suddenly see each other for what they really are. During this period, you attempt your first sessions. The training teaches both your conscious and subconscious to perform separate tasks and then requires them to put the results together to come out with a viable session summary. Suddenly, the two isolated neighbors within you see something good, helpful, and worthwhile in each other. The first sessions you perform are usually very good, because your two minds do their jobs, as the training requires.

The student rarely realizes that the end goal of those first sessions is not to get the target. The real goal is to have the two minds work together on a common task. Sometimes, it is the first time in the student's life that this has really happened.

In the third phase, the newness wears off and the two minds again become uncomfortable working with each other. Each tries to take charge and dissension breaks out as they try to establish their separate roles and responsibilities. They try to rebuild the wall that has always kept them apart. What they do not realize is that, in working together to rebuild that wall, they are still working together.

When I was growing up, my brother and I used to fight like cats and dogs. Our house was one of those old houses where the rooms are large, the ceilings are high, and everything in them is oversized, as was the style of an even then bygone age. Our house had large, glass-paned double doors between the living room and dining room. Each door had a few dozen square panes of glass. When my brother stubbornly refused to see my way (I was always right), the fight would begin. My mother, not always patiently, would pull out two bottles of Windex and a couple of cloths and make us get on each side of the closed glass doors. We had to clean a single pane at a time, and neither was allowed to go to the next pane until each agreed that the other's side was finished. My brother and I would glare at each other through the closed glass doors. We would shout at each other, shake our fists at each other, and make faces. It soon became a contest to see who could make the worst face at the other. That soon turned into laughing, and the end of the hostilities, at least for a little while. We fought like cats and dogs, but remained best of friends. Our mother had the cleanest glass doors in town.

All these decades later, it dawns on me that, as a remote viewing trainer, I am only doing what my mother taught me to do. When the conscious and subconscious start a war, I put them on either side of a target and make them work on a single aspect of that target until it is finished before going on to the next. Neither can jump ahead, and neither can take credit for a clean glass pane until both have done their part of the job. In the process, the hostilities cease, at least for a little while. During this phase of the training, I ask my students to stay in touch with me through phone calls or E-mail, so that we can work out any problems that arise. This phase is the crucial one that determines whether a student continues or gets lost.

This phase of the training shows a flattening of scores, which is almost defeating to most students. There will be from ten to twenty-five sessions where the scores are a total embarrassment. No matter how well I have explained that this is a natural and constructive part of the process, the low scores still feel like failure, and sometimes that failure can make a student give up. But if a student keeps trying, those two neighbors keep meeting face to face and working together on tasks. Each finally sees that the other is there for them and can be helpful to them. One day the struggle for dominance ends and a dialogue starts over the fence again.

If the student sticks with it, in the fourth phase he becomes friends with himself. I mean, true friends. During this phase fairly strong life changes begin to take place.

In the military life, the saying goes that your friend is someone you can trust with your life, your wife, and your wallet. It is easy to find buddies who can be trusted with any one or two of those things, but finding someone you can trust with all three is not easy. In like manner, people may trust themselves to do well in, say, business, but not in love, or they may trust themselves to do well in love, but not in public speaking. It is this phase in which people learn to trust themselves in all things.

In the fourth phase of development, remote viewing scores rise again because the two neighbors come to an agreement and begin working together once more. Students also start developing that attitude toward all facets of their existence that is only held by those who have a true, secure friendship in their lives.

Then comes the fifth phase, where the two mind neighbors forge a lifelong working relationship. This is not always a smooth road, and the two will find themselves in a fight, often over new tasks and differences, and often over old, forgotten slights of the distant past. But they have become friends. Each is the other's "other half." I have never seen anyone reach this phase of development who has not been totally happy with the path they have chosen.

This is the real reason I am in this field. Teaching people the ability to do psychic spying is the least important part of the work I do.

Since I have started training people to become more sensitive to the world around them, I have seen their creativity and happiness soar, their marriages and parental relationships improve, as do their work situations, life paths, and spiritual closeness with God. It's been a thing of joy for me, just seeing the joy in others.

But you can't become more sensitive to the world without also becoming more sensitive to the sorrows within it. While that may not be pleasant, it is nonetheless an unavoidable side effect, so let this be a fair warning.

Those who finish my advanced remote viewing course work on at least ten missing-children cases. For some people this may be their first experience of man's inhumanity to man on a real, experiential basis. It can be a traumatic and cathartic experience. But once they have worked on ten cases, they will have been instrumental in helping bring home at least one child. The satisfaction of having made a difference in the life of a child and his/her family brings enormous satisfaction, even if it sometimes means locating the body of a dead child so the parents can have closure and get on with their lives.

Several years after retirement, I was asked to work a missing-child case outside the U.S. When I began working the case, I found the child alive, but in the most horrible of circumstances. The child had been kidnapped and sold to a paramilitary group as slave labor. There were many children there. The group used them as servants, sex objects, and punching bags. The children were not cared for and received no medical care. In the end, the child was used as target practice to harden the group members to fire on innocent humans.

Once I had reported my findings, I was asked to get information on the other children. The country where this was located has a very high rate of missing and abducted children. I went back into session repeatedly over the next few months and I got to know each abducted child in the encampment. I did what I could to comfort them when they got sick and died. I became emotionally involved with each tiny life only to watch it be extinguished in pain and suffering. During all this time, I did what I could to find the location of the group, but the work went slowly.

Eventually the paramilitary group was located and eradicated. Two children were retrieved alive. The person who had hired me later commented to me that these two children would be so emotionally scarred that it would have been more merciful to have them die with the others.

Getting over the sorrows a remote viewer meets in session is not easy. In fact, sometimes you don't ever get over it. You just get through it. I'm afraid that even after years of doing this, the wear and tear on me is still very evident. We sometimes take a too cavalier attitude toward this whole field, thinking that we can throw on our white hat and just ride in and save the day. But reality isn't just a movie that we can watch and then go out to dinner. In many subtle ways, reality shoots back at us, and its bullets can inflict many a hidden wound on the viewers. Viewers can, without even realizing it, bleed to death emotionally and never know what hit them until it is too late.

Despite the sorrow, the remote viewer learns that the mind, now given more freedom and control, has a way of taking care of you, no matter what comes your way. Once in Hong Kong (in real life, not in a session), I wandered into the wrong alley, which was evidently the turf of some Chinese underworld gang. I was immediately confronted by a huge Chinese man who pulled a huge knife, about the size of Crocodile Dundee's, and had already begun his roundhouse swing to slice across my abdomen and kill me. Before I could even react mentally, my hand shot forward in a handshake gesture. A huge grin spread across my face and I heard myself saying with the strongest accent imaginable, "Howdy, y'all! Ah'm from Texas!" I must have looked like a character from the TV show *Hee Haw*. The man stopped his roundhouse swing in midair, looked at me as if I was some kind of mentally incompetent idiot, snickered, shook his head, and walked away. Right before that happened, I felt a sudden calm, realizing the situation, but knowing that somehow I would get through it. To this day, I don't know why that worked, but it was probably the only thing in the world that would have. I could never have thought of it myself.

There have been countless times in recent years when a crisis situation has been more than I could handle on a conscious basis. At those times, it has been as though the Divine has come to me and said, "Don't worry. I'll handle this." And, following a momentary sudden calm, it was taken care of.

TEN

PROTECTION

Fear is the main source of superstition, and one of the main sources of cruelty. To conquer fear is the beginning of wisdom.

—Bertrand Russell

One of the major concerns about psychic spying is how to protect yourself from it. With most forms of psychic functioning, you simply decide against access and your subconscious mind will automatically ward off any invasion of privacy, through its own natural defense systems.

Many people imagine a symbolic and protective "ball of white light" around them. Some people have protective talismans. These are meant to be an outward and visible symbol of some inward conviction. They are "string around the finger" types of reminders. However, that symbolism often gets lost, and people start putting their faith in the talisman itself. Therein lies the danger of such a device. When the person starts having faith in the talisman itself, it becomes just the opposite of what the person wants. They begin to feel that, since they have this "protector," they no longer need to be diligent and self-protective. Therefore, they let their natural and internal guards down, and actually become easier to spy on psychically.

In many ways, the art of protecting a target, in this case yourself or your workplace, from being viewed is like protecting a computer program from being hacked. The better you are at writing protection schemes, the better the hackers will become as they learn to break them. The stories we hear on the news about the newest computer viruses are the tip of the iceberg in the war being waged between the software protectors and the software hackers. The protection software gets better every time the hackers find a way around the protection, and the hackers get better every time the protectors find a new way to foil the hackers.

Military codes are much the same way. If there is a way to encipher a message, there is a way to decipher it. When the military security people encipher a message, they do not do so with the expectation that the code cannot be broken. They only do so with the hope that it will take the enemy so long to break the code that the information in the message will no longer be of any value. They also encode messages knowing that only a very small percentage of the code breakers have the talent and ability to decode them. They know, too, that as they develop more difficult codes, they are only training enemy code breakers to a new level of proficiency. Therefore, encryption codes are not measured by how unbreakable they are, but by how long it takes to break them. To put it another way, they know that there is no such thing as real protection

So it is with protecting yourself, your work, your loved ones, your invention, or any other secrets you may have from remote viewing. You may find a way that will slow a mental spy down, or will prevent all but a small percentage of spies from achieving success. But if the spy is dedicated to getting the information, he will simply use that session to learn a new way to break past your protection. In effect, you are not just protecting yourself, but you are also making it harder to protect yourself in the future because you are also creating better psychic spies. Luckily, most of them will quit the session long before they should. They will "go to the site," find only your protection, and quit. It is the really dedicated ones and that small percentage of really experienced and well-trained ones you have to worry about. But what you must come to terms with is that, in the end, there is no such thing as real and total protection.

No matter what you have heard or felt or experienced concerning psychic attack, it is probably 99.99 percent the result of fear and imagination on your part, and has nothing to do with anything someone else has done to you. Sure, it felt real. The illness was real. The "bad luck" incidents that started happening in your life were real. But the *cause* of those things had more to do with your own fear and imagination than with anything or anyone else.

It is not at all unusual for a person who wants power over you to use some subliminal method of convincing you that they already have that power. Then, each time something bad happens to you, they take credit, and it further confirms their power over you. In reality, it is only your own belief that is causing the problems. Soon, any time you feel you have made them angry or you have gone against something they want, you will begin to fear retribution, and will bring the bad events onto yourself as surely as if you had planned them.

I have come to believe firmly that there are only a small handful of people in the world—few enough to count on the fingers of one hand, five people or fewer—who actually have any capability of this sort, at all. The rest only have ways to manipulate you—and that is rarely through psychic means.

I know that people who call me asking about protection from psychic attack often need nothing more than something they can do about the situation. They feel helpless, and simply giving them a slight bit of control will put an end to their fears and thereby stop the psychic attack at its real source: their own minds.

That is not to say that some psychic attacks are not real. Some are very real, and a few are even very effective. But after study and experimentation, I have become convinced that almost all of the psychic attacks are merely the victim's own fear and imagination.

Remote viewing is used only to obtain information about you. It is not a tool for psychic attack. This is especially true of Controlled Remote Viewing. Since the controlled remote viewer only accesses his own subconscious mind, there is never any mental contact with you, so attack is not possible.

There is, however, a formalized method called Controlled Remote Influencing (CRI), which is, at best, only mildly effective for psychic attack. Only a few people are capable of performing CRI, and the names of those people are known, because it requires specialized training.

There is another method called Controlled Remote Control (CRC), which is extremely effective for psychic attack, but there are only two people who know this skill, and they were carefully selected with an eye to their Christian and altruistic nature. You do not need to fear them.

So, in reality, these methodologies are completely the concern of wild, fantastic science fiction and horror story writers. Therefore, I would like to put the idea of psychic attack behind us and move on to protection from psychic spying.

Controlled Remote Viewing is certainly not the first form of psychic spying ever used. It is more the result of millennia of improvement over older and more primitive methods, which did not work as well. It is, in a very real sense, the mind-hacker's newest weapon for gaining information. Just as old protection schemes do not work when hackers learn new methods, old methods of psychic protection no longer worked when CRV entered into the psychic spying picture. In the military unit, we loved to find someone who had faith in a protective "ball of white light" or other form of talisman. They were like the proverbial sitting ducks. It could cut session time from more than an hour to fifteen minutes or less.

CRV cuts past these old protection methods because it does not depend on mental magic or telepathy or competitive mental powers. CRV does not have the viewer actually go to the target; it only asks the viewer to address his/her own subconscious mind and see what it knows about the target. The fact is that the subconscious has the ability to know almost everything about the target. It has the information and is ready to give it. Therefore, anyone who "protects" themselves from the psychic spying of a CRVer wastes time and effort, because a CRVer does not need to access them to get the information he needs.

If the targeted person has some protection, the novice CRVer may view that protection instead of the person, and will therefore be defeated by it. But in later stages of training, a CRVer learns to blow past this smoke screen without even slowing down, much the way an accomplished computer hacker blows past passwords and firewalls without a second thought. With an advanced CRVer, psychic protection is useless.

Getting past protection at the target site is actually so simple as to be almost funny. When the subconscious mind tells the CRVer that there is psychic protection at the target site, the viewer simply asks, "What information is it protecting?" The subconscious gives the answer, and the viewer reports what is there.

There is nothing that you, as an untrained individual, can do to stop another person from sitting down and accessing his or her own sub-conscious mind. This was one of CRV's strengths and one of the reasons it was adopted by the military. For years, we had an unstoppable mind-hacker's tool. No one was able to detect the work we were doing. There were hundreds of ways to collect intelligence, but when we collected it, the target had no way of knowing their information had been compromised. They went ahead and acted on it, thinking that it was still secure.

But because the military is always concerned with worst case scenarios, they knew that once this technology got out and became publicly available, our enemies would learn it, too. We would need to protect ourselves when our enemies use CRV on us.

Although we were never officially and specifically tasked through channels to develop protection techniques, several military viewers set out on personal quests to find ways to develop such detection and protection methods. We did in fact discover a few ways to stop novice CRVers and to drastically slow down the more proficient ones

To understand how to deter being remote viewed, you have to understand the remote viewing process itself. One of the most fundamental processes is called "doorknobbing." It is a trap that most viewers fall into, and in fact, fall into quite often. If there is something at the target location that is very attractive to the viewer's subconscious, its attention will tend to be pulled away from its assigned purpose to the thing that interests it more. An "attractor" is anything in the physical environment of the target that tends to draw a viewer's attention away from the actual assigned target. It can be as simple and innocent as some colorful or intricate whatnot or whirligig. It can be something as imposing and out of the ordinary as a contorted and indefinably shaped modern statue. Therefore, having an attractor in your immediate physical environment tends to draw a viewer's attention away from you. This is the simplest form of deterrent and, at least, it will give you a measure of protection from novice viewers.

To show how attractors provide protection, let us say that a novice viewer is given the target of Pearl Harbor one week before the Japanese attack; the viewer will almost always be attracted to the day of the attack. In a sense, then, the target of a week before the attack is somewhat naturally protected. In the same manner, having a single, strong attractor in your office or workspace will do the same to protect more mundane work and activities from psychic spying.

The normal parts of the location have the natural protection of being comparatively unattractive to the viewer's mind. The viewer has every indication that the session is successful, but wastes all his session time and energy doorknobbing the attractor(s) instead of collecting the requested information.

Many top-secret facilities in the U.S. are very lax about the choice of pictures on the walls and personal items on desks, even though the proper selection of such items could act as attractors to deter the success of foreign psychic spies. They would also make the workplace better for those who must spend their days in windowless buildings and underground facilities.

The Soviet KGB and other foreign intelligence services are very mindful of this fact. For that reason, Russian, Bulgarian, Chinese, and other countries' intelligence agencies are now building many of their most top-secret facilities very near to carnivals, circuses, amusement rides, and other mentally attractive locations.

Expert remote viewer Joe McMoneagle was once tasked to view a location suspected to be a very high-level military meeting place within a targeted foreign country. He was not told it was a meeting place; he was only given a set of numbers. During the session, he described military men of high rank and status discussing military plans. He said that many important group decisions were made in this place. Throughout the session, though, he was attracted to activity on the upper floor of the building. When he was told to move there and describe it, he said that the upper floor consisted of "small rooms where one-on-one business is conducted." Ground intelligence later discovered that the building was, in fact, a special brothel where military leaders discussed military plans downstairs while waiting for other activities upstairs.

But our military knew that foreign psychic spying units would have advanced viewers who would not be stopped by such trivial attractors. Therefore, a system had to be developed whereby we could protect ourselves from being spied upon as we did our own psychic spying work. Further, we would need to find a way that we could protect some other person, place, or activity, as well.

To conduct experiments on such a method, we would need three people: one to be the target person, one to protect the target person, and a third to try to hack through the protection. Getting a viewer was the easy part. We had a unit full of them. Getting a target person was easy. One other person in the unit agreed to be viewed. That left me as the protector. While the targeted person was away doing interesting things and the viewer was trying to view him, I would quietly try out my latest and greatest protection scheme to keep the target person safe from being viewed.

Despite a few very minor successes, we had one repeated failure after another. Those sessions that we accepted as minor successes were probably more wishful thinking than anything else. Yet, I was convinced there had to be a way.

One day, as I was working a real, operationally tasked target, I was required to establish mental access with a certain foreign military leader and report his plans and intentions for the next day. During that session, something happened that, for a moment, threw me completely off target. This may have happened before, but for the first time, I understood the potential significance of it. This foreign military leader had, for a span of several minutes, prevented me from viewing him, and in doing so he had unwittingly provided me with my newest latest and greatest idea.

The next time the unit had some slack time and we were again doing practice targets, I tried this protection scheme. It worked wonderfully. I tried it again and again and it worked each time. The viewers would come back from the viewing building, look at their feedback, and wonder what in the world had gone wrong with their sessions.

I wrote up a report on the method and gave it to the director. The director at that time was a very paranoid man, and I had not made allowances for that fact. He took one look at the report and became flaming angry.

"Who tasked you to do this?" he bellowed, with fists raised and waving in the air.

"No one!" I said. "I have been working on it on my own for a couple of years now."

I was shocked at the response. He threatened to have me thrown out of the unit for taking things into my own hands. ". . . And if I find out that you're lying to me and taking tasking from outside the unit," he continued in a rage, "I'll have you court-martialed!" With that, he took the report to the shredder and fed it into the slot. The golden egg that the government had been wanting for almost twenty years had just been destroyed.

It was not only people who needed protection, but also inanimate targets such as top-secret installations, weapons under development, the Oval Office, and other places where top-level military and political decisions were made. Therefore, after what had happened, I was forced to work on my own time to develop the method further. Working at home, I never kept notes or data, since that would surely violate security. Any information that I gleaned would be mentally noted and then entered the following Monday into a small personal database that only I knew about on the secure computer at work.

The basic principles were sound and the development of protection for non-people targets went very quickly. The method had even proven that it could protect one aspect of the target, and leave other aspects completely viewable. One thing led to another, and I found that I could do the protection sessions at one time and protect against being viewed at another time, and even over a span of time. When the Gulf War started and we began working overtime, my private protection research came to a halt.

However, the hacker-vs.-protection process did not stop there. Now that a method of protection from CRV had been invented, we needed to find out whether or not there would be a way to break that protection. There was one object that I had protected during those experiments, and it became important in the process of learning to break the protection I invented.

This object is a carved stone which had come into my possession years earlier, and which I keep proudly displayed in our bookcase. Only my wife and I know its very unusual history. I would pull out all the stops and do the best job I could at protecting it, then trying to break its protection.

The session to protect this stone from being viewed began on a Friday evening around 11:30 and lasted until the next morning at 6:00. Afterwards, I fell into bed exhausted and slept the entire day, waking up Sunday morning just in time to get ready for church. I protected only the aspects of the stone's history and the long and circuitous route by which it finally came into my possession. To this day, viewers can go into session with nothing but a set of numbers, not knowing that the target is this stone. Viewers can describe it physically in fairly good detail, depending on their own individual abilities. But when they are tasked to describe its history, the session quickly falls into chaos. For some reason unknown to me, this chaotic period is usually accompanied by lots of giggling. Many viewers then quit the session, thinking that they have gone "off target." If they continue, the chaos ebbs and a

story begins to form, leading them to think they are having a tremendously successful session. In fact, it makes so much sense that it soon forms a story. But almost none of the information is correct. If the viewer is given the same target again, another story develops, totally different from the first. For this reason, it has come to be known as the "Story Stone."

I have come to believe that a person could learn CRV and make a living writing fictional short stories, doing nothing more than viewing the Story Stone. The amazing thing to me is not that the stone is protected. I understand the principles behind that, and can see clearly how it works. What amazes me is that I only worked a single session, and the stone has been protected from being viewed ever since. The protection appears to be permanent. Also, its history seems to be safe from all forms of psychic functioning, not just CRV alone.

As for breaking the protection that I placed on it, I have to report that I have been totally unsuccessful at doing that. After retirement, I have given many hours to the attempt, and have not once succeeded. Maybe I am not as good a hacker as I thought I would be.

So when people ask me whether there is any protection against CRV,

I cannot truthfully answer that there isn't, nor can I truthfully answer that, for them, there is. It always seems rude, but a truthful answer can only be, "Well, there *is* a form of protection, but there is no way for any of you to do it, and once it is done, there is no way to undo it that we know of."

ELEVEN

THE HUMAN MIND

"I'm not a smart man, but I know what love is."
—Forrest Gump

Throughout the 1970s and 1980s, the U.S. government spent an estimated $20 million developing and using CRV. Like most governmental programs, there are spin-offs and benefits for the civilian sector other than the military's intended uses. The most obvious spin-off of the remote viewing program is, of course, the fact that the protocols and methods have now moved into the public sector for business and private applications. But for me, there is an even more valuable spin-off. That is what I have learned about the human mind.

My model of the human mind contains a conscious mind, of course. It also contains a subconscious mind, but no "unconscious" part of the mind. I have come to realize that there is no part of the mind that is unconscious. Each part is conscious in a different way, and aware of different aspects of life, but no part of the mind is ever truly unconscious. The human mind also includes a kind of "body mind." This mind makes our heart beat, our stomach digest, keeps track of our circadian rhythms, jerks our hand off the hot stove, and in general tries in vain to keep explaining to us that "Pain is nature's way of telling us we're hurting ourselves."

To that, many people would add a fourth mind, that being the "overmind" or "collective consciousness" or whatever private term they invent for that part of the mind that gives us access to understandings beyond our physical senses. Here, especially, I have realized that the term "collective unconscious" is totally in error. The collective mind is very conscious, indeed. I catch a lot of flak from those students who are in the mental health field because of my use of the word "subconscious" and the phrase "collective conscious" instead of "unconscious" and "collective unconscious." But I stand resolute that every level of brain and mental activity is conscious of itself at its own level. If one level, the conscious mind, is not aware of what is going on at the other levels, that does not mean that the other levels are not conscious of their own activities. I submit that the term "unconscious" should be reserved for deep coma or death. Even in deep coma, there are levels of the brain that continue to be aware of a person's need for heartbeat, breathing, and digestion, so the coma patient cannot be said to be truly and completely unconscious. Actually, I submit that the term "unconscious" is useless and leads many an "expert" as well as many a professional to misunderstand their patients' needs. The term should be done away with. In CRV, we will be working with all levels of the brain and mind, and will need to realize that these levels are very active and aware. This new understanding is necessary for the work we do.

But, for the purpose of this model (and remember, it is only a model), I prefer to view the first three as the main levels of the *brain,* and the fourth as the main level of the *mind.*

With this approach, it becomes obvious why a ghost, if you believe in such things, remains behind, wandering around repeating the same actions over and over. It has a mind that desires some action or needs fulfillment, but it no longer has a brain to think things through and make any decision on what to do about the desire or need. It has no brain to understand the changes that take place around it over the centuries, or even to recognize that it is dead and can move on.

Further, let's assume, for just a moment, that the mind's main access to the brain is not through the conscious, but through the subconscious. That being so, the subconscious would have much more access to the knowledge and understanding of those things beyond our normal physical senses. It is through the subconscious that the information of remote viewing comes.

If the information exists, and it is available mostly to our subconscious, then the real problems remote viewers have with inaccuracies is not getting the information, but processing it. The real problems do not lie in having the subconscious get the information. It is already there. The real problems lie in getting it from the subconscious to the conscious and onto a sheet of paper so someone can see it. People through the centuries have done everything they can to "be more psychic," when they should have instead been trying to devise a way to simply "work smarter." It was this shift in viewpoint from parapsychology to straight psychology that allowed Ingo Swann to develop a remote viewing method that works reliably and well.

There is one point that should be understood before going into the mind of a CRVer. There are things in our conscious mind of which we are not aware, and there are things in our subconscious mind of which we are aware. So, to more fully understand the process of CRV, as well as the mind itself, I would caution you to differentiate between "conscious/subconscious" and "aware/unaware." Also, I will use the word "perceive" to mean that information of which we become aware, no matter from what level of consciousness it stems. Therefore, our subconscious mind can become aware of something in the universe long before our conscious mind does.

We use the conscious mind to perceive the world around us, to think about what we perceive, and to perform logical manipulations of that information and act on it. The conscious mind is where we live our daily lives and take care of our daily activities. At this level, the mind only has access to the world around it through the normal senses of sight, taste, hearing, smell, and feel.

That poses a problem for the person learning Controlled Remote Viewing or any other form of psychic functioning. It sets limits. If we can't sense something with the normal five senses, then we just don't perceive it. And that is important. Our normal five senses not only help us perceive what is around us, but they also determine what we can or cannot perceive. We sense colors, sizes, and shapes mainly through the eyes, but only within the range to which the eyes are sensitive. We sense temperature and texture through the skin, but only within a "bearable" range. Outside that range, we sense only pain. We sense sounds through the ears only within a certain frequency range and only at certain levels. Below that level, we sense nothing; above that level, we feel pain. Our senses of taste and smell are not only limited by the organs that sense them, but also influenced by a set of likes and dislikes developed over time. These two senses interact with the subconscious more than the other sense organs do, simply because of their need for greater interpretation.

The conscious/subconscious can be seen as an office building where the top floor is reserved for the bosses and the floors beneath are for the various departments and the workers within them. The bosses do not have to know what detailed tasks are going on within each department, or at the desk of any one worker. They deal with the generalities—with the "big picture." The workers on the lower (sub) levels remain busy all day, each totally conscious of his own job and activities, but not necessarily conscious of anyone else's job. Very few of the workers at these sub levels are ever aware of the big picture, and therein often lies the source of many of a company's problems.

If a top-floor boss tries to get information from the lower levels, engineering or accounting, say, he will often receive technical answers he may not understand. The boss neither speaks nor understands engineer-ese or accounting-ese. Nor do workers in those departments speak boss-ese. This is a very real problem in many corporations. In fact, many computer companies have created job positions called "interpreters." The interpreter is a person who goes back and forth between the customer and the programmer, translating the English of one into the English of the other.

Basically the same problem exists between the conscious and the subconscious. Whenever psychics want information about a missing child, for instance, they try to learn on a conscious level what the different sublevels know about the child, his or her condition, location, emotional state, welfare, dress, and other aspects of the child's life and situation. Each sublevel has its own jargon, its own very narrow view of the situation, and its own way of handling the information it has. None of them sees the overall big picture and the information from each of them is just as unintelligible to the conscious mind as the conscious mind's question was to them. The end result is a sort of "telegraph game," where the conscious mind winds up reporting what it thinks it heard, and filling in the gaps in its understanding with guessing and imagination. What this system needs is an interpreter.

The body mind can accurately understand the languages of both the conscious and the subconscious. If, for example, I want to raise my hand, I can consciously decide when, and the body responds. If my hand accidentally touches something hot, my hand rises off the hot surface, a split second before I become aware of the burning sensation. It has taken a command directly from another, deeper (sub) level of consciousness.

Ingo Swann said that this is a function of the autonomic nervous system. There are professionals more than ready to argue that some of these functions are handled by the central nervous system and by other body systems. For our purposes, let's just call this whole collection of nervous systems by the arbitrary name of "the body mind." It controls the body by understanding orders from both the conscious and subconscious minds.

Therefore, if we can train the body to act as an interpreter, a line of communication will open up between the conscious and the subconscious, allowing accurate and even intricate information to flow between them. This is the basis of what Ingo Swann developed when he developed Controlled Remote Viewing. CRV is not concerned with "being psychic." It is a physically based martial art with the body used as an interpreter and communicator between the conscious and subconscious minds. It is a martial art in every sense of the word, incorporating a marriage of both body and mind. Where the psychic information comes from is now no longer an important question. The only important thing is to make that line of communication as clear as possible in order to get that information to the people who need it.

Like any other martial art, remote viewing involves practicing a series of physical movements that have meaning. The CRV student practices the same moves over and over until the conscious mind is bored stiff and starts doing other things. At that point, the subconscious takes over and practices the moves on its own. This intentionally boring exercise is called the "ideogram drill," and is the basic set of moves for all CRV. The student develops a move for, say, "land," and practices it until the subconscious knows how to make the body say "land." Then, if there is land at a target, the viewer's subconscious can make the pen hand give the sign for land. After developing this body language, the viewer continues learning more complex physical-based methods to enhance this language. The body mind becomes a more proficient means to allow the two minds to communicate freely and clearly.

Because the body mind does not creatively think on its own, it is very happy to sit and breathe, pump blood, and regulate body temperature all day. It needs to communicate a little, but it only has the most rudimentary language of its own. That language is completely physical, and deals mainly with physical responses to input from the conscious mind, the subconscious, and its physical environment. Because the body mind is unthinking, it also takes much longer to train to do anything. Any pianist, martial artist, bowler, golfer, or anyone who depends on accuracy of physical movement will be more than happy to tell you of the long hours of repetitive practice it takes to hone any skill. If they stop practicing, the body forgets little by little until the skill fades back into obscurity. It is no different with Controlled Remote Viewing. Anyone can dabble with this skill, and sometimes even hit a home run or a hole in one now and then. But for the person who wants to become proficient at it, it takes practice and more practice. That is the nature of a martial art.

In Controlled Remote Viewing, you must be able to tell your subconscious what information you want, then you must be able to get that information from the subconscious and report it. Ingo Swann originally developed CRV by using actual geographic coordinates for his tasking. He used them for training the soldiers as well. But in applications, you cannot always know the geographic coordinates of a target. This is especially true of, say, a hostage. If you knew where the hostage was, you would not need a remote viewer to find him. So, for applications we began using first random numbers, then number/letter combinations, random words, then numbers that would allow for easier databasing of the sessions. They all worked. We continued calling the first cueing "coordinates," but now realized that their main purpose seemed to be that of simply kickstarting the conscious/body/subconscious communication process. The numbers do not really mean anything.

The CRV session begins with the monitor giving the coordinates of the target to the viewer and the viewer writing the numbers down as the monitor speaks them. This gets the viewer's pen moving. It is most important for the viewer's pen to move, because this is the first signal to the body that a conversation is about to take place.

As the viewer writes the coordinates, the body passes the message to the subconscious mind, "What is at this target?" The subconscious mind reads the message and responds with the major gestalts at the target site, passing this information back to the body. The body, which can only give a physical response, moves the pen in your hand, producing an ideogram. The practiced remote viewer has trained his body to give a specific physical response to an inner message. He can then look at it and consciously decipher what it means.

But you then begin to run into a problem, as the following story illustrates. Oog and Ogg were walking through the primeval forest one day when they heard a twig snap behind them. Without even turning around, Oog immediately thought, "Sabertooth tiger!" and ran as hard as he could. Ogg, however, turned around and asked, "Uhhh, what was that?" I will leave it to your logic to determine whose descendants we are.

There is a part of our brain's plumbing that I call the NAG, an acronym for "Namer and Guesser." It identifies things. If it cannot name something, it guesses. If it cannot guess, it makes something up. It has an overwhelming drive to name things. It is what saved Oog's life, and countless lives throughout history. It is bred into our genes. We are compelled to name things.

Therefore, when a perception comes up from the subconscious mind, the NAG immediately grasps hold of it and tries to identify it. It calls on our memories, our fears, and our desires. So most people will jump to conclusions when they get the message that the target has land, water, and something manmade.

"*Ah ha!*" says the NAG. "It's a ship near the shore!"

From that point on, no matter what the target really is, the conscious mind will "build its castle." It will see the incoming perceptions that fit its mental picture, and ignore those that do not.

The task before the viewer, then, is not to identify the target, but to identify the gestalts that are represented by the ideograms. What do those squiggles mean? When this has properly been accomplished, the viewer is finished with Phase 1 of the CRV process.

Phase 2 begins a give-and-take dialogue between the conscious and subconscious minds, still working through the body as a translator. However, the body, now in a different mode, stops using the ideograms. It begins using all its means of communication—the senses. As Phase 2 begins, the viewer may get brief flashes of, say, red color or warm feeling or the hint of an imagined sound. As the line of communication opens further, more and more complex signals such as tastes and smells show up, followed by impressions of ambience and dimensions. Eventually the viewer may get perceptions of "conceptuals," such as "This feels religious" or "This feels scientific in nature." As this line of communications is established, more and more complex and accurate perceptions can come through.

During "setting up the line" time, though, your NAG is still in there fighting and clawing for its say-so. You get valid perceptions of, say, "red," "round," "rubbery feel." The NAG jumps in and says, *Ooh! I know what it is! It's a ball!* When, in fact, it is nothing more than a target site with something red, something round, and something rubbery.

Another analogy illustrates the problem well. Let's say that you are a spy, relaying information back to headquarters. You find yourself in a very dark place. You do not know whether you are in a lion's den, on the edge of a cliff, or in a safe and empty room. You do not know if there is something you might step on or trip over. You feel in your pocket and find a small, narrow-beam penlight. You turn it on and begin shining it around. You shine it upward and see something red. You shine it to the right and see something else that is round. You shine it at your feet and see something that is rubbery. As you relay all these bits of information back to headquarters, someone there is jumping to all kinds of conclusions about where you are. The same is true when your subconscious mind first makes contact with a target site. The subconscious mind relays perceptions back as it gets them in random order. But back at headquarters, the NAG keeps trying to identify the target in as short a time as possible. *"It's a ball!"* the kibitzer yells. At that point, trying to remain disciplined and not think of it as a ball is like the old command, "Don't think of an elephant."

This is the situation every viewer (in fact, every psychic) finds himself in as he begins every session. One of the main rules hammered into every beginning viewer is, *"Describe, don't try to identify."* Most errors in any psychic session are made during the first few moments. If those initial errors can be avoided, the rest of the session will be of much higher quality.

To resume the dark place analogy: As the subconscious continues looking around the site, its panic about possible dangers dies down. It begins to get a feel for the environment, and finally says, "I can deal with this place." From that point on, the subconscious mind will stop waving its light back and forth wildly and will begin to concentrate on specific objects in its new environment. The moment the subconscious quits panicking and begins to seriously concentrate on the different aspects of the target, Phase 2 of CRV ends and Phase 3 begins.

In Phase 3, the viewer begins feeling and working his way around the site, generally sketching what he finds. Relationships between the parts of the target site and how things are arranged become clearer. This is where detailed information begins to flow.

The CRV process then becomes a matter of interview and report. The viewer goes through an increasingly complex series of methods for working with the subconscious mind, still using the body as a translator to obtain information about the target. Throughout the rest of the session, the subconscious looks, smells, tastes, listens, feels, and senses the ambience of the place, the event, the activities, the people, and every other aspect of the target site. It reports its findings back to the body, which translates the information into physical feelings and impressions the conscious mind can understand and record. If the conscious mind has questions, it passes those questions to the body through a physical act (such as tapping around the ideogram), and the body passes the question to the subconscious. The subconscious responds by going to the part of the target site that has the requested information and reporting back on what it finds. In the end, if the process has been correctly handled, the viewer has a complete and accurate description of these target aspects written down on paper

Like any other martial art, gaining proficiency in working with the body so that it will dependably respond to knowledge in the subconscious mind can take years of training and practice. Is it worth it? Natural psychics will be quick to tell you that it is not. They will say, "Just let it happen," and for them, it does. For the average person, it does not.

This is one of the most ignored facts about CRV: CRV was not created for psychics. It was created for nonpsychics, for the "ungifted."

But is all the work worth it? As a parlor game, no. As a self-improvement tool? Yes, but there are many self-improvement methods that are a whole lot faster and easier. But how about as a tool to help your company grow to maturity in the shark pool, a means to help find missing children, a way to diagnose health problems long before doctors can, and to reap the other benefits of having the world open to you? Is it worth it for these things? I can only tell you that for me, for the government, and for hundreds of others who are now using this new science, the answer has been yes.

TWELVE

MIND MELDS

If you don't control your mind, someone else will.
—John Allston

Keeping a good database of remote viewing results helps provide an accurate viewer profile and shows a viewer's strengths and weaknesses. To be more exact, it shows the strengths and weaknesses of the viewer's subconscious mind to do this very unusual job. Sometimes, the results come as a total surprise to the viewer. It did to me when the database began strongly indicating that one of my strengths was mentally accessing people. I am not a total recluse, by any means, but I find great comfort in being alone with only my thoughts and studies. I tend to need massive amounts of "alone time," and if deprived of it for too long, I get sort of "owly" or "squirrelly," to use the common vernacular. I have also always found it very difficult to deal with people. They tend to be too chaotic and make little sense to me.

So along came this database that said that I was able to very easily "get into people's minds" and record their thoughts, feelings, and plans and intentions with a high degree of accuracy. My first thought on learning this was, "There must be something wrong with the database."

But I knew that the data that had gone into the database were pure. When I reviewed my sessions, the evidence was there; the database was correct. I chalked it up to the weirdness of human nature that some part of my own mind would, quite unknown to me, actually like dealing with other humans, and even be good at it.

But I was not the only one who had access to the database. For the intelligence world, mental access of target people has great value. Profilers and psychological analysts who specialize in this craft are highly prized within the intelligence community. They are employed in that part of the intelligence community which is called HUMINT, which is short for "Human Intelligence," or "intelligence derived from human sources." They are credited, and rightly so, with performing the hardest job within the entire intelligence field—that of dealing directly with people.

With CRV, however, it goes several steps further. You are not limited to dealing with a person's outward personality alone. You can get directly into the person's mind at its deepest levels to get your information. You can actually access that person mentally and bring back their most deep-seated thoughts, feelings, emotions, motivations, fears, desires, drives, reservations, and everything else that might be there to drive their actions. It is, perhaps, in this one area where CRV surpasses any other intelligence tool and finds its highest value.

At various times, we were tasked to access a foreign leader and report on the plans and intentions for battle, political aspirations, and upcoming decisions. We became familiar with foreign political and military leaders in ways that were not known to standard psychological profilers, and in ways not even known to the target person's family or even the person himself. Throughout the Gulf War, we mentally accessed Saddam Hussein daily to learn of his plans and intentions for the following day. If there were ever an aggressor who did not stand a chance of success, it was he.

Because of my ability in this area, I was tasked heavily with this bad guy or that drug lord or some crazy military or political leader. Eventually the wear and tear of this work drove me into a very serious mental state of my own.

The situation came to a head one afternoon as I was driving home. I lived seventy miles from Fort Meade. The drive, on a good day, took about an hour and a half. On a high traffic day, it could take two and a half.

On one wonderful spring afternoon, the kind where you drive with the windows down just to enjoy the feel of the world about you, I was thinking about what I needed to do that evening. The mental list included writing a letter, setting out the garbage for the next day's collection, killing Linda, mowing the lawn, and if I still had time . . .

"What?" I thought. "Kill Linda? My wife? Where in the hell did that come from?" I almost laughed that such a stray thought had come into my mind. Yet, as I rode on toward home, I realized that I actually did have plans to kill my wife that evening. The realization of it sent a shock of electricity through me which is impossible to describe. I pulled over to the side of the road and got out of the car. As I stood, leaning against the hood, I thought back on that day's work. I remembered that all through that day's session on a specific target person, there had been a "feeling" I could not quite pick up on. It had bothered me at the time, but I had dismissed it. I was there to get military plans and intentions, and that was what I paid attention to. I now realized that underneath all the military plans and intentions, the feeling I had ignored was the target person's intention to kill his wife.

Mental access at the level provided by the CRV process can be very dangerous to a viewer. The process requires the viewer to begin feeling the target person's feelings and actually thinking the target person's thoughts. In a very real way, you actually become that person, at least partially, for the span of the session. As you continue to access more deeply, you begin to see their personal reasoning, their points of view. You see how right it is to perform genocide to gain political power, to kill and maim in the cause of terrorism, or to molest children and steal people's possessions. You cannot help but experience the thrill and emotional satisfaction a homicidal maniac gets when torturing and killing helpless victims. You feel the surge of pride and victory at casting aside all moral values to destroy anyone who stands in your way. The target person's way of thinking actually becomes your way of thinking as well, or at least for the span of the session.

Often, the end of the session comes and you are left with some remnants of that target person's emotions, thoughts, aspirations, attitudes, and morals. That's why CRV is not a toy. It can be very dangerous. It can totally destroy a viewer's life and mind. I warn all of my students not to try mental access without a good, experienced, well-trained, and capable monitor present to act as a safety line for them. Novice viewers can lose control of the situation even before they are aware of what is happening. This is so dangerous, in fact, that I teach students how to avoid this ability, rather than how to develop it.

As I stood by the roadside, leaning against the hood of the car, I realized that I had gotten "sucked in" to that day's target person. I had to do something to get rid of the last vestige of his mind within mine. Over the next two hours, I managed to clear most of the problem from my head, but I knew that until it was all gone, I could not go home to my family that evening. Nor could I just call home and tell my wife why I was staying away. Security measures prevented it. Something had to be done. I was totally unprepared for this; the Ingo Swann method of remote viewing did not give me a clue to how to handle this.

As I stood there beside my car, I developed a method for "detoxification" from those types of mental access sessions. The detox process became a normal part of every such session from that day forward. Within an hour, I knew that I was myself and only myself again, and was able to safely go home to my family. It often scares me, though, when I think back on how close I came to changing the lives of everyone in my family, losing my wife and probably my freedom, and actually killing the woman I loved. I am still 100 percent certain that, even without knowing why, I would have done it.

Years later, I was teaching an intermediate class in San Francisco, and one of the students wanted to experience accessing a target person to the point of "getting sucked in." I had firmly resisted allowing him to do that. He just was not experienced enough.

I had repeatedly warned him and the entire class that, when the target is a person, you *"Describe, don't try to access."* That is, you should describe the person in terms of physical appearance, location, work habits, dress, mannerisms, and such outward things as would be of interest to the police or anyone trying to find that person from a witness's description. You should never get into that person's mind. In the training stage, no student is experienced enough to handle the dangers posed by CRV when it is used for doing psychological profiling, mind reading, or even the shallower personality assessment.

But this one student persisted in his desire to experience "getting sucked in." I knew that sooner or later, he would try it on his own, when there would be no one there to get him out of it.

It was a fairly large class, so I had the students working in groups of three. Each group would have a viewer, a monitor, and an onlooker. The CRV process looks different from each position, so rotating people through the positions lets them get a more well-rounded understanding of it. Because the class was larger than usual, I was going from work group to work group, answering any questions they might have, kibitzing, watching for errors, and correcting potentially bad habits. In general, I was making a nuisance of myself with all that teaching, while they only wanted to "nail the target."

I was working with one group while at another table, the viewer had finished his session, and now the job positions for that group rotated. The woman who would now be the monitor came up to me and asked, "I brought a target from home. Can I give that to the viewer?"

"Sure," I answered. By the intermediate course, the viewers should be able to handle just about any kind of target, so whatever it was, it would probably be good training. I continued going from group to group, and even went by that table a couple of times. I had not seen the target yet. I was interested in students keeping the proper work structure and habits. I was not concerned about how well they were on target or off target, so it was not necessary for me to see the target.

A few minutes later, the woman who had brought in the target rushed up to me and said that I had better get over to their table quickly. Something was wrong. I looked over to their table and saw that the student who had wanted to "get sucked in" was rapidly doing just that.

I rushed over and grabbed the target. It was a picture of a man being swept away in a watery mud slide and fighting in vain to keep from drowning. People on the sides of the flow watched in helpless horror as the man swept rapidly by them, fighting for his life. The student viewer was gasping and choking and struggling for his every breath.

I did something at that point of which I am not particularly proud, now that I look back on it. He was in a total panic, and finding it hard to breathe, but I knew that he was only in the very first stages of getting sucked in. He had been badgering me relentlessly for quite a while to allow him the experience, so I decided, "OK. You asked for it—you got it." I knew that I still had plenty of time to pull him out of it. I would not let it go too far. I had enough experience, both with the process and with him as a student, to see when his "too far" point would be. So, I let him continue to fight for survival.

Through his struggles, he continued to try working the session. This is one of the standard aspects of getting sucked in. The target becomes such an attractor that the viewer cannot bring himself to quit viewing. It can quickly become so strong that a viewer will face even death (which, by the way, I do not think is possible—we've never tried it that far), all the while grasping frantically at the target to experience it more and more and more.

If you are wondering what getting sucked in looks like, here is an analogy. I used to live in East Texas, where there are many chicken farms. These farms raise the chickens much as cattle ranchers raise cows. Very regularly, you will see a truck going by, which has several hundred small cages crammed full of chickens, headed for the slaughterhouse. Almost every truck that goes by has at least one chicken that has escaped and is now grasping as tightly as possible to the outside of a cage as it gets buffeted by the wind and tossed back and forth by the bumpy truck ride. It hangs on with all its might, not willing to let go. It does not struggle to get free, but to cling for dear life to the cage which will ultimately lead it to its death. I have never seen an instance of getting sucked in that has not reminded me of the scared, helpless cargo of those slaughterhouse trucks.

My student clung to the target for dear life, even after (he would later tell me) he had become convinced that he would not live through the session. He kept getting sucked farther and farther in, until I could see the "too far" point approaching. At that time, I took over his session and got him out of it.

All the other students had stopped their sessions and were standing around aghast. They were afraid that he was having a seizure of some kind. When I pulled him out, I made him end the session, so that he would not start viewing and get sucked in again. People who get sucked in often cannot resist rushing back into the danger which can do them so much harm. When he had calmed down somewhat, I told him that he had finally had the experience he desired. I turned to the class and told them that this is what getting sucked in looks like, and that if they wanted to experience it, too, they should do so now, instead of waiting until they got home with no one there to help them. For some strange reason, no one else wanted to have the experience. For the one student who had experienced it, it was not something he wanted to repeat.

But, truth be told, all target contact is an extremely mild form of getting sucked in. When you get totally sucked into a site, it is called "bilocation" or "perfect site integration (or immersion)," which is usually abbreviated PSI, and called the PSI experience. It can be a wonderful or horrible experience, depending on the target. The really dangerous thing for beginning viewers is getting sucked in when the target is another human.

When you are the viewer, and especially when you are working without a monitor, it is very hard to tell when an uplifting site contact turns gently into that downward slope of being sucked in. The slope gets more slippery as you go, and by the time you realize what is happening, it is usually too late. I have personally had this happen many times, only to catch myself at the very last moment. Sometimes, I have not caught myself. The result has been a PSI experience when the target was a place, event, or manmade object to be spied upon. The result when the target was a person has been to lose myself for a period of time. Once I had developed the protocols for detoxification, this was not a problem, but before that, there were several experiences that were all but life altering.

Once I was given a set of coordinates by Ted, who has been mentioned before in this book. Ted is a rabid UFO fanatic, and liked to sneak UFO targets into our tasking now and then. This was forbidden, but he sometimes did it anyway. I thought that the target on this particular day was an operational target and was not expecting an ET target.

I accessed the site and found a pilot flying an aircraft. I saw that he was worried about something. Still a fairly novice viewer at the time, I rushed in and accessed the pilot's mind to find out what was worrying him.

The pilot and all his passengers had been members of an extremely oppressive culture. They had rebelled against their government, but to no avail. The political leaders of that culture had given them the choice of dying or being allowed to leave and never return. They had elected to leave. They had been provided with the aircraft and allowed to leave without incident. But now that the pilot had found a place to land so they could start a new home for themselves, he realized that something was wrong with the aircraft. It had been fixed to self-destruct as soon as it tried to land anywhere. Someone in the oppressive regime had not been satisfied just to let them go. He wanted to kill them all. The pilot realized the problem, but could find nothing to do about it. He had called his wife and children into the cockpit to watch the landing, fully aware that they would probably die before the aircraft could land. I gave myself a move command to the problem, and found that it was a device that the saboteur had placed within the pilot's range of sight, but out of the pilot's reach. He sadistically wanted the pilot to know and understand before death what had been done to these freedom-seeking refugees and their families.

The pilot tried everything he could think of to procure a safe landing. He went around the world several times (this was my first in-session clue that it was possibly an ET target). Going back up was out of the question, for some reason that I did not investigate because I was getting so sucked into the pilot and his panic. Now, every life on the ship depended on our skill and our creative ability to solve the problem. We finally figured out a way to bring the ship in for a landing. We hoped to be able to land on a mountain top that would be high enough to keep the explosive device from detonating. As we made final preparations for the landing, we turned to our family and assured them of our love, then got back to the job at hand. A moment later, the ship exploded in a great ball of fiery debris.

Once I had gotten sucked into him, it was my family, too. I loved them and ached for them. I felt responsible for their lives and knew that my political actions and beliefs and my desire that they have freedom had caused this situation to exist. In the last moments of their lives, I realized how much they had suffered for my beliefs, and I blamed myself for their dying. Everyone I loved and cared about was to die, and it was my fault.

When the ship exploded, I was thrown violently out of the session, and even fell out of the chair in which I had been sitting to do the viewing.

I found out later that my task had been to find out what caused the Tunguska explosion, which flattened thousands of acres of land in southeastern Siberia, on June 30, 1908. I have always felt (and still suspect) that the explosion was caused by a meteorite, but even if that is true for the particular event at Tunguska, I am certain that what I accessed was a real target, real beings, and a real event. There was no feedback on the target, so there is no way to prove it, but deep inside, I know it for sure.

But, at the time of that particular session, I had no way of detoxing from the target. For almost two months after that session, no one in the office or at home dared to talk to me about any political subject or anything the government was doing. I became so violently opposed to any form of organized government and the oppression it wields that several times I became physically violent, just at the mention of any political subject. I could not listen to the news on the way to work or back home. I could not watch the news on TV for fear of getting so enraged that I was ready to yell and scream and throw things. Over the next two months or so, it slowly wore off, and I could again function normally. But to be totally honest, I found out about two years later, after I had developed the protocols for detoxification, that I still needed to detoxify from that session. I was still harboring very deep and angry resentment toward organized governments of any form, all because of the evil that had been done to the people and family "we" (the pilot and I) loved and cared about so dearly.

Mind melds of this kind can also cause physical effects. There have been times when a targeted person would have, say, a broken leg, and the viewer would begin to limp after the session. At one time or another, this happened to almost every viewer in the unit. I was once tasked to view a person who, unknown to the tasker, had just broken his rib. I came out of the session with a horrible pain in my side which could not be cured by detoxification. After writing my session summary, I decided to go on sick call. The resultant X ray showed that I had a broken rib. At this time, no one was yet aware that the target person had also broken his. Aside from the information gained in viewing, there had been no session pollution, no "telepathic overlay" or unconscious suggestions involved. I would like to believe that on picking up on his pain, my muscles tightened up so much that I cracked my own rib. I do not care to believe that my rib mystically broke itself to match his, or that the two "unified in the cosmos," or any of the occult or magical explanations that might be offered. I was acutely aware of the pain all the way through the session, and I think that I just did it to myself. Such can be the side effects of a CRV session.

For me, these side effects might even involve a change in eye color. I have blue eyes, but in reality, my eyes tend to change color on a fairly constant basis, from blue to green, to very slightly hazel. Once, while I was doing a session to access Saddam Hussein, my eyes evidently turned dark brown. The monitor at the time had not seen such a thing before. I realized later that I had not told her of this during her training. As I accessed Hussein, she saw my eyes turn brown and heard my voice deepen, and she hurried out of the room in a panic. I did not know what was going on, but was concerned about her. I went through a quick detox protocol, and went to see what was wrong. By the time I reached the administration building, she had gone home for the day. The next day, she refused to talk about it for the entire morning, and it was afternoon before I finally found out what had scared her.

I cannot broach this topic without touching on one last item of danger to the viewer. There is also a possible danger of temporary changes in the viewer's religious and/or cosmological belief systems. Thankfully, all such changes are usually temporary, but such changes and the personal actions you might take because of those changes are something that merits serious consideration.

But I would be quite remiss if I left you thinking that these things are a normal occurrence and happen every time someone tries to access someone else's mind. It just is not so. While such occurrences are most certainly possible, in actual practice, they are rare, and only occur when you use specifically Controlled Remote Viewing, and only when the target is a person, and you allow yourself to get sucked in.

THIRTEEN

THE PERFECT SESSION

*"I am careful not to confuse excellence with
perfection. Excellence, I can reach for; perfection
is God's business."*

> —Michael J. Fox,
> quoted by Lorne A. Adrain,
> *The Most Important Thing I Know*

People often ask me about the most exciting session I've ever done, or the most terrifying or the most inspiring. When I think back to answer those questions, though, one of the first sessions I always think of is one that was considered so potentially dangerous that we were told ahead of time what the target was, and asked to volunteer to do it. The tasker's thinking was that it could be a potential suicide mission.

One of our customers needed some intelligence about a Russian particle beam weapon at Semipalatinsk. A particle beam weapon is basically the ultimate ray gun. It destroys everything in its path. Even small ones can blow large holes through solid steel blocks a foot thick within a matter of microseconds. This one was a massive weapon, so large that it totally occupied the building in which it had been built. I do not know how true it is, but it was reputed to be able to blow a large hole straight through a mountain in a few seconds' time. Our scientific customer even referred to it as "a death ray." Our customer needed a single bit of intelligence which could evidently not be obtained through any of the other spy options available to the U.S. In order to obtain that information, they had to know what was happening inside the beam itself. There is, of course, no way to place a piece of test equipment inside a particle beam, since the beam will destroy anything in its path. Even if there had been a way, the fact that it was a Russian classified project prevented access to the weapon or any information about it.

Someone came up with the brilliant idea of placing a remote viewer mentally inside the beam and having him describe what was going on in there. The targeting was effectively rejected by our director at the time, because of possible unknown dangers to the viewers. But the information was of vital importance, so it was explained to our group and a call was made for volunteers. I thought it would be a really unusual target and an interesting experience, so I raised my hand. I was the only one.

Some viewers thought there might be a danger to the viewer's psyche, and in reality, I know that such danger was possible. Because you use your body as an interpreter in Controlled Remote Viewing, you not only get physical sensations, but you can start having physical reactions as well. That can become dangerous.

But the lure of the experience and the information to be gained from this target was just too great for me to pass up. Paul was my monitor, so I knew that I was in good, experienced hands. At the slightest sign of any problems, he would pull me back and abort the session. We decided that I would not be targeted with a location inside the beam, but would first go to the facility, then enter the beam when I felt ready.

The session began like all other sessions. Paul read the target coordinates. I wrote them down as he called them out, and then made my ideogram. As we progressed into Phase 2, I began to get sensory and dimensional impressions. These were impressions of the size of the facility, the shape of the weapon itself, the temperature and weather at the site, and so forth. These things could be checked ahead of time so the monitor could know whether or not I was on target. It also gave me concrete sensory impressions that I could hold on to in order to increase my site contact.

In Phase 3, I began making sketches of the target location, the weapon, and its surroundings. I do not spend a lot of time on graphics while in session, unless the shapes and sizes of the target are both important and unknown. When they are known, any graphics I make only serve to strengthen my tactile contact with the target. This time, I knew that I was getting on target very quickly. There is a certainty about such things that comes from having done hundreds of sessions. Curiosity about a site helps me to make good site contact, almost without fail.

I had just entered Phase 4 when I felt I had sufficient site contact to proceed to the weapon. Paul gave the prompt, "Move to the time of beam activation and describe." There was a sudden visual impression of some large, round, tubular thing about fifty yards in front of me. The impression was not vague, but quite real. I was buying into the virtual reality. At that point, I began sensing only the information coming from my subconscious, and lost touch with the room around me. Without realizing it, I had reached the Perfect Site Integration, or PSI condition. I was standing in an open area outside a building, looking at the large tube, just ahead of me.

I decided to move to the tube. Because I had strongly bought into the virtual reality, I had to walk to get there. I could feel the ground under first one foot then the other as I walked forward. The PSI experience was getting stronger. I began to hear a hum coming from the tubular feature. As I looked closely, I saw that the tube was a light milk chocolate color, and was not solid, but was merely a beam of strange looking energy. The insides of it were moving in a very quick blur from my left to right. Its left end was connected to a piece of electronic and mechanical gadgetry inside a large laboratory-like building. Its right end went out to a large, flat metallic plate, which was in the process of melting and vaporizing. I knew that this had to be the particle beam.

As I studied the beam closely, my full interest in it enveloped me, and I forgot about the viewing room, Paul, and even the task I was there to perform. I didn't realize it at the time, but the Perfect Site Integration had become complete. I moved closer to the beam. I was now standing in front of a sparkling, dancing, horizontal flow of energy, looking into it as a child would look into a toy store window at Christmas. It was totally captivating.

The beam seemed like a constant flow of light brown liquid streaming by at supersonic speeds. It was a perfectly round, horizontal, tubular flow of this energy/liquid, but without any physical tube to contain it. As I put my face nearer to it, I could see that it was different down in the middle than it was on the outside edge.

I put my fingers into the flow, to see what would happen. As my fingers entered the liquid streaking by, the flow parted for only a split second then resumed coherence as my finger melted and streaked off toward the right, leaving a discoloration within the flow. My finger appeared to have become part of the flow, but was still, even in its melted state, somehow a part of me as well. There was a feeling of searing heat and bitter cold, both at the same time. I stood watching my fingers melt and flow outward along the beam, totally fascinated by the process. It then dawned on me that this might be dangerous. I pulled my hand back, and the beam resumed its former shape and color. My fingers were intact. I realized that my hand had not melted at all. It had been placed into an area where time was proceeding at a different speed. It had only appeared distorted because I had seen the hand in that time-space locale from the vantage point of normal time and space.

I again shoved my whole hand into the beam. This time, the searing heat and bitter cold did not seem quite as intense. My hand again appeared to melt and flow out along the beam. I then thrust my arm in up to the middle of the forearm. My wrist became icy and painfully cold and I instinctively jerked my arm back. The beam resumed its former shape and color. My arm was as it should be.

I looked to my left and saw the machine from which the beam originated. There were some men wearing goggles standing around it. They were checking dials and gadgets. I wanted to go down and see what they were doing, but vaguely remembered that I was not asked to make side trips.

"Oh, yes!" I remembered. "I'm supposed to step into it and describe it from the inside." Without any further thought for personal safety and without even remembering what I was to look for, I stepped into the beam.

I experienced something at that moment that I have never been adequately able to explain to anyone. It was something so totally strange and unique that nothing in my life had prepared me for it. I suddenly realized that my body was spread along the beam for what seemed to be endless miles of distance. My back was against the melting metallic plate, but was also a part of the metal itself. I could look forward and backward along the beam and see myself standing at thousands of places within it. Thousands of images of myself were spread along the tube, yet blurred somehow into one image. I was aware that I could see each of the other images from the vantage point of each and every one, all at the same time. It was like something out of a high-budget science fiction movie, but this was real.

Each of my images began to converse with one another, somehow showing different personalities and thought patterns within each, but somehow all unified into a single mind. As my many awarenesses conversed, they quickly came to the same conclusion: I had a job to do.

It was like walking into a strong, gale-force wind, but all my many images finally joined together into one, back at the point where I had entered the beam. They did not all make it, but enough of them did that I was able to turn and face the oncoming beam of energy, to study it from the inside.

The very center of the beam was swirling rapidly in a counterclockwise direction. The outside edges of the beam were coming directionally straight, with no swirl at all. Between the exact middle and the outside edge, the swirl dwindled from the rapidity of a central hurricane to the directional straightness of the edge.

My analysis of the beam ended at that point. I could no longer keep an analytical mind as I looked into the beam. Each particle within the beam was every color of the rainbow, all at once, but never blending into white. The colors were more vivid than I have ever seen, even in the most vivid nighttime dream. I found myself facing an oncoming rush of beauty like I have never seen before. Repeatedly, the beauty of the beam made me lose coherence, and I would separate into a thousand images along it. I would regain physical coherence, only to become totally awe-stricken and lose it again.

To this day, I do not remember the end of that session. I suppose that I must have come out of the Perfect Site Integration experience and finished the session, written a final summary, and gone back to my desk to do other work. I must have closed up for the evening, locked my papers away in the safe, and gone to the car to drive home. I honestly do not remember. The next memory I have of that day was driving into Waldorf, Maryland, almost sixty miles from the office, almost home for the evening. The awe of the beauty I saw at that target did not wear off for weeks to come. I'm not certain it ever has.

Some years after the "death ray" experience, the researchers at Stanford Research Institute decided to test the military remote viewers with a series of targets from around the Palo Alto area. We were tasked with shopping malls, historical sites, and many things around the Stanford campus. They would phone us a set of coordinates, we would work the target and send them the results. They would score the sessions and log the data into their databases. That's where the urgency ended for them, and it would be a week or so before we got any feedback photos, usually by regular mail.

One of the targets I was assigned was the Stanford Linear Accelerator. It is similar to a particle beam in that it takes the individual parts of the atom and sends them flying down a long, straight tunnel into a collection point. With the accelerator, the nuclear physicists at Stanford can study the makeup of the molecule in order to understand the quantum laws of nuclear physics more clearly.

Of course, I did not know what the target was. I was only given some numbers and told to describe what was at the target site. The session began like any other. I worked through the phases but at one point, a perception confused me. I perceived a square that appeared to be made of hundreds of long, flat, sandwiched sensors embedded in a wall. When I went into Phase 6, which is used to clear up confusion by focusing on extreme details, I immediately went into Perfect Site Integration. I suddenly found myself standing in a very long, dark tunnel. The walls right next to me appeared to be made of these long, sandwiched sensors. Off to one end of the tunnel, there was a faint light, but nothing of interest. The tunnel appeared to have a square shape along its length, but it was hard to see in the very dim light. I heard a buzzer of some kind from the direction of the light, so my attention focused there. The light and the sound were easily a quarter of a mile away. I turned toward it, and as I did, a pelting of sand particles began to spray against my face and hands. The number of sand grains quickly grew until I was getting sand blasted from that direction. I turned away from it, and the sand continued to pelt the back of my neck. By that time, the pressure of the sand hitting me became uncomfortable, and I once again turned into the blast to try to figure where it was coming from.

The blast hit my face and hands with a stinging not unlike being in a violent desert sandstorm, but there was no wind associated with the onslaught. It was as though someone were simply shooting sand, by itself, down the tunnel.

I placed my hands in front of my face and began deflecting the sand particles over to the side wall, right into the sensors. By now, the particles were hitting with biting force, but I realized that I could turn my body in such a way as to deflect most of the onrushing sand into the side wall. As soon as I started doing that, an alarm sounded at the lighted end of the tunnel and the sand blasting stopped. I could hear faint voices at that end of the tunnel, muffled, but clearly excited.

After traveling the length of the tunnel in the semidarkness, I came to some equipment. The tunnel had no apparent outlet. When I found that I was trapped there, the Perfect Site Integration ended and I was suddenly back at the viewing table. I wrote down what I had seen. I then gave myself the cue to move to the sound of the voices. The PSI situation began again immediately, and I found myself standing in a laboratory where a young man sat at a machine console. There were two women working excitedly nearby, and a couple of other people—one slightly older—shouting orders to the rest. Clearly, they had been performing an experiment, and something had gone wrong. I looked up at a clock on the wall and saw that the hands pointed in the direction of 10:37. Numbers are rarely ever visible in CRV, and in fact, blur and change much like in a dream. Therefore, if a CRVer needs to find out the local time at the target site, he must find a clock that has hands—not digital—and describe the direction in which the hands point.

It was about a week later when the feedback photos came in and I learned that I had been viewing the linear accelerator. We went over my material and found that the descriptions I had given of the facility, the equipment, the long building, and the surroundings were correct. The "sand" had been atomic particles shot from a cyclotron of some sort. As I thought back on the session, I began to wonder whether or not my deflecting the sand had actually deflected the atomic particles at the real site. If so, I thought, I had not only sensed the site, but had affected things at it, as well. Such things are generally not considered possible with CRV, but no one had studied what happens during the bilocation experience. I checked the session time and found that, making allowance for the time zones between Maryland and California, the time on the clock had been accurate. I went to the director and asked if we could check with the Stanford people to see whether there had been some anomaly with the accelerator that had actually taken place at that time. The director told me in no uncertain terms that we would absolutely not do that. If there had been such an event, and the people at the linear accelerator found out that we had messed up one of their experiments, there would be hell to pay, not only for us, but for our researchers at Stanford as well. Not only that, but our unit had an extremely strict and rigorous policy to collect intelligence passively and never, ever have any active interaction with the site. If anyone ever found that I had actually done such a thing, it could possibly cause us to lose our funding.

I have never been able to get feedback on that event. Of course, if my remote viewing presence had had an effect, then there would be a plethora of questions to ask. Could I actually have had some effect on the target site while I was perfectly integrated with it? If so, did that mean that some part of me was actually there, as opposed to the CRV theory that we are only interviewing our subconscious mind? And if so, could this be developed for other uses at other sites? Maybe wreaking havoc with an enemy computer or guidance control mechanism? Who can say? Our unit had its singular passive, never active, mission, and because of that, these are questions we did not even dare ask openly.

The first Perfect Site Integration experience I ever had came as a complete surprise. It occurred during a practice session Ted had given illegally because it concerned space aliens. Knowing now that he could get into trouble for giving such targets, he had taken up the practice of telling us ahead of time what we would be viewing, thereby making us participants in the blame, if we conceded.

"I think that I've uncovered the location where the aliens have stashed thousands of their young in hibernation," he said. "They're waiting for the day to come when they will wake up and begin taking over. I'll give you the coordinates and you are to describe what you find there. I've already worked it, and found everything, so this is just to check your work for accuracy. I think you'll be amazed at what you find."

This was an insurmountable amount of pollution. I should have walked out of the room at that point. I don't know of a single remote viewer of any kind who can work a session with ease under such circumstances. But it was a practice session and I had work at my desk I didn't want to do, so I decided, "I'll give him what he wants and get it over with. It'll give me an hour's vacation."

During the start of the session, I toyed with the perceptions, not really working a session. I was mainly feeding him what he wanted to hear, and watching him react. It was entertaining.

At those times during the session when I said anything that didn't confirm what he felt the target to be, he would correct me and tell me what I really meant to say. Pretty soon, the whole farce became boring and I wanted to end it. His excitement had reached a peak, though. I had created a monster.

I finally pretended to go blank, a time in a CRV session when the impressions just dry up for seemingly no reason, and you can do nothing about it. It is rare, but maybe if I faked it, it would work. I looked up and said, "Uh-oh. I just went blank."

"No problem" he said, enthusiasm undaunted. "You're underground, in the hive chamber, and I need you to move one hundred feet higher and begin describing what I've found up there."

I sighed and wrote down the move command, thinking, "Will this never end?"

He said something else that I did not quite hear, and when I looked up, I could not see him any longer. I saw a very dark and cold corridor stretching forward, with light streaming into the far end of it.

I did not realize it at the time, but my desperation to get away from the painfully fake session had driven me to escape mentally to the actual tasked geographic location. I had spontaneously bilocated to the *actual* coordinates he had given me—just to get away from the misery of what was going on. To his credit, none of the massive pollution he had given me included the name of the actual location. So, I had no idea where I was.

I walked forward along the corridor. I always work sessions in my socks, and at the site, I could feel sand piled up on stone flooring under my feet. At the other end of the corridor, I stepped out onto an extremely small porchlike structure about 100 feet up the sloping side of a building. It overlooked a vista of land stretching out to the horizon. The sloping side of the building was to my left and right behind me. I turned a little and looked at it. It sloped backwards as it went up. I looked up and saw that the slanted side of the building rose many hundred feet higher and came to a point above the place where I stood.

I looked back at the vista before me. Something was wrong with it. The sun was out and the skies were devoid of clouds. But the sky looked strange. It was much too dark for daytime, and the sun was much smaller and dimmer than it should be. The land looked very rocky and rough and had no vegetation at all. There were some other things that looked like possible ruins of other buildings, but they were far away and hard to make out. They looked as though they were as worn and old as the building on which I stood.

I turned again to look at the building which held the ledge where I stood. It then struck me for the first time that I was someplace other than the viewing room. How had I gotten here? What had happened? As soon as the realization came, I found myself looking across the table at my monitor again. The very act of realizing that I had bought completely into the virtual reality had destroyed it.

"Where have you been?" the monitor asked.

"That's what I'd like to know!"

"Mars," he answered with a smile. "That's where they are."

"That's where who are?" I asked.

"The hibernating aliens!"

Then I remembered what had driven me to mentally leave the room in the first place.

"Oh, yeah," I lied. "I guess that's where they are."

So that no one will misunderstand, I usually enjoy working targets such as UFOs, prehistoric events, the surfaces of other planets, and such other esoteric things. I even have a good amount of faith in the results I get, simply because I have a track record in a database that gives me a dependability rating on my work. In that session, though, right up until the time of the bilocation, I was simply telling the monitor what he wanted to hear. It had become boring and painful. It was not excellent site contact that drove me into the Perfect Site Integration. It was the need to escape.

To be totally honest, though, I had serious doubts about the whole session, and actually convinced myself that I had gone to sleep during the session and had dreamed it all up. It was about two years later, when I was at Stanford Research Institute in California, that I happened to see a picture on the wall. It was a picture of "The Face on Mars." I had never seen that before. As I looked closely at it, I saw what looked like a pyramid far off to one side. I thought back to the Perfect Site Integration incident to remember the locations of the buildings I had seen off in the distance, their shapes and sizes. Studying the photograph even closer, I saw that the coordinates I had been given had corresponded to this location on Mars. Further, my perceptions had had the correct features in the correct places.

I can't really say whether or not there were any aliens hibernating there. However, right before I received the move command, I had already bilocated to a place in which I did perceive forms of alien life much like large segmented worms. They were very active and not at all in hibernation. I had just looked up and realized that there was a way out of the chamber I was in when I received the command to "move up one hundred feet and describe." How much of that part of the bilocation was accurate, I cannot even guess. There was no feedback, and probably will not be within my lifetime.

But what I did see, and get feedback on, was enough to convince me that at one time in my life, I experienced what it is like to stand on the surface of another planet. When I saw pictures sent back from the Mars Lander some time later, my first reaction was, "Been there. Done that."

Too bad the army never gave us travel pay for these sessions.

Every time I have had a PSI experience, it has been on a target of great interest, one that could induce me to give up my hold on the physical reality around me and totally buy into the mini-virtual reality of the CRV session. All except one, that is.

The target, though I did not know it at the time, was a simple picture clipped out of a travel magazine. It was a photo of a town square in a tiny Swiss village high in the Alps. There is nothing spectacular about the town. The only reason it could have attracted me is that I was never able to go to Switzerland the entire time I lived in Germany. Other than that, this tiny town was no different from any of the hundreds of small villages in Germany, Austria, and Switzerland.

I had received about ten pages of information on the target, enough to realize that it was a small town in a place with extremely clear air, bright sunshine, and mountains all around, when suddenly, the PSI experience took over. I looked up from my worksheet at the monitor, but the monitor was not there. Instead, I was looking across a cobblestoned street to see a man and his son coming out of a building. They stopped on the sidewalk and began to talk. A sign on the building clearly identified it as a Bank of Switzerland. I crossed the street to meet the two. When I approached them, I could hear them speaking Bayrish, a southern dialect of German. I spoke to them, but they did not hear or see me. Since I speak German, I began listening to their conversation. The son wanted to go to a store before they returned home. The father said that they had time to go by the store.

The two then walked to their car and I followed along, listening to their conversation. When they reached the car, I noticed that it was a VW convertible, an uncommon car for Germany, and even more so for people who live in the high altitudes of the Alps. The day was sunny and warm, and the convertible top was down. I had realized by this time that they were not able to sense me, so I climbed in and sat on the folded convertible top, behind the narrow back seat.

At about that time, Paul, my monitor, asked me a question and broke the "spell" of the PSI experience. Not realizing that I was having the PSI experience, he thought that I had just gone blank, and was trying to get me started again. I wrote down "sunny," "clear," "people," and half of some other word that I still cannot read. The experience had totally intrigued me, and I slipped back into the PSI experience.

I found myself still perched atop the back of the rear seat. The man was just pulling out of the parking lot. I looked across the street and once again saw the bank building. We turned and went down the street, past a central town square. There was a very ornate fountain in the square with some tourists and an elderly couple sitting around it on benches. As he drove further, I looked up at a street sign and read the name of the street. But there was something nagging at the edges of my attention.

Paul was calling me again, trying to get me to write something down.

My awareness came back to the viewing room. I made a quick sketch of the fountain and wrote down the street name, then slipped back into the PSI experience.

We went about eight blocks. I looked at each street sign and mentally catalogued the street names. I watched for any outstanding stores or sights along the way. Paul was calling me again, and I returned, wrote down what I had seen, and slipped back into the PSI experience.

The driver turned left and went one block. He pulled into a parking space. As he and his son got out of the car, I looked quickly around. Between two buildings, I saw the train station some two or three blocks away. Paul was calling me again.

I snapped out of the PSI experience and flashed a look at Paul that let him know that I did not appreciate these interruptions. I wrote down what I had seen and drew a quick map. I was getting ready to slip back into the PSI experience when Paul asked, "Am I irritating you?"

Oh, no! A direct question! A direct question requires an answer that has to be provided by the viewer's conscious mind. It interrupts access to your subconscious. The monitor should never ask a viewer a direct question. I stopped viewing and answered. The access to the PSI experience was broken and the session was over.

Paul told me that I had hit the target. He pulled out the feedback picture of the town square, and in its middle was the same fountain I had sketched. The feedback picture did not have anyone sitting around the fountain, but the benches were there. I evidently had visited the site location instead of simply viewing the feedback picture. There was no way to get feedback on the street names, the train station, the location of the bank, or any of the other features I had described. But, because of my sketch and the German names and the fact that I had said the location was Swiss, the session was considered a success.

Months later, the session was still eating away at the back of my mind. I knew that there must be some way to get feedback on the details. Finally, I wrote to the town's tourist bureau, asking for information about the town and a town map, if possible. When it arrived, I got the most pleasing reward anyone could get for a CRV session. The map not only showed street names, the location of the town square, and the train station, but also showed the locations of the businesses of the map's various sponsors. One was the bank. Another was a department store. Although I had misspelled many of the street names, they were unmistakably the right names. The bank, department store, train station, and town square were where I had described them. Although the map I had sketched during my session was missing several streets, it was essentially a correct rendering of the parts of the town through which I had ridden on the back of a VW convertible one warm, clear, beautiful day in the Swiss mountains.

For many months, I was tasked to access foreigners of interest to the U.S. intelligence community and report each person's plans and intentions. During one very long stretch, we were working many drug interdiction cases. I was constantly being targeted to find the plans and intentions of various drug lords, Noriega, and many of the other individuals involved in drug trafficking. After several months of this kind of tasking, I went to the director one day and pleaded to get some lighter targeting.

"Give me Mother Teresa or Bozo the Clown or something. I can't take these murderers and trash anymore."

The director looked at me with totally emotionless eyes and said, simply, "Suck it up, soldier. Do your job. Get out of here."

The same kind of targets continued. About a week later, though, my monitor walked up to my desk and told me it was time to do a session. When we got to the viewing room, I filled out the administrative section of the transcript and looked to him for frontloading.

"This one is a personality profile," he said.

Good. It was not a "plans and intentions" session, where I would have to access the person fully, getting deeply involved in the target person's thoughts, emotions, goals, and motivations. I only needed to lightly access the target person and give those superficial descriptions that allow a profiler to do a personality assessment on him.

The monitor gave the coordinates and I began the session. About a half page into the session, I looked up at him and said, "This isn't one of the bad guys." He shrugged his shoulders and motioned for me to continue. A few pages later, I again felt compelled to say, "Whatever evil you think this guy did, he didn't do it." Again he motioned for me to continue.

By the time I had reached Stage 4, I felt an actual tingling to my face and hands. It was the kind of slight tingling your skin makes when you have a slight sunburn and you feel cool air passing over it. I felt as though I were glowing inside. The target person was one of the nicest people I had ever met. I really liked him. He was impressive. I could not find a single thing about him that I did not like. I became so intrigued that before I realized it was happening, the PSI experience began setting in.

I found myself standing beside the man; he faced in one direction, and I faced in the other. I would have been shoulder to shoulder with him, had I not been a few inches taller than he. I looked over at him and saw the side of his face. He did not seem to take notice of my presence. I started to put my hand on his shoulder, to get him to think something, so I could gain better mental access. As my hand touched him, I felt a sudden rush of the most peacefully energetic power I have ever known. He continued to face forward, not taking notice of me, which is normal for the PSI experience. Since you are only accessing what your own subconscious knows about the site, the reality is virtual. No one at the target site ever knows you are there, simply because you are not.

As I tried again to gain better contact, I felt something I remember vividly to this day, but which I will never be able to adequately describe to anyone. He turned to look my way, gave a very slight smile, and then turned away again. He knew I was there. But how?

I tried to remove my hand from his shoulder, but the feeling that filled my entire being continued flowing. I remained standing there beside him, my hand on his shoulder, soaking up the most wonderful energy I had ever known. And I knew that he did not mind me doing so.

When the flow seemed to stop, I still stood there, my hand on his shoulder, but I was now aware more of myself than of him. I sensed the presence of this powerful and perfect person, and was aware of the contrasts between him and myself. He turned to me again, gave the same slight smile, and I realized that he had just done a personality profile on me, as well. Even more, he had caused me to do a personality profile on myself, a totally honest and accurate one.

I was suddenly back in the viewing room, with my monitor smiling across the table at me. He had seen a PSI experience before, and knew what it was like. He had allowed me to enjoy it.

My summary of that session both began and ended with the sentence, "Whatever evil you think this person did, he didn't do it."

We had been working double-blind. In other words, my monitor did not know what the target was either. After I finished my summary, he opened the target envelope and pulled out the task request to see if we needed to get any more information for the customer.

"Huh!" he said. "This was a practice session." He slid the sheet of paper to my side of the desk to give me the feedback. What should have been a tasking order with background information and a list of questions was nothing more than a single sheet of typing paper with one word written in the middle of it:

Jesus

This was the most moving and soul-stirring session I have ever done. I had not only met the Jesus I grew up worshipping, but, probably for the first time ever, I had also truly met myself. I had seen all my shortcomings and failures, but at the same time, I had been found acceptable. Even more, He had let me know that I was acceptable to Him. A quiet glow filled my entire being for months afterward, a glow that returns every time I remember that session.

The Perfect Site Integration experience is the pinnacle of Controlled Remote Viewing, and is a very rare occurrence. All in all, I only had nine PSI experiences during the eight and a half years I was in the military unit, and have had only four or five since. The majority of military PSI experiences dealt with classified targets, and cannot be discussed here. But PSIs are that rare. Many viewers have never had a single PSI experience throughout their whole viewing careers.

Interestingly, Ingo Swann discourages remote viewers from having a PSI experience. The reason, he says, is that when you are having it, you cannot report back. You don't even realize there is any session to report back to. When you do come back from the PSI experience, the only thing you can do is summarize what you experienced. It is much better, Ingo feels, that a viewer be able to report the extremely fine details of the target site as he progresses through the session. I have seen the results of sessions where a PSI experience has taken over the viewer, and I tend to agree with Ingo completely on this point. The quality of reported information suffers greatly when the viewer has the PSI experience. You get summaries, not details.

But to be totally honest about it, I live for my next PSI experience. It is one of the greatest experiences a CRVer can ever have.

FOURTEEN

SLIDING AROUND IN TIME

Before Abraham was, I am.
—Jesus

Remote viewers face a host of problems when trying to view a site. Some, called distractors, are caused by the viewer's own environment. Examples of distractors are the temperature of the viewing room, the viewer being hungry, or needing to go to the bathroom—they pull a viewer's attention away from the target. Other problems are intrinsic to the target environment itself. These attractors, as they are called, are objects at the target site that draw the viewer's attention away from the target. For example, if the target site is a carnival, the viewer may be tasked with the activities at a specific booth, but get attracted to the Ferris wheel. The viewer will get so fixated on the more interesting part of the target that he will not be able to turn his attention to any other part, and therefore will not be able to complete the tasking. The CRV term for this phenomenon is "doorknobbing." It is one of the more devious problems a viewer faces.

In doorknobbing, the viewer gets on target and perceives things at the site. In the viewer's mind, he is working well and doing everything correctly. If the session is double-blind, the monitor will get all the indicators that the viewer is working correctly, too. But in reality, the viewer has been pulled just slightly off target. The end result is that a viewer has a great and highly accurate session, but a useless one, since he viewed the wrong part of the target.

Temporal attractors compound the problem. These attractors pull the viewer off target in time, rather than in space. San Francisco on the day before the big fire is a good example. It is extremely difficult for a viewer to cleanly view any target that is temporally in close proximity to a catastrophic or other major event. The temporal attraction is just too strong.

People often ask whether the viewer will view the target site at the present time or will view it at the time the feedback picture was taken. The answer seems more like a Russian grammar rule than anything else, but it works in actual practice: *A viewer will default to present time, unless there is a temporal attractor that is stronger than the target's present condition. If the site has multiple temporal attractors, the viewer will tend to slide in time to the strongest.*

Another problem, especially for beginners, is the tendency to "view their feedback," rather than the actual site. The feedback picture is what they will be shown at the end of the session, so it becomes the strongest attractor. It is, after all, the yardstick by which their session results (and usually their own evaluation of their fledgling abilities) will be judged. If they describe what is in the picture, they feel success, in spite of the fact that what is in the picture may no longer be at the actual site.

We have found, quite by accident, that if the picture gets mixed up with another and the viewer is given the wrong feedback picture, the beginner will almost always describe the picture they are given at feedback time, rather than the one tasked. A more advanced and experienced viewer will tend to view the tasked site, even if the wrong feedback is given.

This is also one of the major problems faced by well-meaning laboratory researchers who test beginners the same way as they would experienced viewers. Often, the viewer is given "feedback" of a group of five to ten randomly selected targets. The viewer must then look at each target and, thinking back on the information he got in his session, rank it according to which one he thinks is the most probable target, second most probable, and so forth. The order in which he selects the most probable target will determine his final and unchangeable score.

After all these years, I'm amazed that researchers still do not realize that beginning viewers almost always view their feedback. So, if they present, say, five different target pictures to a viewer after his session, all five become his feedback. Elements of each of the feedback pictures will have been viewed. Usually, the viewer will view the most interesting aspects, or attractors, of each picture and meld them together within the session. Therefore, the viewer will have a conflict judging the tasked site, simply because the session contains elements of all five. These are the researchers who make public statements that remote viewing has an accuracy rate of only 10 percent to 15 percent. The problem, they think, is attributable to remote viewing itself. But the problem is really a flawed experiment.

The beginning viewer just naturally tends to view forward in time to the moment of feedback. Moving around in time is not only the simplest thing for the subconscious to do, it is also the most natural.

The ease with which viewers can move their minds through time is one of the major strengths of Controlled Remote Viewing. In CRV, no distinction is made between time and space as far as any working conditions are concerned. It is as easy in CRV to move back ten days as it is to move back ten feet.

But there is one strange factor in all time movement. As far as a viewer is concerned, the viewer always describes perceptions as though he were seeing them at the present moment. It does not matter when the event happened or will happen. The conscious mind only reports perceptions it is getting from the body. It has no idea of any time frame at all. All perceptions and descriptions are made in the viewer's present conscious frame of mind, even though the subconscious may have just been sent a hundred years into the past or future.

Because of this tendency, the CRV monitor is very careful to use what we call a "well-formed question to a psychic." This question is composed of two parts: a task to the subconscious mind, and a way of giving the conscious mind something to do *in present time* to keep it from jumping in and trying to take over the subconscious mind's job.

As an example, a CRV monitor says to the viewer, "Move to nine P.M. tomorrow evening." That is something the conscious mind has no idea how to do. It is a task for the subconscious mind only. The monitor then finishes it up with a task to the conscious mind, "Now, tell me what you are smelling." Note that the monitor *never* says, "And tell me what you *will* smell." The monitor always keeps the command to the conscious mind in the present tense. The same with moving a viewer into the past. The monitor says, "Move back four hundred years." This is the task to the subconscious. "And tell me what's happening, now." The monitor would *never* say, "And tell me what was happening then."

This is one of the spin-offs of CRV's years of trial and error. It is a spin-off because it works with any psychic method. When you are dealing with any psychic, palm reader, or tea-leaf reader, no matter what their methodology, if you couch your questions to them in the format of a "well-formed question to a psychic," their accuracy rate will rise. They will probably not realize that you have done anything different, but the accuracy of the information they provide you will rise nonetheless.

When I am asked by local police for tips on how to deal with psychics, I tell them that they should develop a routine, which on the surface will seem rude and inconsiderate, but will obtain more valuable information from the psychic. The method is to constantly keep jerking the psychic's subconscious mind around the time frame of the crime, but at the same time keep the psychic's conscious mind fixed on reporting in the present tense. This method limits the conscious mind from taking over the process. The investigator asks the psychic a well-formed question and records the answer right up until the time when the psychic starts trying to make logical sense of what he is perceiving. At that moment, the investigator should break in and jerk the psychic's subconscious mind to another time. Here is an example:

Investigator: Move to the night of the crime. What are you seeing?

Psychic: Noise. People noise. Laughing. You know, these people are—

Investigator: [interrupts] OK. Move back to the evening before. What are you getting now?

Psychic: Uh, well, I see some people in a car. I think these people are going to—

Investigator: [interrupts again] Fine. Now, move to an hour
before the crime. Are you sensing anything now?

Psychic: . . . Well, OK. Yes. I smell a strong alcohol smell.
Not like booze, but like medical alcohol. I think I
must be in a—

Investigator: [interrupts again] Good. Move to two P.M. that
afternoon. Now what do you get?

The psychic will be totally frustrated by the end of such an interview. Natural psychics love to build castles and give explanations for what they perceive. When not allowed to do so, they tend to get a little testy, but also produce much higher quality information. In the end, that has to be the bottom line. So never ask a psychic to tell you what will happen in the future or what happened in the past. Ask the psychic to move to the time in question and report what is happening "now." Believe it or not, this simple rephrasing of your question to the psychic will actually cause them to give you more accurate answers, no matter what method they use and no matter how talented they are.

Here is an example of how the time movement can help a viewer (and a client) gain information more cleanly and accurately. This session occurred with one of my students during his advanced class. The feedback picture was of a satellite being built and readied for insertion into a rocket for launch. The caption under the picture told the mission number and date of launch, and all the other pertinent information. The launch had occurred a little more than two years before the session.

Because advanced-level targets can take days to complete, especially when the instructor keeps breaking in and instructing you in the new tools that are available, I try to give my advanced students an extremely complex target which will last them all the way through the advanced course. This particular target was one of those.

I gave the student the target coordinates and let him work on his own into the advanced stages, where new instruction would begin. He started out by giving a very good and detailed description of the satellite itself. Much more detail and he would have surely identified the target. But I did not want him to realize what the target was. If he had, he would have had to fight every stereotype of a satellite he had ever seen. To prevent him from identifying it, I asked him to describe its location. Being an experienced viewer, he had not been attracted to the moment of the picture, nor had he been attracted to the exciting moment of launch. He began describing the present time location: "flying," "darkness," "pinpoints of light," "extremely high up," "no air," "total silence," etc.

Again, I felt that he was in danger of being able to guess what the target was, so I asked him to take a break and receive some instruction on methodology. We began discussing time movements, "timelines" and "threading." When he returned to his session, I decided to move him to a time three weeks prior to the time frame he had been viewing. I did not tell him that he had been viewing it in present time. The associated article had the main dates of the process, so I let him get some new perceptions and then said, "Move back two years and forty-five days from present time. Now, describe what you are perceiving." He began to describe a very clean enclosed space with people wearing spotlessly white uniforms. He began giving details about the preparation area which was also shown in the feedback picture.

I decided to move him forward in time to the day before the launch. "Move forward twenty days and describe what you perceive." He began describing a flat outdoor location and one tall, very thin structure.

"Move forward one year." Again, he started describing something flying through darkness at an extreme height.

I selected random times through the history of the satellite's manufacture, launch, and orbit. I even moved him back to when the whole project was in the planning stage, whereupon he described several men and a woman sitting at a large desk in an office, talking and shuffling many papers around.

His descriptions were accurate throughout the timeline. Yet his conscious mind was so confused by the entire wide range of locations, situations, activities, sounds, and smells, that he never guessed what the target actually was. It was only at the time of feedback that we drew a line and placed each perception he had made into its proper location on the line. When we did, the story came into focus and he finally realized what he had been describing.

Novice viewers have a tendency to slide around in time. Keeping your footing while sliding around in time is largely a matter of practice, but there are certain things the monitor and the viewer can do to ensure a little steadier stance.

The monitor should be very careful about the cues he gives to the viewer. In one session dealing with a hostage situation, I was describing the present location of the hostage. The monitor told me to "Move back to the beginning and describe." He meant, of course, that I should move to the beginning of this hostage crisis. But that is not what he said. My subconscious mind, seeing the way out of doing yet another hostage target (there were many of them in those days), did just what it was asked to do. I suddenly found myself back at the formation of the planet Earth, watching meteorites rain down on a steaming, seething ball of poisonous gases and molten rock.

If the monitor knows that the viewer tends to slide around in time, or is not experienced enough to resist temporal attractors, he can simply give a cue now and then to "Move to [the desired time] and describe." The first time I had to do this, it came as a surprise. My monitor had earlier told me to move to a time two years back from the present. When he cued me again to move to a time two years back from the present, I thought he had not been paying attention to the session and had forgotten where in time I was.

"You've already moved me there," I told him.

"But I'm not sure that's where you stayed," he said. "Let's take the cue again, just to be certain."

We did. It was a wise decision on his part. I had been sliding around in time at the target site and getting many aspects of different historical events all jumbled together. He gave the same cue several more times throughout the session. If he had not done so, the results would have been a mixture of every historical event that had ever happened at that target site. Timewise, I must have looked like the Keystone Kops on a bed of banana peels.

The monitor can also anchor the viewer to a specific aspect of the site, which is fixed in time, and have the viewer continually relate to that aspect. Instead of giving a series of move commands in the following manner . . .

"Move one year forward in time and describe."
"Now, move six months forward and describe."

. . . the monitor would instead give the same series of moves as:

"Move one year forward in time and describe."

"Now, move back to the target."

"Now, move one year and six months forward in time and describe."

This would tie the viewer firmly to the single target aspect.

For me, CRV is serious business. It was always a job during the military. Now I use it to help find missing children. I also do sessions for corporations to help them in their business planning, R&D work, financial projections, and executive decision making. There are many times when I sit down to do a session and realize that something inside me just does not want to do it. It wants a vacation. The obvious answer is to leave the pen and paper and head for the hills to hunt for gemstones—my personal hobby. But the job needs to be done, so once again I leave the virgin hillsides unravaged and do what is necessary to make a living. When the work sessions are over, I get busy with the other demands of life. My wife has "honey-do's" for me, the yard needs mowing, and my study looks—once again (still)—like a tornado hit it.

A student recently said, "You can go anywhere and do anything with this stuff!"

I agreed.

The student then asked, "But do you?"

The situation suddenly came crashing in on me. No. I don't. When I started learning Controlled Remote Viewing, I would quite often do a session on the weekend to learn something about my ancestors or about some exotic place I have always wanted to go. Should I live long enough to someday get to Australia, I will get the feedback for the many sessions I have done, just so I could spend some time experiencing the Great Barrier Reef, Coober Pedy, and the badlands of western Australia. I have longed to go there all my life, but Fate has stuck its hand in every time and stopped me. No problem. I could go there and experience it in my mind. And I have often done that. But not lately.

The point is that CRV can become so important that you can get lost in the importance of it. You can forget that it can also be a thing of great joy and entertainment. You can vacation anywhere you would like in time or space. The days of the dinosaur and the days of travel to the stars are just as close as the present. No feedback? That is OK. Vacation is a state of mind, anyway.

One of my students was in a bookstore one day and saw a book about one of Adolf Hitler's aides. It was a biography of the man's life and his experiences during the Nazi era in German history. My student thought, "I've never heard of this man, and here is a book about him. It is probably all the feedback I would ever want, if I were to do a bunch of sessions to find out everything I possibly can about the man." The student bought the book and stuck it on his shelf at home. To avoid contaminating the remote viewing sessions he planned to do on Hitler's aide, he would not read it or even open its pages. Over the next several months, he performed sessions on the target person whenever opportunity allowed.

The student learned about his social status, the family in which he was raised, and the family he made for himself later in life. He even found that the person loved horses. He sought to learn all he could about the man's brothers, sisters, children, pets, the number of marriages, background, jobs, interests, hobbies, and any other facet of the man's life that could be found. He even sought physical descriptions of the man's father and mother, relatives, wife, children, and other related people. He tried to get details about the man's military uniform that differed from the stereotype of a German uniform. What was the exact form of this man's collar insignia? How did his uniform fit his body? Did he wear a uniform at all?

After several months, the student set aside his stacks of completed sessions, and began to read the book for feedback information. The accuracy rate of his findings was in the high 80 percentile range.

Previously, my student had no major interest in the Hitler years, in German history, or even in war or politics. Yet, through the remote viewing process, he connected with a specific time in history in a way that few other people in the world can do. There were parts of his sessions that, if the history book were accurate, would logically be true, but which were not exactly recounted in the book. There were other aspects of the person that were not mentioned or even implied in the book, but about which my student has some feelings of certainty. In his opinion, he met this historical figure and learned more about him personally than any history book could ever record.

Along those same lines, I was personally approached one day by a government official who was also a historian. (This was not work for the military unit.) He asked me to solve a historical puzzle for him. In order to keep from polluting my findings, I told him that I did not want to know what the task was. We had no project manager or monitor to act as a go-between, so I told him to simply ask the very basic question he wanted to know, devoid of all site-related information. He thought for a moment and answered, "The question is *why?*"

It was not much to go on, but I worked three sessions for him. In the first and second sessions I obtained the background information that would cause my tasker to ask his question. In the third session, I would answer the question itself.

During the first session, I found a bunch of farmers and some family members, all meeting in one place and doing non-farm-oriented work. They met in an area that appeared to be a city, but it had no permanent inhabitants. I decided to do a small side investigation of this odd fact, but nothing spectacular came from it. I finally realized that this place was simply a set of buildings where people came to perform public service. The farmers would go out as members of road crews, would repair edifices, would plaster and paint, and do many of the hard-labor jobs of manual workers. The family members would sew, weave, clean, beautify, and do other jobs people consider to be "women's work." Also, while they were in this location, there were religious services for them.

Their public service activity continued for a span of a couple of weeks, and then everyone went back home to their farms. On the way home, they met other people who were traveling toward the citylike location to perform these same labors for the coming few weeks.

As far as I could tell, there were no outstanding events taking place that might be of historical importance. Nor were there any aspects of the target site that might confuse a historian and make him ask, "Why?" As far as I could tell, the whole process was neat and orderly and uneventful.

During the second session, I told myself to "Move to the event of historical significance and describe." All I found were more farmers and their families. This time, though, I found them returning home. There was nothing notable about the trip, the countryside, or anything else.

I decided to access one of the farmers. He was worried about something, so I delved further. I learned that he was worried about the fact that they were not meeting anyone on the road headed toward the city-like location. There would be no replacements to do the work within the coming weeks.

"That's it?" I asked. I continued a little further in session, but could find nothing more of any significance, so I finally quit. The farmer and his family were headed home, and no one else was coming to the city to replace them. That was all.

What could be of any historical significance to that? What was the whole importance behind the seemingly nonsignificant events I was finding? What about all this would cause a historian to be confused enough to go to a remote viewer for answers? It felt like a waste of viewing time.

There obviously were no historical records of the supposed event, or the historian would not have asked for my help. That probably meant that there would also be no feedback for my sessions. However, the historian was an important man in government, and had sought me out individually, so feedback or not, I felt obligated to do the work. Besides, he also was extremely influential in swaying appropriations committees for our unit's future funding. So, I worked the sessions very diligently in order to answer his question: "Why?"

In the third session, I concentrated on the "conceptuals," the purposes, hidden concepts, general topics of concern, and other kinds of esoteric information not readily discernible to the viewer. During this session, I kept getting the phrase "They didn't have money." Each time I got that perception, I wrote it down. A viewer should write every perception down, whether it makes sense or not. Because of that phrase, I began to assume that the farmers had gone to do public work because they were broke and needed the income to survive. Yet, the information I had already found in the session did not validate that conclusion. They had seemed healthy, happy, and prosperous. I had found them well equipped, well dressed, and not poverty-stricken at all. Now, I was as confused as the historian. Still I kept working, trying to find out the answer to the question, "Why?" In the end, all I could get was the answer, "They didn't have money."

One day shortly thereafter, the historian called me at work and asked for the answer to his question. I apologized to him and said that I had tried, but had not found anything important. I told him about the farmers, and that the event was simply that one day, no one came to replace them. All I could get for an answer was, "They didn't have money."

He was not at all satisfied with that answer. I had expected that he would not be, and felt that I had totally failed with his request. He hung up without telling me what the question had been about. Usually, when people don't tell you something like that, it means you had a total and absolute failure. That's what I assumed in this case.

But about a year later, I heard from him again. He was excited and bubbling with enthusiasm. "You know that answer you gave me last year?" he asked.

"Yes, sir," I answered. "Sorry about that. Would you like for me to try again?"

"Hell, no!" he answered. "That was exactly the information I needed."

"It was?" I was surprised to hear that.

"Yes. It answered a historical question that has been around since my childhood, and one that I have never been able to find any logical answer to."

I asked him to tell me what was behind his question, and he related the following:

"The wording of your answer bothered me and has nagged at me for almost a year now. I wondered why you said, 'They didn't have money' instead of 'They didn't have *any* money.' The second way would have meant that they were broke or poverty-stricken in some way. It has taken me a year, but I finally realize what you meant by not putting the word 'any' into the sentence. What you meant was that they didn't have money!"

I was totally confused by his explanation but he continued:

"Historians have always wondered why the Aztec and Mayan cities emptied out overnight and what happened to all the people. The answer has been there in front of us all along, and you brought it to light. The Aztec and Mayan cultures did not have any such thing as money. Therefore, the people could only pay their taxes and support to the government in the form of public service. Much like our National Guardsmen, groups of them would go for two weeks of service, and then go back home, only to be replaced by another group the following two weeks. They did this because the Aztecs and Mayans did not have the concept of 'money.'

"We had always thought that some catastrophe caused the cities to empty out overnight, but in fact, the people doing their public service just went home at the end of their weeks of service, and the following week, nobody came. Evidently, at one point, the governments had crumbled to the point where no one was in charge of scheduling the public service periods and deciding which groups would come the following week. So, after the last scheduled group went home, the public service gathering places were empty of people. What we thought were cities weren't even cities at all, but just places of public service.

"You're great," he continued. "Why didn't you explain all this to me a year ago?"

I thought quickly and tap-danced, "Well, sir, I knew that you are a good and thorough historian, and that you would understand it when the time was right."

Funding for the unit was not a problem that year.

Viewers often found very important and previously unknown historical information when performing remote viewing for more immediate and time-sensitive information (such as a hostage's physical condition, etc.). But such information never made it into any final governmental reports. In the sequestered records of the military unit, there are more than likely volumes of "history book revising" information of this kind. This information, because it was not important to the task at hand, was usually ignored. It is a shame that the contents of these sessions will probably never be made publicly available to historians and writers.

Some years after I retired from service, I received a call from an investigating officer at a local county-level police department. His department had an old "dead" case that needed reopening. He wanted to see whether or not a remote viewer could help provide information they had not been able to find during the years when the investigation was ongoing. The case had been cold for years, and there was now very little likelihood that any new evidence would be found. He needed a witness and had heard that my remote viewing business, PSI, could assign one.

I was very busy on other cases, so I called another remote viewer, Dave Morehouse, to come in and "honcho" the case. Dave had been working with a producer of the television show *20/20* and let them know that we would be doing the case. Dave called and received permission from the police department to have the process televised. Dave set up a date for the filming, and he, Mel Riley, and I showed up to do the sessions and to be interviewed for the *20/20* show.

The three of us were briefed by the investigating officer and then moved into separate rooms to do our sessions. I was busy with some paperwork, so Dave and Mel went into interrogation rooms that had one-way mirrors. The film crew shot their footage through the mirror. After they were finished, the producer wanted to see a monitored session, so Mel monitored my session.

When I started, I wrote my name on the top of the paper, and laughed out loud. "This is going to be a great session!" I told Mel. I had spelled my own name wrong. Traditionally, this was a sign of a good session.

The police had unsucessfully been looking for a piece of evidence for over nine years. Dave, Mel, and I were tasked to draw different aspects of that evidence's location, in hopes of finding it. After our session, we placed our three maps together and the lines on the edges of each map took up where the lines on the other maps left off. The police and the television people were visibly impressed.

But the investigator needed more. He needed an account of the events of the night of the supposed murder. I knew that Dave was the best man for this kind of job, much better than I. Dave began working the problem, and I kept giving him minute-by-minute time movement commands, starting with the last known location of the victim to the point where the victim's body could be found. Dave described the path the victim and her assailant had traveled with the surrounding landmarks along the way. In the end, the investigator was able to identify the landmarks and trace the route on a map. The specific history of a single event was revealed using a tool not previously open to historians or investigators of any kind. And it worked. The police already had bits of evidence that showed that the trail Dave found in session was accurate. In the process, he uncovered more information which proved to be of later use for them. The case is still ongoing at this time, because it involves some complex interdepartmental politics, but the investigating officer found enough evidence from Dave's session alone to return the case to active status.

*   *   *

I am fascinated by the new technology of virtual reality. In doing research on it, I have found thousands of references to the phrase "buying into" the environment. That is, at some point in the interaction with the computer, the user's senses accept it as real-world surroundings. His mind accepts the virtual reality as a real reality.

In CRV, the question arises about whether or not the experiences are real, even if you are only forming a mini-virtual reality in your mind. Let us say that you are tasked to visit a civil war battlefield during the height of battle. Your actual environment is a comfortable chair and writing table in a quiet room. But I can tell you from having been there, and from having monitored other people who have been there, that the experiences of the war are both real and historically accurate. This is especially so during a bilocation or Perfect Site Integration experience, when you have bought into your own mind's mini-virtual reality to the point where you cannot tell that you are not at the target site. The experiences you have at those times are very real.

So is experiential time travel possible, even if physical time travel is not? The answer is a resounding, "Yes, but . . ." The "yes" indicates that CRV is possibly the Carnegie Hall of the remote viewing world. The "but" brings back the one phrase that students everywhere dread. As the old joke goes, "How do you get to Carnegie Hall? Practice, man, practice."

Because of remote viewing, I no longer view time the way I had been taught to in school. When the time experiences started, early in my training, I quickly accepted the New Age belief that "Time is not linear. It is happening all at once." Now, after years of experience, I realize that that, too, is just as incorrect as the scientific theory it was meant to replace, which would have you believe that time is totally linear, going in a straight line from past to future. I have come to believe that time really is linear, that every cause has an effect and every effect has a cause. But I have come to realize that the progress of time can go in any direction. That explains why we can sense the event ahead of time. It is as though a rock thrown into the pond of time sends ripples out in all directions— each tiny arc expanding from the "plunk point." Part of it even comes backward toward what we have traditionally called the past.

There is an old paradox that says, "An infinite amount of days and an infinite amount of years must span the same amount of time—infinite." In CRV, traversing a microsecond is exactly the same as traversing a century or a thousand centuries. Increments become only markers and measures, and are otherwise insignificant. To a large extent, the passage of time depends more on our perception of time than anything real and tangible.

Over the many years, I have used CRV to answer some of the most difficult questions in my own life, and even questions about life itself. Much of this work came about accidentally or incidentally during tasked sessions against government targets. In one such session, the task was to collect information about "the target person's perceptions of life and time," although all I received was a series of coordinate numbers. As happens in many sessions where the target is complex and conceptual in nature, the answer came in the form of an analogy. As I progressed deeply into the session, I found to my surprise that my target was a molecule of water in a vast ocean. The water was calm and still, and the molecule drifted without awareness, without bumping into other molecules, and without change.

But then a wave came along and the energy of that wave pushed the molecule up into the air. The molecule rose, peaked, fell again to the surface, and then went back into a quiet state, waiting for another wave to lift it again. Yet, during the rise and fall of that molecule, I sensed some awareness from it. It had somehow imparted to me the sensations of newness, eagerness, peaking, then a growing tiredness as it dropped back down, losing energy as it went.

Then my session ended. I had either received an answer to the assigned task or botched the session. I had no way of knowing at that point. So I wrote the session summary and went on to other things. Later, I learned that the analogy was related and appropriate to the assigned task. It was a good session, after all.

But somewhere, in the back of my mind, I knew that I had experienced something profound. There was something more which had not wound up in the summary, and I had no idea what it was. Then, one day a year or two later, relatives came to visit. We took them sightseeing around the area, including the old lighthouse at Lookout Point, at the southern tip of Maryland. I was standing, looking at the dark and choppy waters of Chesapeake Bay, when my wife's niece walked by and commented that the waves looked alive. I looked out and saw a small spot of foam on the water. As the wave rushed past underneath it and moved quickly on, it merely rose, fell, and settled to a spot on the water only slightly different from where it started. An endless succession of waves made the same thing happen again and again until the speck of foam finally reached the shore. The analogy of that forgotten session came flashing back and I finally understood what my deeper self had tried to tell me. It was a perception that my good Baptist upbringing had not allowed me to even consider.

Picture yourself as a molecule of water in a vast, limitless ocean. You are in a single place on that ocean, and as long as nothing drastic happens, you stay where you are. You do not sense the rest of the ocean, nor do you sense anything else. There is no movement for you, no change. In essence, you are dead to the world about you.

But then comes a wave. Its energy lifts you up, and you are suddenly alive. You experience the upward lift of life; the change; the exhilaration of suddenly relating to the world about you in new ways. You have a sense of newness, a sense of becoming. And then, the wave peaks, passes by, and you slowly settle down to a trough between lives. The wave moves rapidly by, but you moved very little.

Some waves are small and move you only slightly. These are lives where you are a farmer, living in the same home and manner as the unchanging generations of your predecessors. You are born, live a set life, and die not having ventured far from your small valley. The small swell that gave you that life only moved you a fraction of an inch or so across the vast ocean. Yet during that life, you did learn some small something. There was some change and movement there, no matter how small. The next swell finds you in a slightly different place, the place where the former swell left you.

But now and then there comes a larger wave. When that wave lifts you into life, you experience a wilder ride. In this life, you are a traveler and scholar. You learn things that alter your being and at the end of this life, you have been moved a good deal farther.

Now and then comes a mighty, crashing wave, which lifts you even higher, and you become part of the frothy whitecap. It hurls you farther than a thousand small swells would have. In this life, you are a soldier, yanked from your home and thrown into the uncontrollable and unfathomable chaos of the world gone mad. This life is tossed by the violence of drastic social and economic affairs. The world around you changes so rapidly you cannot keep up with it, must less control any part of it. All you can do is hang on to this life and experience and learn more from it than you can even realize. The chaos and energy of this wave toss you about frantically and it deposits you, at the end of that life, far from where you started.

And so you move across the ocean of time and space, one swell at a time, one wave at a time, toward some distant shore. The waves roll by underneath you, each lifting you into life and then settling you back down into nonlife. Each time, you are slightly changed, as are the other few molecules that manage to accompany you on this journey. With each wave, you find yourself in a somewhat different location and surrounded by mostly different others. The waves roll on forever. They seem to be the very stuff of life itself.

But it is not the waves that allow there to be water. It is the water that allows there to be waves. The waves are not life and time. They are merely the experience of life and time.

And so, one wave after another surges up underneath you and then rushes away to be quickly forgotten. But you remain. Even when some wave finally deposits you on the farthest distant shores of time, that which is you remains.

FIFTEEN

THE AFTERLIFE

My grandfather was a Methodist minister and my parents were Baptists, so I was raised in both the Methodist and Baptist churches. There are major differences between those two churches, but in the Southern Bible Belt, where I grew up, there was really only one discernible difference between them and that was the difference in the volume level of the singing at the Sunday and Wednesday night meetings. The two denominations often have "dinner on the grounds" together, give joint choir recitals at Thanksgiving and Christmas, and in general, have found a great and peaceful coexistence. Small towns in the South grow up around the church, and it is a very important part of the community's life. If you grew up in one of those two churches, you were "home folk."

I grew up like most Southern boys, with the church a very major, integral part of my philosophical life and religious life, even if not always a major part of my day-to-day life. For the most part, I have always said that everything that has ever truly helped me in life, I learned in church. I have also always said that everything that ever truly hurt me in my life, I learned in church.

One of the things I had learned, but never really realized how dogmatically it had become ingrained into my psyche, was that when you die, you get judged according to your deeds, and from there get sent to Heaven or Hell. If, in life, you had accepted Jesus as your savior, you were saved from judgment and went straight to Heaven without your past deeds even being considered. But of course, while you were still alive, everyone on Earth had already been judging your every deed to determine whether you had truly accepted Him or not, so either way, you had to really watch out for those deeds. They'll get you every time.

That was an integral part of the unconscious mental framework I carried over into my military project. My "out of arm" experience at the Monroe Institute, which I described in Chapter 1, confirmed that I had a soul, and reassured me that what I had learned in Sunday school was probably true. Yet, it also opened the door to many questions that had never been posed to a young boy growing up in the conservative, rural South. Could the soul and body part ways for an hour or so without dying? Could it happen when you were "out of body"? Could some other soul jump in and take your place?

As time went on, I became more and more acquainted with this psychic field and the many and various people within it. Yet, an integral part of the Southern Baptist belief system is that psychic functioning is evil, and you will go to Hell for doing it. Though you might act upon any spontaneous act of psychic awareness, you should never give credit to it or admit that it happened. So the introductory talk Skip gave me when I was to do my first remote viewing session shook me to my very core. The restraints that had burdened me and held me down for a lifetime were suddenly lifted. The relief was enormous.

One day at our weekly office meeting about three years into my military assignment, a discussion took place that dealt with individual viewers' strengths and weaknesses. Since I ran the database, I had access to those data, and ultimately, the conversation came around to me, to give a listing of the strengths and weaknesses of each viewer sitting there. As I listed off the ones I knew for certain, I came to my own. I said, "One of my own strengths is that I can access people mentally better than everyone else, but I can't seem to access people who are dying. I guess the rule holds true that 'Anything you'll turn your eyes away from, you'll tend to turn your mind away from, too.' "

The person who was then training officer heard me say that and over the next three or four months, he fed me dozens of targets of people dying. He picked targets of people who were dying slowly of illness, suddenly and unexpectedly in car crashes, explosions, war, and a hundred other scenarios.

I could not tell the difference between this and other mental access targets, because all I got was coordinates. In normal sessions, the monitor would have me access the person at a known time and then give me move commands to the time the person could provide the information we needed. For those targets where I was, say, picking up on a foreign leader's plans and intentions for the next day, such a session format was normal.

But for these dying person targets, the monitor moved me up to and through the moment of the target person's death and out the other side. I call this the "spinach period" of my training. I know it was good for me, but it certainly wasn't pleasant.

During this time, I successfully accompanied people through the death event and over to the other side about sixty-seven times. What I learned about death through these sessions changed my entire outlook on the subject. Through all the experiences, one of four things usually happened on the other side. By "the other side" I mean the end place—after the "tunnel of light," being greeted by long-dead loved ones, etc. Those experiences did happen to most of the people I accompanied into "Heaven," but not all. I would say that the experience was not present in about one third of these people. It never happened to any of the ones I accompanied into "Hell," nor any of those I accompanied into "oblivion." It only happened three times to those who wound up "reincarnated."

Those four things I have arbitrarily labeled "Heaven," "Hell," "Oblivion" and "Reincarnation." I no longer have access to the unit's database, so do not have any way to determine which of my targets went where. That is not really important, as there was seemingly no rhyme or reason to the types or number of people who met the different ends. Also, the people targeted were all subjects of intelligence interests, so I doubt that the data would be statistically significant for the general population, anyway.

1. *Heaven.* There were a number of the people who died and wound up in a place that had all the physical attributes of the real world, except that everything there was perfect. There was an ambience of absolute and wonderful bliss. The sky was the deepest and most beautiful blue, every tree was perfectly formed, the grass made a perfect carpet, and there was an overwhelming sense of joy and happiness. I was never allowed to stay long in this place, but was, in effect, gently "ushered out" of the session by some unseen force after only a minute or so of being there. I was not able to reaccess the person who "passed over" in "pres-

ent time viewing" again to find out what happened after that. This led me to assume that once there, they stayed.

2. *Hell.* A good many people went through the death experience and immediately wound up in a place so dark that I can only describe it as "a glowing blackness." The blackness was so strong that it had its own presence. There was always the visual experience of a very dull and sinister orange glow with no real form or shape, just out of sight ahead. A good look at the dull orange glow was always blocked by some person-like "thing," which stood there, eagerly awaiting the just-dead person. I find it very hard to adequately describe the experience, which never lasted more than about a tenth of a second. The entire experience of the place was one of total and complete horror. I never actually saw anything that would cause the horror, but I was suddenly and helplessly overwhelmed by it nonetheless. After such a session, the fear and horror accompanied me home, into my dreams, and into my daily thoughts, and it was usually a week or more before I could do any effective viewing again of any target of any kind. I hated these targets. I was never able to "detox" from this experience

3. *Oblivion.* The third class of "places" where people went after death was no place at all. I would follow the person through the death experience and suddenly there would be no person at all. I could move back in time to before their death and would still be in touch with them, so I knew that I had not lost session contact. But if I moved forward again, beyond the moment of death, there was simply no person there. I've made searches for these people, but never found one of them again. They just stopped existing.

4. *Reincarnation.* A fourth fate appeared to be reincarnating into another life. The person would suddenly have other physical characteristics, different surroundings, different life situations, etc. There was a very strange and unexpected aspect about this type of person, though. I have always thought that reincarnation would involve the person coming back as a baby and beginning the life process all over again. This was not the case for those whom I accompanied through this process. Every one of them suddenly became a child of around twelve or thirteen years old. One of these even had the awareness of his new status as well as memories of his old life, and was, for a moment, very confused about it. I remember that this person had been some sort of political leader in

the previous life, and at the moment of death, he suddenly found himself standing out in the front yard of a modern suburban-style American home. He found himself wearing a cowboy outfit, complete with furry chaps, cowboy hat, and all. He was standing with a cowboy pose and looking across the front yard at his parents, who were taking his picture and laughing. He did not know these people. He looked to his right and saw a younger sister. When he realized what had happened, he accepted the situation and I lost contact with the "him." I had accompanied him as he became a new person.

In a later session I tried to access the originally targeted foreign leader "in present time," and found a young, American boy. When I gave the command to move back past the moment when he appeared in that body, I got the originally tasked political figure. This kind of session made me wonder about the bar mitzvahs, bas mitzvahs, and many other "coming of age" rituals of the various cultures of humankind.

There were other types of "ending up places" that I began to look for as I worked these targets, but never found. I thought that I would find at least one soul that "got lost" and stayed on as a ghost. But within the group of targets I had been given, none did. And not one wound up reincarnating as animals or as species of beings on other planets.

I also learned something else. I had always thought that when people who believe in reincarnation talk about past and future lives, they meant past and future in time. From the people I followed through the death experience who reincarnated, I have come to believe that this is not so. I now think that people who believe in reincarnation are using the wrong terminology.

Many people believe that you reincarnate to learn a specific lesson. What if the best place to learn your next lesson is in the past? Your "next" incarnation could be in a past time, and your "previous" incarnation could well have been in our future. Of the people who were given to me as targets, one of those reincarnated did so into surroundings that I could clearly tell existed in a past time, and not the present or future. This person wound up as a skinny young boy standing on the front porch area of a wealthy looking marble home overlooking the sea. He was dressed in a toga and had every appearance of being a member of a

Grecian culture. Later, out of session, I found that his dress and surroundings were Minoan.

These targets had no hard and fast feedback, however, and I could have been imagining them all. But I was no longer a novice viewer at this time. I knew from my track record in the database what percentage of my findings were accurate. Although I have no absolute proof, I am confident of my experience in these sessions.

Once this series of sessions was completed, I no longer had any problems viewing targets that included death and dying. But what effect did all these targets have on me, personally, especially in the realm of my good Baptist upbringing? It certainly did not provide me with any firm answers. It did, however, make me consider—almost to the point of a conviction—that anyone who says that there is no afterlife might be just as correct as the person who says there is. The person who says that there is only one life on Earth may be just as correct as the person who says that we are reincarnated hundreds or thousands of times before moving on. The person who says that there is no Heaven or Hell may be just as correct as the person who says that those places do exist. Such considerations may not be logical, but they do seem to be true.

A couple of times, I looked up the personal history of the targeted person, after receiving feedback and learning, in session, what happened to that person after death. I wanted to find out what kind of people go to Heaven, what kind go to Hell, what kind get reincarnated, and what kind just cease to exist. Written records of people's lives are never revealing enough to determine such things, and I never felt that such investigations really did me any good.

There are those people who believe in Heaven, but don't believe that there is a Hell. There are those who believe firmly in reincarnation, and those who believe that there is no soul, and only oblivion awaits them. I have often wondered whether, at some subconscious psychic level, we don't all have some hunch of what will happen to us individually. I do not know. But of one thing I am certain: For some people, there is a Hell, and I know that I absolutely do not want to be one of those people.

SIXTEEN

THE ASSIGNED
WITNESS
PROGRAM

Early in 1993, about a year after I left the military unit, I was called to work on a missing-child case by a local police department. I had worked with the investigator before. He is the type who does not know what he wants, whose case has gotten so tangled up with conflicting evidence and contradicting accounts that he just does not know where to begin untangling it. The first step of the process—getting him to tell me what information he needed from remote viewing—would be difficult. I explained for the tenth time that we needed one single question to begin the process. I would need to task the viewers with the one question that would get his case back on track. He gave me a "massive multiple-tasking" question, which included the child's location, the location of any and all evidence, the names and addresses of anyone involved, the condition and health of the child, and "any other pertinent information you come up with."

"No," I said. "I need to know what one single question you need to have answered in order for you to get the investigation going again. We do not solve cases. Our job is to provide information to get you on track, then we get out of your way and let you do your job."

He thought for a moment and finally said, "What I really need is a witness."

"We can assign one," I answered.

This took him by surprise. "Do you mean that you can assign a viewer to witness a crime that has already happened?"

The enormity of what remote viewers can do had finally dawned on him. "Yes," I answered. "If you had a witness, what is the first single question you would ask him?"

"Is the child OK?" he answered.

"Then that is where we will start. I will have my viewers find the answer to that question and get back to you."

From that conversation came the name, the Assigned Witness Program (AWP). At that time, I did this work as a public service of my data analysis company, Problems Solutions Innovations. I was doing most of the work myself but did have a couple of volunteer viewers, and we were doing what we could, as we had the time and opportunity.

We used only trained CRV people in the beginning. But as we began to get more and more requests for help, the demands on my personal time and resources became overwhelming. In 1999, I decided that I had become the bottleneck in its operations, and that I needed help in the form of talented and trained personnel, administrative help, and funding. I separated the Assigned Witness Program from my company and made it a 501(c)3 nonprofit organization. In theory, this would allow for grants and public funding, as well as for the inclusion of non-CRV people, such as dowsers. A very fine group of people volunteered as board members.

Getting through the paperwork process was a nightmare, taking almost three years to complete. The standards of the AWP are extremely high, demanding that each person who works as a viewer have an established and documented track record before he/she can work on actual cases. We keep detailed documentation on the viewers, and in fact, demand that they prove themselves over and over again before working on any real-life case. Then, because all their work is databased, they are selected for work on any one case according to their strengths and how those strengths meet the needs of the question at hand.

Some viewers, for example, seem to always get colors correctly, but are not so good at getting shapes. Some are good at shapes, but not sounds, mechanical aspects, or other information. So if, for example, an investigator needs to identify a weapon, we would not ask the person who is good at colors to work that question. We would ask the person who is good at shapes. The viewer, then, does not "solve the case." He only describes the shape of the weapon—that is what viewers do. It is the investigator who takes that description and identifies the weapon for himself. That is what investigators do.

With the formation of the nonprofit organization, the goals of the Assigned Witness Program also expanded. There is a great need for standardization of work among those groups that perform this service. Since no other group has been able to create a set of standards, the AWP has taken that task as one of its major goals.

REPORTING IS THE MOST IMPORTANT STANDARD. Most groups or individuals report the information they get in the words and phrases used by psychics. No wonder the police do not want to use them. Reporting should be done in "police-ese." That is, in the terminology needed by a police investigator. The investigators do not care a fig about the color of someone's aura or about the victim's spiritual condition. Psychics need to answer the question posed by the investigator, and to provide that answer stripped of all the "voodoo" and "woo-woo." There are many psychics in the world who are good and would be a very valuable asset to any police investigation, if only they could learn to speak the language. The Assigned Witness Program has made this one of its highest priorities.

WE USE ONLY QUALIFIED PEOPLE. The majority of groups working for police simply take anyone who feels they are psychic. There are no tests to find out whether a person is qualified to do the work or not. There are no standards. Each person in the group just works his own way and comes up with whatever occurs to him. There is no way to analyze the person's work for meaningful imagery, allegory, or truthfulness regarding known fact. The resultant information from such a group can be as contradictory and tangled as the case that requires it.

WE ALSO SEPARATE OUR VIEWERS. Police often separate eyewitnesses and interview them separately to make certain that the statements of one will not color or change the statements of the other. It is a known fact that you can change a person's recollections of what he saw, simply through suggestion of something else having taken place. The same goes for viewers. If they work together and one excitedly announces that he has found something spectacular, the others will be influenced by the excitement and will tend to see it, too. Whether it is true or not makes no difference. I have seen this happen in groups working together. One person "finds" some exciting thing, and announces it to the group, and within minutes, the entire group has become so excited that their imaginations are completely in control from that point on. The Assigned Witness Program does not allow the viewers to know what other viewers have found. This eliminates the possible contamination of information.

WE DO NOT USE CONSENSUS ANALYSIS AND EVALUATION. Many groups solve the problem of contradictory information by providing only information for which there is "majority rule." This is self-defeating, especially when groups work together, because any and all information is shared among the members of the group. They want their findings reported, so they will tend to agree with each other, no matter whether it seems correct or not.

By keeping a database, we have found, for example, that nine viewers can say the car is green, and one can say that the car is red, and the one viewer will be correct. Consensus evaluation and reporting may work at times, but cannot be depended upon for accuracy.

Consensus reporting is an attempt to solve the case for the investigator. The Assigned Witness Program does not do that. It is a central location where the investigator can call on the best, most thoroughly trained and tested, databased, and proven talent available. He can get information to assist him in his work. It is a tool he can use when needed. It is a tool that will not try to invade his workplace and do his job for him, as most psychics and psychic groups do.

WE DO NOT "CONTAMINATE" THE VIEWERS WITH CASE INFORMATION. Most psychics who work for police departments want to know everything they can about the case before they work. They begin their sessions already having conjectured on the answer. It is rare, then, that they find an answer that contradicts what they suspect. The Assigned Witness Program does not allow its viewers to be contaminated in this way. The viewer will not be told any of the known information about the case. In fact, he is not even told what type of case it is, who the customer is, or any other information that might drive his imagination. He is given a set of numbers, only, and sometimes not even that. For example, the tasking to a viewer may be nothing more than *"The coordinates are: 010918 / 018051."* From that information, alone, they are to provide the information the police need to kick-start their investigation. If the viewer works correctly, this is enough.

WE USE TRAINING AND A PROVEN TRACK RECORD. The importance of standardized training followed by databasing and documentation of results cannot be overemphasized. Without these two factors, the group is nothing more than a bunch of civilians getting in the investigator's way.

Ask psychics or groups of psychics for proof, and they will tell you at great lengths of their successes. Ask for actual data about the person's or the group's pass/fail rates, their "less than spectacular" work, and you will generally get a story or two, filled with deduced reasons for any errors. Some may give you a statistic for their success, such as "We've been ninety-seven-point-three-percent accurate." But if you then ask to see the data, you find that the statistic was made up from a personal estimation. Like the old saying goes, 83.47 percent of all statistics are made up on the spot—even this one. What you will not get is accurate data, such as their success rate where blood and guts, murder and mayhem are involved, as opposed to cases where such emotional factors are not involved. You may get an estimation of strengths and weaknesses, but you will not get proof.

The Assigned Witness Program trains all its workers to report in standard formats, so perceptions can be databased. Every viewer must perform sessions on at least forty already solved cases before being allowed to work on a live case. This is to establish their track record and evaluate their strengths and weaknesses before using them.

When they start work on live cases, the AWP requires unbiased feedback from the investigator for continued evaluation purposes. When the live case is finally solved, the AWP evaluates and scores each perception each viewer had given against the feedback from the investigator. We database the results, and keep an accurate and up-to-date evaluation of each viewer's abilities. These self-imposed requirements are very labor intensive, but have been proven to make the difference between a bunch of psychics and a useful investigative tool.

The Assigned Witness Program, then, is an organization of elite and proven professionals, working together for the maximum benefit and highest dependability possible. It is nonprofit and seeks neither publicity nor public recognition for its work. In order for a family or individual to enlist the aid of the AWP, they must go through the police department that is working on the case. It works *with* the police, not around them.

SEVENTEEN

PROVING IT

*"You have the best doctors on the planet," Cormira
assured him, "Just look at all their diplomas."*

*John barely glanced at the diplomas posted on the
wall. "Every doctor in the galaxy has diplomas on his wall."
He answered, "Show me one who'll post his report cards, and
then I'll be impressed."*

—Cormira in *Gravity Can
Be Your Friend*

Millions of people have had personal experiences or been involved in events that can only be explained with the term "psychic." They have known, without any way to know, that a son or daughter was in trouble across town or in another city. They have found out later that they were right. There have been thousands of accounts of someone seeing a ghostly apparition of a friend or relative who should not have been dead, only to find out that the person had just died in some distant location. There have been millions of accounts of people reaching to answer the telephone before it rings. Just as many accounts exist of people inexplicably dodging just in the nick of time before something goes flying by, which would have hit them had they not ducked. Billions of recorded or verbally passed stories exist throughout all history of times when someone suddenly "knew" something for which there was no sensory input, and for which there was no other explanation than the word "psychic." So are these things really psychic? Most people believe that many of them are. I, personally, believe that many of them are just exactly that. But we can easily fool ourselves into believing almost anything. The real question is, "Can we prove it?"

There are a lot of things that pass for being psychic, but that are really something else. Previously I discussed how a person's sense of ambience is quite often mistaken for the psychic sense. In fact, I ventured an unfounded guess that probably more than 90 percent of everything that passes for psychic is merely a good sense of ambience. I'll stick by that estimate. From what I have seen during the more than seventeen years I have been working with some of the world's best psychic spies, I have come to the conclusion that the psychic sense is very elusive and rarely ever used. I have also come to the totally unshakable conclusion that it does, in fact, exist. But then I am obligated to face the question—can I prove it?

Yes and no.

Thanks to the electronic age in which we live, there is a new form of proof which goes beyond the simple anecdotal eyewitness account or the remembered experience(s) of things that happen to us. There are data. Specifically, there is the database, which is the electronic term for good, old-fashioned "record keeping."

There is a problem, though. Any data entered must be accurate, or the entire database suffers. "Garbage in = garbage out" is the rule. For example, how do you accurately judge whether something is a hit or a miss? Let's say that I give you a target site sealed in an envelope. Your task is to describe the targeted site, and when you finish, we will take the picture out of the envelope and see how well you did. You do whatever psychic thing you have learned to do and come up with the following results:

"There is a two-story white house partway down on a hill. It is steep and grassy. It has green shutters. There are chicken sounds."

When we pull the picture out of the envelope to see how you did, the picture shows *a one-story white house on top of a hill. The hill is not steep at all but it is covered with grass. The house has blue shutters. We cannot tell from the picture whether there are chickens there or not.*

Herein lies the problem. If a single perception is wrong, a debunker will rejoice. He gets to reject the whole summary on the basis of a single wrong perception, saying, "See? If PSI were real, it would be one hundred percent accurate, one hundred percent of the time!" He will conveniently ignore the fact that no human endeavor has ever been 100 percent accurate 100 percent of the time. He will make his claim with all authority and conviction, totally disregarding the fact that the same debunker cannot give a 100 percent accurate report of a car wreck he witnessed just one minute earlier. Yet, let one single perception of the psychic be incorrect, and to the debunker, it justifies throwing out the baby with the bath water.

The Amazing Randi once appeared on television to prove that PSI ability does not exist. As one of his bits of proof, he said that he had given the task to a bunch of psychics to predict earthquakes. One psychic predicted an earthquake in a certain town on a certain day. The earthquake did happen in that town, but a day later than predicted. He predicted an earthquake in another town on another certain day. The earthquake did happen on the day predicted, but in a town by the same name in another country. "See?" Randi proudly announced, "There is no such thing as PSI."

On that same show, Randi challenged another psychic to hold his hand over oil drums and determine whether they were filled with sand or water. The challenge was to predict the contents of ten drums correctly. Then, if that were accomplished successfully, the psychic would have to do it again two more times, for a total of thirty drums. The purpose of having him do it again was just to show that the first ten were not dumb luck.

The psychic declared the contents of the first three or four drums correctly. Yet, this proved nothing. On about the fifth drum, the psychic declared the contents incorrectly. Randi immediately jumped in, declaring that here was proof positive that there was no PSI at work, and the experiment was over. Success means nothing—failure, even in the slightest, means everything. It is this kind of illogic that Randi provides to the general populace as "scientific proof." He makes a living pulling "sleight of mind," totally unrealistic tricks on the public.

But he does have a point. There is a good deal of deception in the psychic camp, too, and more people are guilty of that kind of deception than Randi is of his. There are a lot of people who will take that psychic's first four successes as proof that PSI ability does exist and totally discount the failure as though it never happened at all. For them, success means everything and failure means nothing.

One of the problems in this field is that the burden of proof has been left to both the zealous believer and the zealous debunker, while the rest of the world goes on about its business, not caring strongly, either way. Until the advent of the computer, there have been no impartial judges.

But that leads to another big problem. Psychics do not tend to produce data. At worst, they tend to produce volumes of disconnected utterances, and at best, they produce essay-type session summaries—usually verbally. Random utterances are hopeless losses. They have no context, so each can have hundreds of meanings. In actual practice, the psychic produces these disconnected phrases and hopes that one of them will trigger something in the customer's unconscious that will cause an already known answer to bubble to the customer's conscious mind, providing the "psychic" answer. Random utterances not having a definite meaning can always be twisted and reshaped to mean virtually anything that fits the situation. There are many "psychics" who have taken this type of gibberish to a finely honed skill.

A written essay-type summary, on the other hand, requires that the psychic make definite statements, and that the statements are made in context with the whole set of findings. The psychic has to state things clearly and then stand behind each statement as it relates to the entire body of perceptions and their collective, overall meanings. In the military unit, we had a rule that went, "If you didn't write it down, you didn't get it." Our entire reputations went on the line with every perception and every summary to every customer, every day of our career.

Written summaries are fine, but in fact, they are still not data. Computers deal in numbers and statistics. It is extremely difficult to reduce a narrative summary to numbers. For example, when the psychic says, "The target is a light green Ford convertible sitting empty on a steep, paved slope," and the feedback shows a dark green Chevrolet convertible sitting empty on a slight, unpaved incline, is the psychic's entire sentence to be considered incorrect because some parts of it were wrong?

Breaking down the narrative into data that can be entered into a computer yields the following:

1. The color of the car was correct   1 point
2. The tint of the color was incorrect   0 points

3. The make of the car was correct	1 point
4. The fact that there was a car was correct	1 point
5. The fact that it was a convertible was correct	1 point
6. The fact that there was a hill was correct	1 point
7. The slope of the hill was incorrect	0 points
8. The hill was not paved	0 points
9. The fact that it was sitting (not moving) was correct	1 point
10. The fact that it was empty was correct	1 point

The computer would therefore judge this narrative as having six correct perceptions and four incorrect perceptions, for an accuracy rating of 60 percent on that particular target. Over hundreds of such targets, a viewer will establish a track record, or "dependability rating."

Reducing a narrative to numbers is not the daunting task it appears to be. It can be accomplished by following a few very simple steps:

1. Write your summary.
2. Rewrite the summary, putting only one perception per line.
3. Judge each line on its own merits.
4. See what percentage of perceptions were correct by first subtracting the number of perceptions for which there is no feedback (and therefore cannot be judged) and then dividing the number of correct perceptions by the total number of perceptions that can be judged.
5. Do this for every session the psychic performs and wait for a profile of that psychic's strengths and weaknesses to appear. Once you have done this, you will have that psychic's dependability rating. That is, you will know how dependable that viewer or psychic is, and how much faith you can put into his/her work.

That is not an oversimplification. The steps are actually very easy to do. As an example, let's continue with the "white house on the hill" illustration we started above. First, we rewrite the summary with a single perception per line. Let's also use indenting, so we know what each perception relates to. That is, we will indent the descriptors of the house under the line for "house," and indent the descriptors of the hill under the line for "hill." The viewer's summary now reads:

There is a hill
       which is steep
       and grassy
There is a house
       on the hill
              partway up
       which is white
       and has two stories
       and has shutters
           which are green
There are chicken sounds

Note that "partway up" is indented farther because it describes the location on the hill, not the house itself. Also, "green" is indented beneath "shutters" because it describes the color of the shutters, not the house. The last perception (chicken sounds) does not directly describe the house or the hill, so it is placed alone as a separate idea.

Each perception can now be judged as either correct (Y), incorrect (N), or "can't tell" (?). The result would now look like this:

There is a hill	Y
which is steep	N
and grassy	Y
There is a house	Y
on the hill	Y
partway up	N
which is white	Y
and has two stories	N
and has shutters	Y
which are green	N
There are chicken sounds	?

To come up with a score, simply count. The chicken sounds are not considered since we cannot determine whether they are there or not. We cannot, therefore, count them as right or wrong, because we do not know. That leaves ten perceptions, six of which were correct and four of which were not. The information provided by the psychic—at least that which we could score—was 60 percent correct.

So what does that mean? Does that mean that the person is 60 percent psychic? No. But if, over hundreds of sessions, that psychic consistently and repeatedly averages 60 percent, then we can begin to say that he has a dependability rating of 60 percent. That is, you can depend on 60 percent of the information he provides to be accurate.

The question must then be asked again whether this proves the person is 60 percent psychic. The answer is, again, no. It is the end result of the process of gaining psychic information, correctly understanding and summarizing that information, and reporting it in a way that can be understood. There are many pitfalls to losing valuable information at every step of the process. This score simply says that the viewer can be depended upon to perform the entire process with an accuracy of 60 percent.

But this also provides a way to tell what a viewer's or psychic's strengths and weaknesses are. We can look at his work and see what type of information he gets right, what type of information he gets wrong, and what type of information it is that he reports that we can't judge. Let's add another column to the summary we've been building, one that specifies the type of information involved, whether it is an object, shape, texture, color, sound, etc.:

There is a hill	Y	Object
which is steep	N	Shape
and grassy	Y	Texture
There is a house	Y	Object
on the hill	Y	Relationship
partway up	N	Position
which is white	Y	Color
and has two stories	N	Measure
and has shutters	Y	Object
which are green	N	Color
There are chicken sounds	?	Sound

If we now look at the summary, we find that the viewer got every one of the objects correct, but only half of the colors right. You will need many more sessions to make proper generalizations about his strength or weakness in the other categories. Over time, a profile of that person's work will emerge. Perhaps it will show a 99 percent dependability in naming objects and 50 percent dependability in colors. Therein lies the proof.

But even still, the question must be asked, "Proof of what?" Is it proof that this person is psychic? No. There are far too many variables involved. For example, if you are describing an airplane and you say that "There is red on it," you will stand an extremely good chance of being correct. Many airlines have red as one of their signature colors. If you are describing an airplane and say, "Metallic," you will almost always be correct. There is nothing psychic about that. Some people provide descriptors through logic, some through psychic abilities, some through just, old-fashioned good guessing.

So what is it proof of? It is proof that overall, you can depend on this particular person's ability to name an object correctly, but you can't really depend on this person to give you the correct color, so you have to take anything he says about color with a grain of salt. Therefore, if the police want to know what the murder weapon was, I will ask this person to do the psychic work and tell me what the object (murder weapon) was. But if the police want to know, say, the color of the getaway car, I'll look into my database and find someone else who is good at colors.

So, what is it really proof of? It is merely proof of that viewer's reliability to give me good information. I don't have to care where it comes from, as long as the information is good. It is proof of the viewer's ability. It is not proof of the existence of PSI.

The fact is, I don't really care whether there is PSI functioning or not. I only have to care about using the correct person for the job. Whether he is truly psychic or only fooling himself does not have to be my concern. If he can dependably help find the missing child, free the hostage, predict the next day's battlefield activity so we can save our soldiers' lives, the next week's weather so I will know what to take on the trip, or the next day's stock market so I will know whether to buy or sell, then I don't care whether he is psychic or not. If a person can perform those tasks with a dependable accuracy at a level significantly above chance, then we need him.

I find the whole debate about whether or not PSI abilities exist to be pretty tiring. Who cares? I do not have to believe in electricity to turn on a light switch and banish the darkness. I do not have to believe in the ability of digestive juices to turn matter into energy in order to eat food and feel stronger. The whole issue of the existence of PSI is, for all general purposes, not an issue at all. If you can do better than chance, then you have a talent someone needs.

But the fervent debunker will jump in at this point and ask, "What really does 'better than chance' mean?"

Debunkers love to both hide and ignore the truth. They will generally declare that, because a psychic perception is either right or wrong, chance is 50 percent. This is one of those "sleight of reasoning" tricks. Do not fall for it.

Take all the advertising cards and jokers out of a deck of cards, then shuffle the desk thoroughly. Now, predict which color of card you will pull out of the deck. Pull a card at random and turn it over to see what color it is. What are the chances it will be a red suit? Fifty percent. If you continue to do that for every card, the chance probability that you will name the color correctly is always going to be 50 percent.

Now, do the same, but instead of predicting color, predict the suit. The fervent debunker will still say that you are either right or wrong, so chance is 50 percent. But in reality, your chance probability of correctly naming the suit is 25 percent.

Let us say that a psychic has reported that a getaway car is blue. The debunker will say that the psychic is either right or wrong, so chance is 50 percent. But then the car turns out to be, say, sky blue. "Ah!" The debunker says, "He said it was blue! Not sky blue! See? There is no such thing as PSI!" Using the judgment of this debunker, the psychic had virtually "the snowball's chance in Hell" of getting the color correct.

But let us assume further that the psychic had actually said "sky blue." You can revel in that psychic's success all you want, but it still brings us back to the question of what the chance score was for such a prediction. You could begin with the number of colors that exist in the world, but how many are there? That is unrealistic. More accurately, how many colors are there in the psychic's personal vocabulary? If the psychic, for example, cannot distinguish the color heliotrope, he will never use the word. The chance for a heliotrope-colored car to be described correctly is nil, in his case, where a pure yellow color may have a large chance of being named correctly.

But arriving at a chance score is still not as simple as that. It is a fact that there is actually a greater number of, say, red cars, than there are mauve or greenish purple ones. So, the number of samplings in the environment also affects the definition of chance. As an added example, what if you are predicting the color of the next traffic light you come to? Mauve, heliotrope, and greenish purple are simply not valid choices. You are now limited to red, yellow, and green. You would think that you have a one in three chance of getting the correct color, no matter how wide your vocabulary is, so you would think that the answer would be 33.33 percent. Not so. Red and green lights stay lit longer than the yellow caution light, so the chance of your being right if you predict red or green is better than if you predict yellow.

The point here is that comparing a psychic's score to chance is nothing more than a smoke screen that serves no purpose. It is, in the end, meaningless.

I hate to admit this, but I would have to agree somewhat with Amazing Randi and ask, simply, "Did you get it right or did you get it wrong?" I would not throw up the smoke screen that he does, claiming that it is some kind of scientific attempt to compare your score to chance. In the end, my only concern would be, "Did you help find the missing child or didn't you?" The answer to that question, when it is repeatedly yes, is much more important to me than the arguments about whether or not there is proof of PSI's existence. The proof, for me, at least, will always be found in the act of returning the child home to his parents. When something works, and it works reliably, I have all the proof I need. I have seen that the method used by the AWP works, and aside from all other arguments, that, to me, must ultimately be the bottom line.

EIGHTEEN

ONE FINAL STORY

. . . and above all, Lord,
please deliver us safely from
idiots in high places.

> —An often repeated prayer
> of Lyn Buchanan

I was sitting at my desk one afternoon when the director walked into my cubicle and handed me a slip of paper with two six-digit numbers on it. I knew that these were session coordinates.

"We need the answer ASAP," he said.

I stopped what I had been doing and went over to the Operations Building. There was an empty room, so I entered. The entire room was battleship gray in color. The windows had been boarded up and painted the same gray to match everything else. I closed the door and sat down in a gray chair at a gray table. An assortment of pens and a ream of blank paper were the only things on the desk, and in fact, the only things in the room that were not gray. I began to arrange them to my liking. The track lighting overhead was brighter than I liked, so I adjusted it to suit my working style.

I filled in information about myself and about the session I was going to do, and then carefully wrote down the two six-digit numbers. As soon as I had written them, my hand twitched and made an ideogram which, to a trained Controlled Remote Viewer, provided the major bits of information about the far distant location that was my target for the day. After that, the information about the target began to flow.

After about an hour, I returned to the Administration Building with a sheaf of papers in hand. I went to my desk and wrote up a summary of the information that had come to me as a result of writing down the two six-digit numbers and working the remote viewing session.

The information I obtained involved an explosion in a home. There would be death as a result of the explosion. I had noted that the death would be of international importance and would make a minor change in history. During my work in the Operations Building, I had also drawn a sketch of what I "saw" in my mind's eye. It was a living room with a heavy beam fallen down across the couch. The room was in shambles. I turned the summary in to the director and went back to my other work.

Two mornings later, I arrived at the office, grabbed a cup of coffee, and went to my desk to begin a normal workday. Minutes later, the director arrived, newspaper in hand, grabbed his cup of coffee, and headed for his office. He always read the morning paper as soon as he arrived, so we did not normally see him for about the first half-hour. This morning, though, he came out of his office after about only fifteen minutes. He threw the front section of the paper down on my desk with the headlines visible: U.S. BOMBS KHADAFI'S HOME.

"Here's your feedback for the other day's session," the director said. "Good work."

The picture that accompanied the article showed Khadafi's living room with a huge beam lying across the couch and the rest of the room in shambles.

I grinned broadly.

"Too bad Khadafi wasn't home at the time," he said. "If you hadn't predicted a successful raid, the mission would have been called off. If we had thought to include whether he would be home or not in the tasking, we might have gotten him." The director turned to leave and added, "Too bad about the girl."

I read on through the article to find that Khadafi's daughter had been killed in the raid. My joy at having had the successful session abated. According to the director's comment, it had been my session results that had told someone that the raid would be a success, so they went on with it. It had been one of the very few times when something concrete had actually happened as a result of one of our unit's sessions. I had done some very good and very important work—and a young, innocent girl was dead because of it.

To this day, I understand that I was innocent in the matter, and that I have no reason whatever for guilt. I just wish it would feel that way inside.

If the reader will permit me a moment of pure, unadulterated frankness, I would like to make the following as clear and unmistakably to the point as possible, so some strong, army sergeant language is required.

AN OPEN LETTER TO MUAMMAR KHADAFI

Sir,

I feel the need to say that I support the U.S. having taking action because you were dealing in terrorism and deserved to die. You were supporting the destruction of innocent human lives. I see you personally as a soulless bastard who deserved punishment in the most severe degree, and you got it in type and kind as you gave it. You learned first-hand how the families of those innocent victims of your terrorists have felt. To a very small extent, justice was served.

You are now trying to sue the U.S. government for your loss. You act as though you have been wronged terribly and want someone to pay. When will you pay the thousands of others for the loss you have caused them?

But I also feel compelled to say that your daughter should not have paid for your crimes at our hands any more than innocent victims around the world have paid with their lives for your political and religious callousness at the hands of the terrorists you support.

I have always been proud to serve in the U.S. military, except in this one event. If there is anything I will ever hold against the U.S. government for my time in it, it is simply that, at this one point and in this one act, it stooped to your level and took me unwittingly with it. We should have attacked your operations tent or your car along the road. We should have found your military location and bombed it. We should have killed you in retribution for the many thousands of others you have killed. But we should not have bombed your home and family. We gave you a taste of your own medicine, but we lost a tremendous amount of prestige and honor as a nation in doing so. Some pitiful excuse for a military commander in our government, who is just as craven and sick as you, gave an order that was against all the laws of God and man. I will always resent the fact that he used me as a tool for his injustice. Pigs wallowing in mud are the only beings at the level you two people inhabit, and I resent being dragged down to it.

I feel grief for the many families that have suffered under your acts of terrorism, so please don't think that I am taking your side in any way. You deserved to lose a loved one. That is what you have been making other people do, and your loss is only a taste of the bitter meal you have dished out to others. So, it is not for any comfort to you, but only for my own comfort alone that I say, "I'm sorry about your daughter. I have grieved for her, too."

EPILOGUE

I had some business to do in New York City, so I decided to deliver the manuscript of this book to my literary agent in person. That morning, George Thorndyke, one of the officers of Problems Solutions Innovations, who met me in New York, hurried into my hotel room and told me to turn on the TV. Something had happened to the World Trade Center. It was September 11, 2001. We hurried to the meeting we had scheduled just four blocks from the twin towers, not knowing whether anyone else would show up. Later, after delivering the manuscript to Sandra Martin at Paraview, we made our way to see Ingo Swann, who had been on the roof of his building all morning, looking the few blocks across at the World Trade Center as it burned and collapsed.

What happened that day made me more eager than ever to put my remote viewing skills to use. Like an old firehouse dog, I might not be riding the trucks anymore, but when the alarm goes off, I still feel the need to do a lot more than just bark. It was virtually impossible to get through to any of my still-active contacts within the government, but slowly, I let them know that I was available and eager to be of help. Before long I was contacted by three individuals within different agencies, asking for help.

President Bush had instructed various agencies that, in view of the situation, they should allow their agents to "think outside the box." Of course, when an individual agent asks for help from a remote viewer—quite unofficially, of course—the agencies can honestly say that the agency itself is not using remote viewers, but can also boast that their agents are using every means possible to accomplish their investigations. What could be a public relations disaster thus receives a very positive spin, and everyone comes out looking good. In politics, spin is everything.

The viewers who work for Problems Solutions Innovations, those who work for the Assigned Witness Program, the few hundred new viewers we have trained, and those retired military viewers with whom we work will continue to dedicate our services and help in any way we can. We want the message to get to terrorists everywhere that no one attacks our country and kills our people and gets away with it. We can, and we will, find you.

A WORD OF THANKS

I am one of those people who hate the idea of "drop what you're doing and do this other thing first." When I sat down one day to write this book, it quickly became my sole job. Everything else, to some extent, became a distraction, to be met with some small amount of unpleasantness. There are many people who have had to bear with me and with that unpleasantness in its varying degrees during that time. I would like to thank them first and foremost for their patience and understanding.

To my wife, who has seen more of the back of my head than the front, and has somehow still managed to mistake the glow of the word processor as a halo, I offer thanks and love.

To my students, who have written E-mails and made phone calls, and not had them answered for days, weeks, or months, I offer my thanks with apologies.

To the people who have helped by researching the correct dates and names, I offer thanks in lieu of actual cash payment.

There are those who have been impatient with me for not dropping everything to immediately work on their personal project instead of my own, who have yelled at me, cursed at me, and crossed me off their lists. To them I offer thanks for the positive impetus to work faster, a wish for success in their efforts without me, and a sincere wish for the warmest of eternities as well.

I thank George Thorndyke, who tore the original manuscript to pieces and made it infinitely better in the process, and Mike Shinabery, a newspaper reporter and remote viewer, who, after the book was checked and rechecked, spent a considerable amount of time and effort alerting me to stylistic errors that the word processing software could not even begin to catch. There were hundreds of errors, and not being a writer by trade, I could never have caught them without the help of these two very fine and helpful friends.

I thank the computer makers of America for the seven computers I have gone through while writing this book. I would also offer a suggestion that a computer that has more features is great, but I think it would be better for the public at large to make a computer that does not crash, instead.

I would like to offer a special word of thanks to five particular people in this field:

To General "Bert" Stubblebine, who had the faith in me to assign me to the project and to later become the very best of friends. Throughout and after military service, he became like a second father to me, and I am filled with admiration and respect for this very great man.

To Joe McMoneagle for selecting me as his replacement in the remote viewing unit, and Brian Busby for adopting me into the project and seeing to my education, training, and advancement.

To Ingo Swann, who has looked more deeply into the mind of man than have most scientists, and who has come back with a working methodology of how to use it. To him, my thanks are intertwined with a strong sense of awe. Even more awe inspiring is the fact that he would meet an upstart like me and call me a friend.

And finally, very special thanks to Skip Atwater, who one day led me to understand that the ability within me was not of Satan. I will always stand in deepest gratitude. It was he who, on probably the most pivotal day of my life, led me to accept myself for what I am—to realize the one most important fact that I hope I have imparted in the pages of this book:

It really is OK to be psychic.

A REMOTE
VIEWING
SOURCEBOOK

The following sourcebook will not teach you how to do Controlled Remote Viewing. That is a science in itself and will require professional training. This sourcebook will, however, provide you with a great deal of the terminology, structure, and theory behind the Controlled Remote Viewing process. It will also provide you with materials that will allow you to organize, standardize, and gain more control over your own methodology, no matter what methodology you are using. It is offered in the hope that this field can gain some unity, some standardization, and thereby some of the honor and respect it has been missing for so long a time.

APPENDIX 1

TERMINOLOGY

There is presently no standard terminology for all the interactions and processes involved in the field of remote viewing. Each authority creates terms for his specific methodology. The terms used here have grown during several years of practical use in the operations and training of my company, Problems Solutions Innovations (PSI). They are plain, earthy, and definitely unscientific. Most come from comments or slang names used by the viewers and students. It is a live, evolving body of language. Though the terms listed here may be slang, and are therefore transitory, they represent those fundamental and permanent principles, problems, actions, and aspects of Controlled Remote Viewing that can also be considered generic to the entire problem of using parapsychology for gaining useful information.

PSI's objective has not been to create a definitive set of proprietary terms which will become the community's standard. Our objective has been to use words and phrases that are utilitarian, highly accurate, and easily understood and remembered by those people who come into contact with PSI, whether for training, or for acquiring information, analyzing and/or reporting it, or acting upon the information produced, either repeatedly or on a one-time basis. The terms included here have served that purpose well for many years.

The terms have been divided into five main areas of concern:

1. Tasking,
2. The Controlled Remote Viewing process itself
3. Analyzing the results
4. Reporting what has been found
5. Record keeping

BASIC DEFINITIONS

Remote viewing: The action taken by a remote viewer. If that sounds like a vague definition, it is. Such is the present state of the parapsychological world. "Remote viewing" is presently a generic catchphrase, which can mean almost anything dealing with parapsychology and therefore causes much confusion. When a person claims to be a remote viewer, it does not signify that he/she is a *controlled* remote viewer. In fact, it signifies only that the person is a practitioner of some undefined parapsychological method, often self-devised and completely uncontrolled. In such a case, saying that a person is a remote viewer does not tell you anything about what they do.

Controlled remote viewing (CRV): A scientifically developed methodology that allows a person to emulate the work of the most talented natural psychics, and in some cases, surpass their abilities. Perhaps one of the greatest and most widely accepted myths about parapsychology today is the belief that "It can't be done in the laboratory." In actual fact, it can, and with just as great accuracy as outside the lab. There are certain common problems that have caused this myth:

1. The psychic is normally unaccustomed to the controlled lab experience, and therefore does not perform normally. One answer to this problem is to train the person within a controlled environment. That person will then work normally within the lab environment.

2. In the laboratory, all the "waffling," "BS," and "pumping the client for information" is blocked. The psychic, who has grown accustomed to having these "aids," finds that he/she must actually perform *pure* parapsychological functioning—and finds him/herself incapable of doing so. The charlatan often blames his failure on the lab conditions or on the myth that "this cannot be tested." He rarely ever admits to less than pure personal habits.

3. The researcher is not trying to do anything of practical value, or dealing with interesting, one-time problems. He usually gives the psychic tasks that are repetitive and dull, and against which all but the most dedicated person will rebel, if not on a conscious level, then at least on a subconscious level.

4. The researcher decides ahead of time what the answer to the re-search should be and devises the lab setting to test for and prove that answer. In short, the researcher most commonly performs directed testing of a theory instead of open-minded research. Even if a miracle occurs, the psychic who does not meet the re-searcher's *stated* goals is considered to have failed.

5. Many more such problems exist to cloud the issue and to further the myth that parapsychological functioning cannot be tested or analyzed accurately. It is still just a myth.

Taking the entire parapsychological process, no matter what form it takes, to its most basic elements, it consists of only three parts:

The tasker:	The person who has a question.
The source:	That undefined and hotly debated source of the answer.
The conduit:	The person who finds the answer and delivers it to the tasker.

In parapsychological work, it is rarely possible to place controls on the type of questions posed. The tasker, for all general purposes, can-not be controlled. We do not even know what the source is, much less can we control it. We are left, then, with only one part of the pro-cess that can be controlled: the conduit. In the case of the CRV pro-cess, that conduit is the remote viewer and the controls are the process with which and the environment in which he/she works.

Controlled remote viewer (CRVer): Perhaps the best way to define a CRVer is to explain what one does. The CRVer (one who works for PSI, at least) receives tasking to find out some information that can-not be gained through normal means. In other words, to go to a per-son, place, or event, and describe it. Then, *in a completely controlled environment,* through a combined process of mental concentration and scientific, organized work habits, he brings the information from the source to the tasker in as unpolluted and accurate a condi-tion as possible. In effect, he provides an eyewitness account via mental *and physical* means.

The tasked site may be hundreds of miles away or years removed into the past or future. The CRVer can, for example, be assigned to witness a crime for which the police have no other witnesses. He can witness and describe places so inaccessible or so hostile that no other form of data collection is possible. In the most extreme example, he can enter a guarded building, pass beyond bolted doors, and search locked file cabinets to read papers no one is supposed to see—all without tripping alarms, being spotted by guards or dogs, or featured on closed-circuit TV. He can then report back without leaving a single trace that security has been compromised in any way. He can see into the body of a child in Manila, to aid in a medical diagnosis there. An hour later, he can peer below the surface of the Sahara to aid an archeologist in the search for mankind's history.

Most people who believe that parapsychological functioning is possible also feel that the talent is held only by seers, shamans, spiritual mediums, or other "gifted" individuals. Experience indicates otherwise. The talent appears to be nothing more than a natural ability, which probably served primitive man as a means of self-protection. Proper scientific training can make the most of whatever vestigial ability lies dormant within each person. That is true for even the average man or woman on the street without an interest in the paranormal. In fact, a person who dives wholly into the mystic or occult is prone to accept anything without scientific method or empirical proof. As a result, he or she appears to have less of a chance to acquire a logical, structured mastery of the ability than the average person who is more grounded in reality. As with playing the piano, very few have its mastery as a natural gift. Most of us, however, can take what ability we do have and develop it. For most of us, mastery of the skill requires proper training and lots of disciplined practice. As in all other areas of life, the person who has less talent and strives hard to master the art will usually perform with a greater precision than the person who has the natural talent but no discipline or training. The training that PSI provides is directed at the development of a normal person's latent remote viewing potential, rather than seeking natural "superstars."

CAVEAT

The person who is interested *only* in inner self-improvement or gaining "a soul link to the universe" can undoubtedly gain a great deal by learning Controlled Remote Viewing. PSI, however, is not the place for such training. PSI is dedicated to developing and providing trained, qualified CRVers who are willing to put their skills to work in such areas as finding abducted children, aiding in the advancement of science and the healing arts, acquiring otherwise inaccessible information for investigative and other information-acquisition agencies, and providing actual, concrete help in areas where no other help exists. The targets used by PSI are concrete in nature, providing provable feedback to aid the student in the learning process. No ethereal, mystic, or unprovable targets are used. PSI does not train students to "achieve other planes of existence," to contact extraterrestrials, "sub-space entities," or spirit guides, or to "develop inner awareness of their own chakras," "spirit-energies," "inner wellsprings of eternal Oneness," etc., ad infinitum. The PSI definition of "*Controlled* Remote Viewer," then, is much more specific and down-to-earth than the generic term, "remote viewer."

While training to be a *Controlled* Remote Viewer does expand a person's awareness and sensitivity and will change a person's life for the better, when used for these purposes alone, it has been likened to joining the Marines just to learn how to fold your underwear. There are much quicker and easier ways to achieve a sense of Nirvana than to go through the rigors of CRV training.

TASKING TERMINOLOGY

Project management personnel: There are so many ways the CRVer can be led astray by contact with the tasker's information that having a *well-trained* and dedicated "go-between" is not only a good practice, but virtually necessary for proper treatment of the CRVers, and for getting reliable results. This is true for the police department working with only a single psychic investigator, as well as for organizations that employ teams of CRVers. "Well trained" means knowledgeable in all aspects of the Controlled Remote Viewing process on a first-hand basis. "Dedicated" means a person who is adamant about keeping the viewers clean of any information that might influence their work or eventually affect its credibility.

The project management personnel must review the tasking before it is given to the CRVer. If there are any possibilities for misunderstanding (unintentional double meanings, vague wording, etc.), if there is any hint that the customer is "tasking a CAT" (see page 221), or if any background information has made its way into the wording of the tasking questions, the questions are reworded to be neutral in nature. The reworded tasking is then checked with the customer to be sure it asks for the information that is really wanted. The goal of rewording is to ensure that the question will not provide any information that would lead the viewer in any way.

PSI's CRVers are trained to recognize and reject any tasking that is not neutrally worded. Normally, it is the viewer who objects most strenuously to any tasking that provides information. PSI strongly advocates that the viewer has both the right and the obligation to call an end to any session in which information is "fed" to them, and places a strong responsibility on all project personnel for protecting the viewer from such information.

Neutral wording: The actual wording of the tasking may have emotional, political, or other overtones that would lead the viewer to erroneous perceptions. The process of wording tasking correctly is a difficult job. The CRVer and project personnel must work together to make certain that all wording used in the CRV session is neutral of such overtones and hidden burdens for the viewer. Examples:

Loaded	Neutral
criminal	person
stripper	person
child	person
raging bull	animal
duty/job/task	activity

Tasking the answer: It is usually the case that the tasker has a feeling or an idea about the unknowns of the task. Extreme care must be taken to make certain that the tasker's ideas are not expressed in the actual text of the question. Example: *"My patient, an anorexic twenty-four-year-old female Caucasian, has vague and periodic symptoms of cirrhosis of the liver, but no other symptoms of this illness are found. I think her problem is totally psychosomatic. Am I right?"* In this example, the tasking itself tells you what the doctor wants the viewer to find. It introduces so much additional information into the session that the viewer will find it impossible to keep a clear mind and be totally open to other possibilities. If such wording were inflicted on the viewer, there would be very little reason to conduct a session. Customers rarely know the mechanics of dealing with a viewer and will often task the viewer to find that answer the customer wants, rather than tasking the viewer to find an absolute truth.

Manipulative tasking: Sometimes the tasker will, either overtly or covertly, tell the CRVer what findings are desired. This situation is usually easy to detect. Either the tasker has a preconceived belief and wants it confirmed, or may have some hidden political agenda that would be best served by certain findings. In such a case, it becomes the project manager's job to deal with the situation.

The test: It is rare to find a customer who will not slip in a test question, just so the viewer can do a "dog and pony show" without knowing it, and prove him/herself to them. This is not only rude but useless. The customer must be educated to the fact that *a good or bad performance on one question does not mean that an equivalent quality of result will be obtained on another question.* The test only proves how well the viewer can do on *that* question.

Prep sessions: This is very similar to the test question, except it is done to the CRVer by his/her own people. It is done in one of two ways:

1. By running a CRVer through one preparatory target after another until he/she begins to show good results, then introducing the real target.
2. By running the viewer on a single test target to see how good he/she is doing that day, then judging the results of the real session according to how well he/she did on the prep target.

Prep sessions do not work. They only tire the viewer, waste psychic energy, and degrade the overall performance. Besides, as previously pointed out, a good or bad performance on one question (target) does not mean that an equivalent quality result will be obtained on another. A prep session (prep target) may sound like a good, logical idea, but in practice, it is bad for the viewer, and for the resulting product. Don't do it.

The lie: This may sound ridiculous, but it has happened so many times in practice that it has earned a place in the Horror Hall of Fame. A tasker will often give an outright lie as tasking. I once worked five viewers for a full five sessions each, getting nothing but garbage and contradictions, only to find out that the tasker had tasked us to describe facts about a crime that had never occurred. When confronted, the tasker replied with a straight face, "If you were really psychic, you would have known I was lying."

MMT (Massive Multiple Tasking): For the great majority of viewers, a single tasking question should be given for each session. If any other information is found, which answers any of the other tasked questions, the analyst can note it and place it in the correct frame of reference. MMT is a tendency of almost every tasker. They try to ask for the answer to every possible question, every possible ramification of those questions, etc. Example: *"Will the expected event happen during the span of this year or next, and, if it does happen at all, when and where will the major indicators occur leading up to it, and who will be the people involved? Give any names and descriptions you can get. If it doesn't happen, what factors will contribute to it not happening, and what else will happen in its place?"*

Such tasking must be dealt with in three steps:

1. Separate the tasking into single, intelligent questions and weed out the questions that are either superfluous or should be answered by some other means than Controlled Remote Viewing.

2. Call the customer and check your revisions with them. See how many of the questions you can get rid of. See if the tasker actually knew what question he wanted to ask in the first place. Then, educate him about what tasking style is needed in the future.

3. If multiple questions remain, rank them in terms of their importance (check this with the customer) and make a logical ses-

sion work schedule, in order to *give each CRVer only one question per session.* If, in the course of any one session, other questions than the one tasked for that session become answered, delete those questions from the viewer's work schedule.

Paradoxical tasking: This is tasking for information about a future event with the intent of preventing it. The result of paradoxical tasking is to make the viewer's perceptions wrong. The best way to explain paradoxical tasking is by example: Say you are asked by the police to describe the location of a criminal at 9 P.M. You describe Joe's Bar and Grill. At 8 P.M., the police arrive and hide in the bushes to catch the criminal when he arrives. At 8:30, the criminal arrives and is apprehended on the spot. At 9 P.M., the criminal is in jail. Everyone is satisfied that you have done your job. Thanks to you, the criminal was caught. However, your subconscious mind isn't happy with the turn of events. It was made wrong. The criminal was not at Joe's Bar and Grill at 9 P.M. He was in jail.

It is logical to assume that the subconscious mind would have foreseen this and given a description of the criminal's 9 P.M. location as a jail cell. However, if the subconscious mind had given that as a location, the police would not have known to go to Joe's Bar and Grill, would not have apprehended the criminal, and the criminal's 9 P.M. location would not be the jail cell, but would, instead, have been the bar. Either way the subconscious mind performs, it is destined to be wrong. The subconscious mind does not take these things lightly. After many taskings of this sort, it will begin to refuse to work under such circumstances. After that, the viewer only produces garbage in any situation where paradoxical tasking might occur again. Paradoxical tasking can ruin your viewers.

The solution to paradoxical tasking is simple: Change the tasking in such a way that it will not cause a paradox. For example, in the above case, the tasking could have been changed to: *"The target is the location where the police will be able to catch the criminal, if they act tonight."*

The frontloading that would then be given to the viewer would be: *"The target is a location. Describe the location."*

IN-SESSION TERMINOLOGY

*For the most part, the in-session vocabulary
presented here is given in the order in which it
naturally occurs within the session.*

TAME CAT (Transfer of Accessed Mental Energy to Consciously Accessible Thought): This is every CRVer's main purpose for working: the perception that is accessed from a truly psychic source. As you will see, it is usually only identified as such after feedback has been received.

Attractors and distractors. Both attractors and distractors ruin a session, simply by drawing a viewer's attention away from the target.

POCA (Previews of Coming Attractors): This is a quiet and insidious form of attractor! Before the session starts, a fleeting thought occurs about what the target might be. If not set aside (see SA, below), this becomes a SCWERL (see below) and can turn an RV session into a nightmare.

POCD (Previews of Coming Distractors): This is neither quiet nor insidious. This is the knowledge or feeling that a distraction is about to happen (for example, a phone call is expected, and might come in during the session). If not set aside (see SA, below), it becomes a distractor in its own right, and the viewer becomes incapable of performing a session at all.

SA (Set Aside): "Setting aside" an attraction or distraction is not always an easy task. The viewer must honestly identify the problem, face the cause, and then make an agreement with him/herself that, for at least the next few minutes, the offending thoughts will be set aside in order to get a job done. It is important that the matter be taken up again after the job is done. If not, the subconscious will not agree to set things aside during the session, knowing the conscious mind's promise will not be kept.

Magic words: Those words that signal nonperception aspects of the session's processes. Two examples follow:

When a viewer is setting aside any problems (POCAs and POCDs, for example), there may come a time when he/she does not want to write the problem down for all the world to see. This involves such things as menstrual cycle difficulties, other physical problems, personal problems with the monitor or administration, etc. At such times, the viewer is allowed to write the word "yes" under the set asides. It is commonly understood that no one has the right to ask the viewer what that means or stands for. It is an acknowledged private set aside, for the viewer alone to know about.

Another example of a magic word is the word "move." Any time the monitor uses the word "move" it signals that the viewer is being given a move command to move from one area or aspect of the target site to another. The viewer, on hearing that word, automatically stops viewing and starts taking dictation in order to record the monitor's directions. This is important so the monitor, viewer, and analyst all have a written record of where the viewer is at the site, at any time throughout the session.

Frontloading: After (and only after) a CRVer is well skilled at handling attractors and distractors, it is possible to frontload a session by giving some information ahead of time. *This information must be both general and neutral in nature.* The purpose of this is to save the CRVer the hours of session time it takes to get on target. The following rules of frontloading *must* be strictly observed:

1. The frontloading must consist of a very small, previously determined vocabulary, which has been worked out between the CRVer and the monitor. The most basic set of frontloading phrases is:

   > The target is a person.
   > The target is a "manmade."
   > The target is a location.
   > The target is an event.

2. The frontloading must consist of only neutral words. For example, it would be destructive to tell the CRVer, "*Yesterday evening, a six-year-old girl was gang raped, thrown into the trunk of a car, and kidnapped. Describe her present physical and emotional condition.*" It would be permissible frontloading, however, to tell a CRVer,

"The target is a person. Describe the present-time physical and emotional condition of the target person."

3. The monitor must always remember that the purpose of the frontloading is to save the CRVer time and work, not to tell the CRVer what he should find. For example, it would not be permissible to say, *"Describe whether or not the target person is dead."*

There is a specific format to the frontloading, and tradition has developed subtle meanings within the words used. For example, "target" means everything at the site. Therefore, the frontloading *"The target is an activity. Describe the target"* would mean that the viewer is supposed to describe the entire target as it relates to the tasked activity. However, if the viewer were given the frontloading of *"The target is an activity. Describe the activity,"* the viewer would know that the only thing the customer is concerned about is the targeted activity itself. When the frontloading *"The target is a location. Describe the location"* is used, the viewer knows that he is to describe only physical aspects of the location and nothing else. When the frontloading *"The target is a location. Describe the target"* is used, the viewer knows that he is to describe the location and everything connected to it. In other words, the viewer understands that he is free to virtually roam about the site describing whatever interests him.

"A well-formed question to a psychic": This consists of two parts: The first part is the task to the subconscious and the second part is a present-tense directive to the viewer's or psychic's conscious mind to perform a specific task in order to keep it out of the way of the subconscious. This technique helps increase the accuracy rate and should always be used in tasking any psychic question.

Examples of well-formed questions to a psychic are:

"The target is a location. Describe the location."
"Move one hundred feet above the target. Now, tell me what you see."
"Mentally touch the target. Tell me its temperature."

Each of these questions has two parts. The first part is something the conscious mind cannot perform. The second is a task it can perform, and is couched in present time. The present tense of this second part is very important, as the conscious mind works best in present tense. Such questions as "Move one hundred years back in time and *tell me what happened then*" cause the viewer or psychic to begin analyzing the past in terms of his preconceived notions about it, stereotypes of it, and so on. But the question "Move one hundred years back in time and *tell me what you see, now*" cause the viewer to immediately probe its input from the subconscious and begin reporting what the subconscious tells it.

Target: Using CRV, the viewer is able to describe all aspects of any location, activity, event, person, or object in all of time and space. He is also capable of describing more complex aspects of those targets, for example, their purposes, any theoretical or conceptual principles behind them, any causes that led up to an activity or event, or any ramifications that follow from it. Any of these site aspects can be tasked to a viewer. The target, then, is basically the tasked aspect of the site, with perhaps all its associations.

Hard target: One for which there is or will be provable feedback. Such targets as objects, concrete and witnessable activities, and physical locations qualify as hard targets. The future actions of a targeted person can also qualify as a hard target, since one only needs to wait for the action to take place to have provable feedback.

Esoteric target: One that neither has nor will have foreseeable concrete feedback for scoring the session. Examples include civilizations or cultures on other planets in other galaxies, whether Jesus had a mustache or not, the location of the Ark of the Covenant, alternate-universe entities, a dead person's real feelings about some historical event, and so on. The *only* way one can have any faith at all in the results of sessions on esoteric targets is to have a track record for the viewer performing the session. If that track record does not exist, the session may be entertaining and produce stirring and fantastic perceptions, but these people are not reliable. It is often said that if multiple viewers get the same results, the results must be true. Such an assumption is totally incorrect in practice, due mainly to general social feelings on the targeted subject, and a factor called "the neighbor's cat" (see page 226). Esoteric targets are for entertainment purposes only.

Double-blind session: One in which neither the viewer nor the monitor knows what the target is. The purpose of a double-blind session is to make certain that the monitor does not contaminate the session by trying to lead the viewer to find what he knows about the target. In reality, there is no such thing as a double-blind session. Once the viewer has given two or three descriptions, the monitor will almost certainly form a mental image of what he thinks the target might be, and from that point on, the contamination and leading exist, whether the monitor has knowledge of the real target or not. Double-blind sessions are conducted in the laboratory for experimental purity. In actual applications work, the need for double-blind conditions is not paramount, and may slow the session down or make it useless by allowing the viewer to fixate on a part of the target site that is of no importance to the customer.

Leading the viewer: A monitor will almost always lead a viewer to find what the monitor thinks the target is. Even with highly trained monitors, the most subtle, barely perceptible reactions to any one of the viewer's perceptions can lead the viewer astray. Some people even say that, if a monitor is absolutely perfect in his performance and makes no perceptible reactions whatever, he will react with pheromones to those perceptions that he feels to be correct or incorrect. The viewer will unconsciously pick up on these pheromones and be led in the direction the monitor believes the session should go.

For these reasons, there is much controversy about whether the monitor should take part in a session at all. Because of other jobs the monitor performs, however, the monitor is usually considered to be an invaluable asset to the viewer, in spite of any unintentional leading that may occur.

Signal line or matrix: Two terms used to indicate the source of the psychic information. In reality, both essentially mean, "I don't know where the information comes from."

Coordinates: In CRV, the viewer begins his actual session with an arbitrary set of numbers or letter/number groupings that will stand for the target. This allows the viewer to work in a blind condition so his imagination does not get in the way. In reality, it provides much greater accuracy with less frustration on the part of the viewer.

The number groupings are called "coordinates" because Ingo Swann, who developed CRV, originally used geographic coordinates for this purpose. Once the technology moved over to military and governmental usage, it was not always possible to give the geographical coordinates (for instance, of a hostage), because they were not always known. Therefore, either random numbers or "structured" numbers were used. A structured number is one that has nothing to do with the target, but allows the databasing of target information in a more orderly manner. For example, the coordinates for a specific task might be 994412 / 018051. Such a structured number is made up of various database fields, to wit:

99 = A session done in 1999.
44 = Done for customer #44.
12 = This is the twelfth project for that customer this year.
018 = This session performed by viewer #018.
05 = On the customer's fifth question for this project.
1 = This is the first time the viewer has worked this question.

The information contained in the numbers will not provide the viewer with any information about the target itself.

Ideogram: A physical, graphic representation of a basic, or gestaltic, concept. It requires extensive training on the part of the viewer, and is very much a martial art. The graphic must be produced in response to an instinctual reaction to a concept in the viewer's subconscious mind. When I explain this to students, I usually tell them that it is the "-iness" of a word. For instance, the subconscious may produce a flat line, a wavy line, and an angle. This could be the subconscious mind's way of telling the viewer, "I don't know what's at the site yet, but I know that there is some land-iness, some water-iness, and some manmade-iness to it." It is the viewer's first contact with the target site.

Airogram: An ideogram that is made in the air because the viewer does not have his pen on the paper when the instinctual reaction takes place. Another type of airogram is one in which the viewer has his pen so firmly planted on the paper that the pen tip does not move. The reaction then shows up on top of the pen as it circles and turns above the paper.

ANS/CNS: There is a fair amount of debate about whether the trained knee-jerk response comes from the autonomic nervous system or the central nervous system. Both systems carry out various automatic functions within the body. As far as the viewer is concerned, the trained knee-jerk response that produces the ideogram is simply the body responding to some target knowledge located within the subconscious mind. The viewer needs to worry about training accuracy into the response, rather than worrying about which internal system is doing the job.

IAB Sequence: When a viewer makes an ideogram, he must then analyze its component parts to figure out what the subconscious mind is trying to tell him. This is a two-step process, labeled step A and step B. The complete ideogram A-B sequence is the major working component of Phase 1 of a CRV session.

EA (Emotional Attractor): Some parts of a site will hold an emotional attraction for the viewer. They are pleasant, safe, or simply interesting. The task at hand becomes unimportant as the viewer turns aside for the wonderful experience the EA offers.

ED (Emotional Distractor): This tends to be unpleasant and creates an anxiety CAT (see below). If the ED is not set aside, the session will trail off into confusion and contradictory impressions as the viewer tries to avoid the perception that holds the unwanted emotion.

NAG (Namer and Guesser): This is that part of the mind that sits on the fence between the conscious and subconscious and plays guardian. No sooner does half a perception appear in the subconscious than the NAG tries to identify it as friend or foe. It blurts, "I know what that is!" and gives the perception a name. The NAG has allowed us to survive as a species, but most often it guesses before getting the full facts. It tends also to guess more on the side of safety and accuracy. This is the origin of almost all STRAY CATs.

STRAY CAT (Subconscious Transference of Recollections, Anxieties, and Yearnings to Consciously Accessible Thought): One of the most persistent problems the CRVer faces is an impression that comes from his/her own memories, fears, desires, or imagination, and is indistinguishable from a true psychic perception. *But just because an impression is a STRAY CAT does not mean it is wrong.*

"Winking about the site": In the earliest stages of site contact, the mind is frantically looking around the site to get its bearings. As an analogy of this problem, let's say that you suddenly find yourself physically at a new and strange location in total darkness with only a small penlight to help you see. You don't know if you are standing on the edge of a cliff, under something about to fall, or if there is some other danger around. Your focus of attention (and your penlight's beam) immediately darts back and forth around you to try to take in all the elements of the location. You point your beam up to the right and see something red. You point in front of you and see something rubbery. You point to the left and see something round. If this happens physically, you will naturally understand that the elements are separate parts of the location. However, when your subconscious mind is doing the same, and reports back that it sees "red," "rubbery," and "round," your NAG jumps in and says, "Oooh! I know what it is. It's a ball!" In the earliest levels of CRV, the viewer should not try to make sense of what he/she is perceiving as the subconscious "winks about the site." Patience is the key.

Aesthetic impact: In early Phase 2 work, the viewer will get random perceptions. A growing dimensional awareness of the site develops that will end in an awareness that comes when the viewer begins to "feel" a relationship to the site. Then there will be a sense of relief (or some other emotion, if there is danger at the site), after which the viewer will slow his/her mind and start looking at each part of the site in depth and detail. The point at which a relationship is established with the target site, accompanied with the emotional reaction, is called aesthetic impact. It is a milestone within the CRV session. At this point the "winking about the site" subsides, and the viewer can begin to successfully begin making sense of the target site.

Up until this time, the operant rule must be: "There is no session above the line you're on." Any perceptions received before this point must be forgotten and the viewer must proceed on to the next one. If you try to carry them forward through your session, the resulting burden will cause your session to fail. During Phases 1, 2, and 3, the best rule for working effectively is: "Get a perception—write it—forget it. Get a perception—write it—forget it."

Cues: When the viewer lags or begins getting entrained during the session, the monitor can utter a cue word. The cue must always be neutral and must not be used to lead the viewer toward any target information. It is only a "poke in the ribs" to get the viewer moving.

Standard cues: These are neutral words that will give the viewer a type of perception to reach for. Such cues must be neutral in meaning and must not be used to lead the viewer. Examples are "colors?" "shapes?" "sizes?" etc. The viewer is not supposed to answer these questions. To do so requires conscious thought. The monitor simply keeps "poking the viewer" until the viewer begins viewing again. The monitor then stops cueing.

Action cues: At times, the monitor can ask the viewer to interact with the site in some way or another and report back what happens. Action cues must be given in the form of a "well-formed question to a psychic." Examples: "Mentally touch your tongue to the target. What are you tasting?"

Move commands: The monitor can request the viewer to move around the target site, either in time or space. When this request is made, the viewer notes the move on his session transcript so everyone handling the transcript will realize when and to where the viewer was moved during session.

Threading: Move commands can be tied together, much like tying a thread to your starting point so you do not get lost. Through the use of threading, a viewer can be moved from almost any target to any other target, even ones they would not normally be able to view because of fear or repulsion. Also, when a viewer knows one target so thoroughly that he cannot work that target without contamination, a monitor can give the viewer a completely different target, and in the middle of it, give a series of confusing move commands in order to "thread" the viewer to the desired target long enough to get the sought-for information.

CAT: This is the short name for STRAY CAT. It is the generic name for any of several types of impressions that result from the output of the NAG, rather than from the "source." Examples are anxiety CAT, memory CAT, yearning CAT, etc.

CAT chasing its tail: This is a "wrapped around the axle" situation where a viewer gets an impression and has a fleeting thought of "No, that's probably a STRAY CAT," then a contradictory thought or feeling of "No . . . it felt like a valid impression." A mental struggle ensues in which the viewer's attention is drawn away from the task at hand in order to decide whether a perception was real or created from his own desires, etc. (a STRAY CAT). Soon the decision process itself becomes the distractor. There is only one way to break this hypnotic situation. The viewer must be verbally reminded: *"It is a STRAY CAT! But remember, the fact that it is a STRAY CAT doesn't mean that it's wrong. So just write it down and move on."*

The responsibility for giving this reminder falls to the monitor. Therefore, the monitor must be ever watchful for this situation because the viewer is usually mentally locked up in the struggle and does not verbalize it. It happens frequently. If this condition is not stopped, the "CAT chasing its tail" becomes either "castle building" or a condition called a SCWERL (see below).

Castle building: A mason starts a castle wall by finding a sturdy stone, and having put it into place, then looks for another stone to fit onto it. If the second stone doesn't fit, he tosses it to the side and looks for one that does in an attempt to make a smooth, seamless surface, which is strong and will resist attack. CRVers are prone to do the same with perceptions. When a viewer begins castle building, he/she will even begin to filter out those impressions that do not fit with the preceding impression. The tendency is to say, "If X is true, then Y can't be right!" The result is a well-constructed STRAY CAT. Not only are these results almost always wrong, the viewer will feel increasingly certain that he/she "has really nailed" the target. This initiates a spiral effect that leaves the viewer more prone to filter out any contradictory information and actively seek reinforcing perceptions.

SCWERL (pronounced "squirrel") (STRAY CAT Wrecking Everything, Running Loose!): This acronym accurately describes the problem. An uncontrolled STRAY CAT stops the session, then begins a destructive rampage by casting doubts about everything that has been perceived before. The more the viewer chases it, the more evasive it becomes. Soon all the viewer's time and energy are taken up trying to trap and control it, and in the process, the viewer does as much—if not more—damage to the session as the STRAY CAT itself. In short, a SCWERL ruins a session, usually beyond repair. The best action to be taken if a SCWERL gets loose is to end the session and start over, if necessary.

Tasker's CAT: Because the tasker usually has a "feeling" or an idea about the unknowns of the task, extreme care must be taken to make certain that the tasker's ideas are not expressed in the actual text of the question. Example: *"My daughter is missing. What does the man who kidnapped her look like?"* In this example, the tasking itself introduces information into the session that the viewer will have to fight: "kidnapped," "the man." Of course, it is possible that neither of these is true. However, if this wording gets to the viewer, it becomes a STRAY CAT the viewer will rarely be able to overcome. The monitor will need to reword the tasking before the viewer is allowed to see it. The wording of the tasking should be as neutral as possible.

Monitor's CAT: Whether the monitor has background knowledge of the site or not, there are almost as many times during a session when the monitor's NAG jumps to a conclusion and yells, "I know what it is!" If the monitor is not able to set aside these impressions, the session should be stopped. If it is not stopped, the monitor will begin injecting cues, leading statements, and/or physical mannerisms into the session that will lead the viewer to find what the monitor wants to hear.

Analyst's CAT: The analyst must go through the session transcript and make an analysis of the findings. Any preconceptions the analyst may have about the target site will influence the interpretation of the viewer's findings and may even distort them. To prevent this, the analyst should check his/her interpretations of the session results with the viewer and the monitor.

Reporter's CAT: The report writer's preconceptions about the target site influence what gets stressed and what gets minimized. The report writer often feels responsible for the report. If the report writer's reputation hinges on the contents of the report, an otherwise perfect (set of) session(s) can be lost.

Customer's CAT: Though the customer supposedly comes to us to learn the truth, in fact the truth is not always well received. If the customer only wants confirmation of strongly held preconceptions, all efforts are wasted, unless, of course, the customer's preconceptions were correct—then you're the hero.

Neighbor's CAT: Although the term was invented as a joke, this type of CAT is one of the viewers' favorites. Basically, a viewer says, "It wasn't that I was wrong, I was just picking up on what somebody else (the tasker, the monitor, another viewer, etc.) was thinking about the target. They were the ones who were wrong. Mental telepathy, you know." Unfortunately, research and data keeping have shown that such a CAT actually does exist. However, it is not as common as a viewer would like to have it be. (See Waffling, below)

Doorknobbing: Quite often, a viewer will get so attracted to one part of the site that he/she accepts that part as the designated target and completely misses the assignment. In this situation, the viewer literarally can't see the forest for the tree. The term originated one day after a session when the viewer and the monitor went to the actual site for actual feedback. The viewer walked up to the door, pointed at the doorknob, and said, "There it is! That's what I was seeing! It was a doorknob!" "And that's exactly what you spent an hour describing," the monitor said, "but the target was the house."

PSI (Perfect Site Immersion): There are times in a session when contact with the site is so strong that the viewer experiences actual presence at the site: full sound, sight, tactility, smell, and all other sensory impressions. This is extremely rare, and most exciting.

Site orientation problem: There are times when the viewer at a site will find himself/herself "mis-oriented," either leaning over to one side, upside down, lying on the side, or even more bizarre, an inch or a thousand feet tall. The viewer, not realizing that something is wrong, will accept this orientation and begin describing the site from the new viewpoint. But the skewed orientation means that the viewer's imagination kicks in that much sooner, trying to make sense of it all. Therefore, a football may look like a dirigible, a flagpole may look like the lance of a knight going into battle, or New York City may look like a small ant hill. Until the viewer can become reoriented, serious viewing errors will occur.

Micromovements: When the subconscious mind is trying to report a truly psychic impression, it is often interrupted by fears, anxieties, and memories from within other parts of the mind (the NAG). These impressions get passed to the conscious mind and either color or are mistaken for the psychic impression that triggered them. However, the subconscious mind rarely gives up without a fight. Some "indicator" of its displeasure will be generated; these can be as subtle as pupil dilation or a change in handwriting or as open as a display of anger where the viewer gets up and walks around the room. Because these indicators form habitual patterns, it is possible to study them to gain a better understanding of which associated impressions come from true psychic sources (TAME CATS), and which are generated within the viewer's own mind (STRAY CATS). For CRV purposes, these fall into two different categories, natural micromovents and CRV micromovements.

Natural micromovements: These are the ones that the viewer brings with him/her from life. For example, a shaking of the head when there is doubt about what is being reported, a bouncing of the feet when the viewer is in conscious mode rather than subconscious mode, enlarging of the pupils when the viewer is getting a sexual perception, contraction of the pupils when the viewer is getting a visual, etc. These are fairly standard among viewers, and can be studied in books on body language.

CRV micromovements: Once a monitor has worked with a viewer long enough and has gotten to know all the viewer's natural micromovements, the monitor can begin to set up CRV micromovements, which provide the monitor with information directly from the viewer's subconscious mind (without the viewer's conscious mind ever knowing that the messages are being passed). Such messages allow the viewer's subconscious mind to tell the monitor that the things being written down are not at all what the subconscious mind is getting, or that things are exactly on target. The monitor can then watch the viewer for micromovements rather than listening to the content of the viewer's perceptions—thereby helping to prevent "the monitor's CAT."

Graphics: Because CRV is a graphically oriented martial art, it allows the viewer to create a wide range of graphics for various purposes.

Ideograms are graphic representations of gestaltic concepts.

Pictograms are ideograms, once they take on relational aspects of the target and become more like a 2-D sketch. The CRV sketch is ideogrammic in nature. This is the way the subconscious sees the target; the target is not seen as the eyes would see it.

Models are 3-D ideograms. Using modeling clay (Play-Doh works nicely), the viewer can construct how his subconscious mind sees the target in true space. The model can also be used allegorically for more conceptual aspects.

Timelines are straight lines that represent a span of time. The viewer is directed to find events and or activities along the line. In this way, the viewer is able to view not just events, but also series of related events, and find their placement in time. The timeline can also be used allegorically to stand for more conceptual aspects of the target. For example, a timeline can become a scale of sizes or relationships.

Graphs, timelines with a second dimension, show the interaction of two related aspects of the target.

Maps provide the viewer with 2-D spatial relationships. Maps are generally of two types, each worked differently. A "blank" map may or may not actually be blank. It is called blank because it does not have the targeted locations on it. The viewer works this type of map actively, drawing in the details progressively. A "printed" map has the details of an area already on it. The viewer works this type of map passively, recording impressions he receives as he is moved about the map. Like the other graphics, maps do not have to be spatial, but can also be used to work more conceptual aspects of the target, such as social and political boundaries, demographics, and the like.

ANALYSIS AND REPORTING TERMINOLOGY

Consensus analysis and reporting: Agreement between the findings of several viewers provides a measure of reliability. If something is perceived by four out of five viewers, it is given more importance than something perceived by only two of the five. Anything perceived by a minority or by only one is usually not even reported.

Also, if one reported fact does not jibe with the other reported facts (in other words, if it does not make sense to the analyst or report writer), it is usually thrown out, no matter how many viewers reported it. In one example, the information sent to the analyst clearly described a desert setting, although several viewers reported a ship. Most of the other perceptions by the viewers (even the ones reporting the ship) gave desertlike descriptions. The ship perception was thrown out of the final report because it did not make sense to the analyst/report writer. In this particular case, the actual location turned out to be a quite well-known desert mesa shaped like a ship and bearing the name of Shiprock. If the ship description had been reported to the investigating police officers, in spite of not making sense to the analyst, it would have narrowed their search time by days.

While consensus reporting makes for a well-organized and well-written report, it has proven time and again to be extremely error prone. It is not at all unusual for ten viewers to perceive one thing, with an eleventh perceiving something that contradicts them, and to find out later that the one was correct and the ten were wrong. The excuse usually involves the neighbor's CAT; the ten were "picking up on each other's thoughts." Consensus reporting is error prone because the analyst or report writer usually knows many of the facts of the case and tends to pick through the viewers' information, pulling out and reporting only that which fits his predetermined beliefs (STRAY CATS) about the case. Consensus reporting just does not work.

Statistical analysis and reporting ("analytic filtering"): In analytic filtering, a viewer's every impression is evaluated against feedback for correctness, and then associated with any indicators (micromovements) recorded at the point in the viewer's session that produced that impression. In time, an increasingly dependable profile of indicators and their meanings emerges for each viewer. Through painstaking analysis and a thorough knowledge of a viewer's individual set of indicators, those parts of a session transcript where the viewer is imagining can be separated from the portions where he/she is reporting valid information, and the information that shows the least probability of being correct can be expunged from final reporting. The result is a report that contains less information, but of highly increased accuracy.

As an understanding of a viewer's individual work patterns emerges, new session transcripts and reports are filtered against those patterns, perception by perception, word by word, to test, retest, and refine the accuracy of the indicators database for that viewer. The more sessions the viewer has performed, the more accurate the filter becomes, and the more correct the resulting information presented in the report.

Long-term analysis of these indicators has also proven valuable for training new viewers. Many of the more common indicators are actually trained into student viewers, helping them gain a higher dependability factor much faster and more easily.

True Reporting: It is most often the case that the report writer will try to figure out what the target or answer is, and then write the report according to his own interpretation. Aside from the fact that this negates the need for viewers, it also usually distorts the viewers' findings and invalidates their results. The report writer does not have complete knowledge of the target, and therefore should not do his own personal analysis. The following "report what you were given" format was created to prevent this from happening.

The report writer makes a list of the customer's tasked questions:

1. What is the condition of the hostage?
2. When will the most opportune time be to enact a rescue?
3. Etc.

The report writer then goes through the viewers' summary to glean any information that would answer the first task and adds this information to the report:

1. What is the condition of the hostage?
   a. Viewer XXX reports that the hostage has a broken leg, but is otherwise well.
   b. Viewer XXY reports that the hostage . . .

The question arises, of course, about what happens when two viewers do not agree, or outright contradict each other. In such a case, it is not the report writer's job to decide who is right and who is wrong. It is only his job to report. The customer, who has much more knowledge about the target than was given in the tasking, is the one best capable of judging which viewer's perceptions should be trusted. This reporting method not only gives an accurate report of what the viewers found, but it also makes each viewer responsible for the quality of his/her own results. It also allows the customer to come back and ask for that viewer who has produced the best results for this project to do more in-depth work.

Waffling: An attempt to redefine the viewer's findings in order to make them fit the feedback. In practice, it is often any reaction to the feedback that begins with the word "Well . . ." The tendency for waffling is as common among CRVers and their supporting staff as it is for other psychic practitioners. For example: In one session, a viewer reported, "The criminal is driving a yellow car." The feedback shows that the criminal was riding in the back of an unpainted hay wagon. The viewer replies, "Well . . . yeah! When I said car, I meant a vehicle of some kind, and when I said it was yellow, I was no doubt seeing the hay. I got it right!"

The practice of waffling not only cheapens the results, but does so in such a shallow manner as to rob the viewer of the respect of his/her peers It is interesting to note that the people associated with the viewer are usually more guilty of waffling than the viewer is. The viewer will normally want to know when he/she got something wrong, and try to figure out why, and tends to be harder in the judging of his/her own results than others. The viewer may not always voice his/her displeasure, but will almost certainly feel deeply offended by another person's attempt to cover up mistakes by waffling the findings. Viewers appreciate honest appraisals.

Checking back: The analyst should check back with the viewer to ask, "This is what I think you said. Am I right?" The report writer should do the same before typing up the final copy and providing it to the customer. Sadly, this is not always the case.

RECORD-KEEPING TERMINOLOGY

Database management: The proper database management for training and analysis of the viewer's work should include at least the following information:

Viewer. The viewer's name, some identifying number, or whatever is necessary to show which viewer did the work in any one session.

Session. The date, time started, and time ended.

Target. The name of the target, a project number, a complete, exhaustively detailed description, or whatever is deemed necessary for record-keeping purposes. It should identify the target site in some way.

Findings. Multiple fields that separate the categories of work you do, including basic information categories. Tracking information in categories will help you identify your strengths and weaknesses. For example, many people are good at getting information on colors, textures, etc., but very poor at getting information in other categories, such as smells and sounds.

Other than these bare essentials, useful information to keep in the database includes:

Length of session
How the viewer felt that day
Weather conditions
Moon phase
Biorhythm ratings
Types and lengths of breaks (and where they came in the session)

Database: This is a computer program that allows you to record randomly gathered bits of information as they happen. Once entered, the individual bits of information are compared, contrasted, collectively organized, sorted, and studied to gain overall information about the subject at hand. For example, if George's session scores are collected and entered each time a session is graded, the information may be as follows:

	Mon	**Tue**	**Wed**	**Thu**	**Fri**
Week 1	87.93	84.55	93.76	65.65	82.73
Week 2	84.32	88.77	89.99	73.25	81.76
Week 3	85.00	83.98	91.23	70.02	83.84

What might seem like a jumble of numbers, when massaged by a database program, gives accurate information about a viewer's work habits. While the viewer may feel bad on Monday mornings and feel that his worst work is done on Mondays, the database will show that his worst day is actually Thursday and his best day is Wednesday. Data collected into a database program can be utilized to analyze and better understand the confusion of information that occurs with normal work.

Field: A field within a database is any single and separate category of information. For example, in the normal database, you would want to put a person's name, street address, city, state, and zip code into different fields. By so doing, you could look up someone by name, could find out who lives in a certain city to which you will be going, who lives in a certain state or zip code to which you want to do a mass mailing, etc.

Record: Think of a record as a filled-out questionnaire. While each question on it is a separate field, the entire sheet is a record. The information in each record stays together no matter what you do with the record. For example, your name and address are separate fields, but since they are parts of the same record, they never get lost from each other.

The two major rules of databasing:

GIGO (Garbage In = Garbage Out): As you put data into the database, *always* remember that putting false or sloppy information into the database will produce output that is incorrect, unreliable, and worthless.

Partial Data = No Data. If you only enter your good sessions into the database, you may be able to use the database to find your strengths, but it will be useless for helping you find your weaknesses. It will also not be able to show you what you are doing right and wrong when you are having a bad day, versus when you are having a good day. Always remember that there are a lot of things in life that you can't learn by succeeding. You have to record and analyze your failures to learn them. That goes for learning remote viewing, too.

APPENDIX 2

WORKSHEETS

The following worksheets are designed for Controlled Remote Viewing records and databasing. Explanations of the fields and uses of these worksheets precede each one. The enclosed forms are for reproduction and use in your work.

While you may be tempted to draw up your own worksheets from the examples given, I would caution that doing so will tend to make your records incompatible with the records of other people. Unless you use some methodology that requires drastically different fields and data, it is best to use these forms, as they are designed to serve the most people in a standardized manner. Also realize that, if you want to add more categories of perception types, you will be making the data you collect incompatible with the standardized databases. If you want your information to be compatible, stick with the standardized fields as much as possible.

There are, of course, other worksheets that are used specifically for CRV work, but they are introduced in the specific courses. These worksheets are also useful for any other remote viewing methodology.

THE SESSION DATA WORKSHEET

The CRV Data Worksheet is the basic form for session work. It is used for recording the data which can then be put into the database. It also serves as a very useful cover page for your session transcript and feedback. The fields on the form are:

Viewer ID: Your name or viewer number (if you have been issued one—do not make one up on your own).

Target #:   For most purposes, the coordinates with which you began the session.

Location: Not for the city and state where you live, but where you do your work, i.e., the kitchen table, your desk at work, while carpooling, in a café at lunch, etc. After a year or so of sessions, you can compare your results at the various locations and see where you do your best work.

Date: The date of the session. If your session spans dates, enter the date you started.

Start: The time you begin your session.

End: The time you end your session. For those who continue to view the target while they are writing their summary, the time they are finished writing.

Actual site: A brief identification of the site. This entry will not be important on the date of the actual session, but may become very important at a later date, in a comparison of old and new sessions at the same place.

Perception categories: After scoring the session, transfer the information here. Any perceptions for which you cannot clearly distinguish a category should be put into the "other" category. Use the Notes area at the bottom of the page, if necessary.

Scoring: Follow the simple six-step process to find out what percentage of the perceptions was correct. This provides an overall score of the remote viewing session.

Notes: Make notes about what you learned during this session, suspicions about what went right or wrong, strange perceptions, and so on. This information can be valuable later on.

REMOTE VIEWING DATA WORKSHEET

Problems>Solutions>Innovations
37 Camino Ranchitos
Alamogordo, NM 88310
(505) 437-8285 e-mail: rviewer@netmdc.com

Viewer ID: _____   Date: __/__/__
Target #: _____   Start: _____
Location: _____   End: _____

Actual site is:_____

Category	PERCEPTIONS			Category	PERCEPTIONS		
	Y	N	?		Y	N	?
Alignment	___	___	___	Objects	___	___	___
Ambience	___	___	___	Patterns	___	___	___
Biologicals	___	___	___	Positions	___	___	___
Colors	___	___	___	Purposes	___	___	___
Composition	___	___	___	Relationships	___	___	___
Conceptuals	___	___	___	Shapes	___	___	___
Density	___	___	___	Sizes	___	___	___
Directions	___	___	___	Smells	___	___	___
Emotions	___	___	___	Sounds	___	___	___
Luminance	___	___	___	Structure	___	___	___
Meanings	___	___	___	Taste	___	___	___
Measures	___	___	___	Temps	___	___	___
Motions	___	___	___	Textures	___	___	___
Numbers	___	___	___	Weight	___	___	___
				Other	___	___	___

Scoring   **Perceptions**
1. Enter the total number of perceptions (Y + N + ?)   ___
2. What is the total number of unknowns? (?)   ___
3. Subtract Line 2 from Line 1. This is the total scorable. ___
4. What is the total number correct? (Y)   ___
5. Divide Line 4 by Line 3 (Y/total scorable)   ___
6. Multiply Line 5 by 100. This is your overall score.   ___

Notes

THE MONITOR'S WORKSHEET

This worksheet helps the monitor keep track of virtually everything of importance during the session.

Date:	Day, month, and year of the session.
Viewer:	Either the viewer's name or number.
Coordinates:	The cueing numbers given to the viewer to begin the session.
Frontloading:	Any frontloading given should be recorded in order to check for potential contamination at a later time.
Pages:	It is the monitor's job to keep track of the page number of the viewer's transcript so the viewer will not have to do so. By making tick marks in this blank, the monitor can keep track of the viewer's page number without having to try to read it upside down from the viewer's previous page. At the end of the session, the total number of tick marks in this blank should match the number of viewer's pages.
Time:	There are four types of time listed in this column. **Start** is the beginning time of the session. **End** is the time the session ends. **B** is the time any break starts and **R** is the time the viewer resumes the session after each break.
Cues:	The viewer will report perceptions which the monitor can use for further cueing or for getting the viewer started again after a "stall." The monitor should write each of the major gestalts here as well as any word that appears to elicit an unusual response from the viewer as he works the session. In short, any word the viewer perceives that could act as a cue later should be listed in this column. It will keep the monitor from having to look through the viewer's transcript for cue words.
Page:	This column accompanies the next one on notes and observations.
Notes/ observations:	When the session is over, you may want to discuss certain observations or questions about something in the session. Refer to this page rather than leafing through the session transcript, trying to find things.

Monitor's Worksheet

Date	Viewer				Pages
			(#)		
Coordinates	Frontloading				

Time	Cues	Page	Notes / observations
Start:			
End:			
B:			
R:			
B:			
R:			
B:			
R:			
B:			
R:			
B:			
R:			
B:			
R:			
B:			
R:			
B:			
R:			
B:			
R:			
B:			
R:			

APPENDIX 3

FRONTLOADING

The issue of frontloading is hotly debated in the remote viewing community, and for good reason. For some people (usually beginners), saying anything to them at all before the session kick-starts their imagination into high gear. For them, frontloading is an unfair and unwelcome burden.

For the more experienced viewers, frontloading can cut an hour-long session down to twenty minutes or so. It gets them to the target sooner and more solidly. It helps them go in and get the information the tasker wants, and prevents them from wandering around the site, viewing anything and everything which may catch their interest. For them, frontloading is a blessing and highly desirable.

Whether to have frontloading or not is totally up to the viewer in operational work. In research work, frontloading is seen as contamination and is not used, whether the viewer wants it or not.

Frontloading, when done correctly, is a method of telling the viewer where to put his/her efforts without providing any information about the target. It is a tool the viewer can use to focus his/her energies for the best effectiveness. When done incorrectly, it is an unnecessary and often destructive pollutant to be avoided at all costs.

THE TEN COMMANDMENTS OF FRONTLOADING

It is clear that different people have different ideas of what constitutes frontloading. I would like to suggest a few rules for proper frontloading, a sort of ten commandments, if you will, in the hopes of bringing some cohesiveness to this subject.

Rule 1: Frontloading must *not* impart target information.

What is frontloading *not?* If frontloading lets the viewer know something about the target, then it isn't frontloading. It is, at the very least, leading, and at the very worst, cheating. It is also very destructive to the viewer's session, and to the viewer's self-confidence. Let's take a couple of examples of frontloading that impart information.

Example 1.1: "The target is the location of a criminal who abducted a young girl."

This is a total disaster. There is not a viewer anywhere who will not immediately find himself/herself battling with personal stereotypes of a criminal, of a child abductor (and probably child molester), and of a location where we would expect such a person to hide in order to do their malevolent deeds. In addition, the viewer is immediately set upon by strong emotions. What if, in reality, the child was taken by her very loving mother, who becomes a criminal in the process? While the monitor may think that this kind of information helps the session and the viewer, it doesn't. It only hurts.

Example 1.2: "NEAR spacecraft landing event on the asteroid Eros, on February 12, 2001."

While there is no emotional triggering or even stereotype pollution, the above would actually serve to confuse the viewer's subconscious. First of all, you have tasked the viewer's subconscious with the answer it is supposed to find. What is the question here? What is the unknown to search out information about? Unless the viewer has absolutely no clue about the NEAR project, the total burden of describing is placed directly on the conscious mind. The little bit of information that is gained through viewing will get lost in the known facts. The viewer may know something about the project, but not know what the craft looks like. In that case, the dimensionals will need to be viewed, but even then, the viewer will have personal doubts about how much is actually coming from memory and previously forgotten knowledge (eidetic memory).

Example 1.3: "The target is the location of my car keys, lost on or about January 20."

This is not any better. A viewer faced with such information will immediately begin to mentally sort out possible locations where the tasker would have been, and all the possible places where car keys would normally have been misplaced or forgotten.

As a last example, let's take one of the most subtle types of unintentional pollution.

Example 1.4: "The target is a manufactured object. Describe it."

In this sentence, you tell the viewer not only the manufactured quality of the object, but you also tell him/her that there is only one. True, you have narrowed the tasking down to about forty quintillion possible targets in space and time, but you have still inadvertently polluted the session, and it will show up as problems for the viewer. The bottom line: *If you impart any information at all about the target site, then you are not frontloading—you are polluting.*

Rule 2: Frontloading must *not* "task the answer."

Simply stated, tasking the answer is a condition where you task the viewer to find what you want him/her to find. You have generally already decided what the target is, and now you want a viewer to agree with you. You aren't allowed to do that during a session, so you use something like the following for frontloading.

Example 2.1: "The target is a specific man. Describe him."

In this example, let's say that you are a police detective and you are looking for the perpetrator of a crime. You have already decided that the target is male, and you are asking the viewer to find what you already suspect. What if you are wrong?

Rule 3: Frontloading must only tell the viewer where to put his/her best efforts.

Let's say that the targeted location is a hotel with a beach, sailboats, volleyball game, refreshments kiosk, kiddy pool, beach umbrellas, parking lot, amusement rides, and people all over the place. Let's further say that I only want you to describe the winner of the volleyball game. If frontloading is designed properly, it will only tell you where to put your viewing efforts.

Example 3.1: "Describe the activity part of the site."

The end result of this frontloading is that the viewer will still, in the early stages of the session, pick up on the buildings, the sailboats, the people, the smell of candy, suntan oil, etc. But as the viewer stops "winking about the site," which is inherent to the early stages, he/she will begin to get site contact and will focus on that part of the site that is of interest to the viewer. The session goes much faster and the viewer is not worn out by the end of it.

Let's face it. Every site has a lot of things to describe. Not everything at a site needs to be described, thought it's fine to do so in a practice session. But realize the pitfalls. Do you want people to spend all their energies on inconsequential parts of the site? By the time they get around to the main part of the target, they will be tired and ready to quit. They won't be doing their best work on the most important aspects of the site.

In real-life session, where a tasker wants to know something specific about the site, you can't have a viewer dallying about for hours at the target site. You need the viewer to focus in on the important part of the site and get the necessary information. You need a tool that will allow the viewer to access that part of the site only. Frontloading *may* be that tool. Many people will respond that frontloading is still not necessary, since the monitor can "guide" the viewer to the desired part of the target, once the viewer is into session. But they should realize that if that happens, then your major pollution is not the frontloading, but the monitor's "middleloading." Monitors should not lead. This is another problem entirely.

To FRONTLOAD OR NOT TO FRONTLOAD: Are there times when frontloading is useful instead of harmful? If so, here are the deciding points regarding when to use frontloading and when not to.

Rule 4: If you cannot frontload without polluting, then don't frontload.

Rule 5: If the viewer wants or needs frontloading, then give it. But make sure it is properly done.

There are times when a viewer feels insecure and actively wants frontloading. In such a case, frontloading provides the viewer with a mental security blanket and actually helps the viewer by putting him/her at ease to work the session better. When the viewer wants frontloading, but the session is being conducted double-blind, the proper frontloading for this situation is:

Example 5.1: "The target is unknown. Describe the target."

Rule 6: If the viewer does not want frontloading, then don't give it.

It doesn't matter whether the monitor or project manager likes frontloading. If the viewer does not want it, then it should not be given. The viewer will know whether frontloading of any kind will be disruptive to the session or not. The viewer will also know whether the monitor can be trusted to give frontloading properly or not. If the viewer does not trust the monitor to give proper frontloading, then even if the frontloading is given in squeaky-clean purity, the viewer will be suspicious, and that worry will, by itself, pollute the session.

Rule 7: If the viewer wants frontloading, but is totally incapable of receiving it without polluting the session, give frontloading as though it were a double-blind session.

Many viewers who want frontloading, either for security or because they think they can handle it, don't realize how badly it can pollute their session. In that case, follow Rule 5 and give them frontloading, but provide absolutely no target information and absolutely no information on where they should put their efforts.

Example 7.1: "This is your first target of the day. Describe it."
Example 7.2: "This is a practice target. Describe it."
Example 7.3: "I won't tell you anything about this target. Describe it."

Such nondescript frontloading will often be sufficient for someone who only wants frontloading.

Rule 8: If you are doing a session for research, don't give frontloading.

It is possible to use the results of real-world operations for research and use the results of research for real-world operations, but it is rarely done. Research and operations exist in separate worlds.

Research demands pristine controls and a pristine environment, only known variables, and no pollution. Frontloading, even at its best and purest, is a type of pollution. So in the lab frontloading is neither recommended nor should it be permitted. The object of a research-oriented session is to test the viewer, a new protocol, or the field of remote viewing itself.

In real-world applications, however, the object of the session is usually to get in, get the necessary information, and get out with the greatest possible efficiency. In that respect, frontloading is sometimes a very useful tool to get the job done more efficiently.

In general it's the researchers who are adamantly against frontloading of any kind, and the applications-oriented people who say that there are times when it is needed and useful.

Rule 9: In all other cases, don't provide frontloading unless necessary.

There is nothing magical about frontloading in and of itself. It should be used wisely and only when needed. It isn't the hammer that fixes everything, nor should it be used as the first tool out of the box. Just like the hammer, don't use it unless the job calls for it.

Rule 10: If you provide frontloading, make a written record of it.

In CRV, the viewer writes down, word-for-word, any frontloading given. Thereafter, there is no question about the purity of the frontloading. It is there for all to see.

APPENDIX 4

EXERCISES TO DEVELOP AND ENHANCE YOUR REMOTE VIEWING ABILITIES

The following exercises are given to every beginning Controlled Remote Viewing student who goes through the training provided by Problems Solutions Innovations.

There were many attempts in the military unit to devise exercises to "make us more psychic," but for all general purposes, they failed. The only exercise that was ever kept within the unit was to purchase a copy of a book called *Drawing on the Right Side of the Brain,* and go through the workbook fully and carefully. I would advise anyone who is serious about the field of remote viewing to do the same.

For the most part, though, exercises to enhance your psychic ability are useless. This is especially true of computer programs that use the computer's random-number generator to create and have you control supposedly random events. In truth, the random-number generator in a desktop or laptop computer does not produce random numbers at all, but produces a string of "randomly appearing" numbers. That is, the numbers are hardwired into the computer's program, and will produce the same series of randomly appearing numbers time after time. The program starts when you turn your computer on, and only appears random because you access the chip at different times in its stream. But when you do access it, what you get from that point on is a canned, mathematically rigid series of numbers which only appear random. Computer programs that are designed to enhance your psychic ability using this method do not work and are not worth bothering with, much less buying.

Like all other "learn to be psychic" exercises, the exercises that follow do not enhance your psychic abilities. They are designed, instead, to get rid of those inhibitions that normally prevent you from using the psychic talents you are not presently using.

The first exercise, the ideogram exercise, teaches you how to allow your body to become a translator between the conscious and subconscious mind.

Exercises 2 through 5 have been designed with the consideration that, if you cannot adequately sense the world immediately surrounding you, there is no way you will be able to sense the world at some far distant target site, no matter how much psychic talent you may have. They train you to be sensitive to your surroundings, and in the process teach you to be sensitive to the surroundings at any targeted remote viewing site.

Exercise 6 is designed to teach you some very important realities about the problems you face when you, as the only one who knows something about the target, set out to impart that knowledge to others. Repeated practice of this exercise has been of tremendous benefit to remote viewers, businessmen, sales personnel, artists, and writers. It should be taken very seriously and practiced often.

THE IDEOGRAM EXERCISE

The ideogram is the most fundamental feature of Controlled Remote Viewing. This physical act initiates the line of communications between the conscious and subconscious in every session. It is the equivalent of the most basic of moves in any martial art. My company, Problems Solutions Innovations, has a computer program that helps greatly with this exercise, as it calls the words out to you over the computer's speakers.

Exercise 1: Ideograms

You know how people always say, "Psychic ability is inherent to everyone! Anyone can do it!" Then you notice that everyone *is not* doing it, and in fact, most people doubt that they can. Ingo Swann and others once decided to accept the idea that everyone can do it and began to look at the problem in that way.

Through a series of questions and answers, a new starting place was developed to allow people to develop the ability.

Question: If everyone has access to the information, where does it come into their minds?
Answer: Everyone generally agrees that, in the framework of human sciences, the answer appears to be "through the subconscious mind."

Question: If everyone has psychic information available to their subconscious minds, why can't they access it consciously?
Answer: Because the conscious and subconscious minds don't talk to each other. They don't even speak the same language.

Question: If they don't speak the same language—and even after eighty to one hundred years of living in the same body, can't seem to learn—then what can be done to get the two talking to each other?
Answer: Get an interpreter.

Question: Who or what can understand and speak to both the conscious and subconscious minds?
Answer: The body. You can consciously control the body, and your subconscious and autonomic minds can control it, too. Through the physical senses, you can pass information to the conscious, subconscious, and autonomic minds. It evidently speaks and understands them all.

In effect, there is no need to develop one's "psychic ability." Whatever ability you have is already there and working. All you have to do is develop a way to get to the information it has access to. That is not a psychic problem, but a language problem. So the correct training is not to be found in the mysterious, the occult, the psychic, at all, but in other fields, particularly linguistics.

What if we could form a language the body could use as a "Rosetta Stone" which the conscious, the subconscious, and the autonomic minds could understand? Swann and others have looked into the already well-researched fields of psychology, psychotherapy, and psychophysiology, as well as linguistics, to find the answers, and they were there.

First of all, since the language is for the physical body only, it has to be completely physical: no pronunciations, no processing, very basic grammar, etc. Since there is no such ready-made language, it is up to you to develop it. Then, as with any other language, you have to practice using it until it becomes a habit or second nature.

Let's start out simply: Let's take the gestalt (basic concept) of "land." We don't care what kind of land: farmland, desert, plains, swamps—just the gestalt of "land." Now, take a pen in your hand and draw the simplest, most basic sketch you can possibly make for that gestalt. Most people draw a straight, horizontal line. Fine. Let's make that the first word in your language. If you drew something else, then you will use that from now on. After all, it's your own language.

Now, sketch something for water. Most people draw a wavy line. Fine. Now, you have a language of two words—or more correctly, two "idea graphics," or as they are formally called, ideograms.

You now need to develop ideograms for "natural," "manmade," "motion," "space," and "life" (or organic/living/cellular/whatever—meaning anything that either has life or has once had life).

Once you have developed the basic set of ideograms, you begin the actual exercise itself. It is called "ideogram drills," and is guaranteed to be almost the most boring thing you have ever done. One person calls out the words in random order, at random speeds, and the student reacts to the word being called out by making the proper ideogram for it. This goes on for long periods of time, until the student has phased out and stopped paying attention. At that time, we know that he or she is doing it subconsciously. In other words, the subconscious mind is now learning and practicing the new language, too.

The ultimate goal of this is straightforward: When we ask a viewer to describe the target site, the viewer's subconscious mind, already having information about the site, will, for example, cause the hand to draw a straight line connected to a wavy line. The viewer looks at the ideogram and sees that the site is a place of land connected to water (a beach, river, island, lake, etc.). First contact with the site has been made, and the session has begun.

CRV training is not just "relax and tell me what you see in your daydreams." That kind of thing has been tried for years with only minor success. That is also what most people taking training in "remote viewing" are doing. It's the same old stuff with a newer name.

Once a CRVer has gotten the basic gestalts of the target site, more detailed information is gained through a secondary language which also includes the physical senses. In other words, the language of CRV starts every session off with basic descriptors, then more involved sensory contact, in preparation for conceptual information about the site, finer and finer details, etc.

THE AMBIENCE EXERCISE

I tell every one of my students that this is the most important part of the entire series of CRV courses. This exercise will enhance your perceptions to the point where everyone will suddenly think you have become a gifted psychic. Yet, it does not deal with psychic functioning at all.

The ambience exercise develops your true sixth sense. (The psychic sense is actually your seventh sense—hence the name of this book.) It will make you so uncommonly aware of your surroundings that you will probably feel as if you have been asleep all of your life.

The ambience exercise consists of twenty separate steps or levels of work. If each step is performed correctly, the total twenty steps should take many, many years to master.

The spin-offs of this exercise include all of the benefits of becoming more aware of the world around you. It will enable you to tell when there is a police radar around the bend by the ambience of the oncoming traffic, or whether a person is lying or not. You will be able to know what a person is going to do before he/she does it, and often before he/she even thinks of doing it. I am convinced that if we could teach this exercise to every policeman in the nation, we could drastically reduce the number of policemen killed in the line of duty.

Here is the first ambience exercise. I cannot stress enough the importance of practicing this exercise as often as possible.

Exercise 2: Ambience

 My years of doing CRV have led me to conclude that our sixth sense is ambience. By ambience, I mean the sort of feeling you get in a large cathedral, for instance. There is no body part to attribute it to, as the other five senses have, but it is there just the same. Not only that, but everyone entering the cathedral will feel it, too. So, in our CRV training, the sixth sense will be a very normal one: ambience. The psychic sense will then have to be the seventh sense.

One of the biggest problems psychics have in describing a distant site is their need to rely on their imaginations to fill in things they can't perceive about the distant site. But the real problem is that they can't even fully describe the location where they are. We are all that way, in fact. When we feel a certain ambience in a room, it is usually very hard for us to describe. There are good reasons for that. English is very sparse in ambience words. Because ambience awareness is not a major part of our language, it is not a major part of our thought process.

That doesn't mean that it isn't an important part of our awareness, however. Think about it: When you first enter a room where there is, say, danger, you are immediately aware of the ambience, even before you are mentally conscious of anything in the room. Before any attention is given to the things in the room, the "feeling" is there. Why, you may wonder, isn't the feeling just as strong whenever you enter *any* room?

The answer to that is found in an old science experiment with frogs. If you place a frog into hot water, it will immediately jump out. But if you place that same frog in cold water, then slowly heat the water to boiling, the frog will sit there and be boiled alive. Humans are much the same way. Once you get used to very hot dishwater, you can stick your hand into water that will scald your skin without instinctively pulling back. The skin will be damaged, but you won't feel the pain or the damage until you remove your hand and it cools off. Humans, like frogs, are much more sensitive to *change* than they are to constant conditions. Therefore, if you leave a room that is safe and enter another room that is also safe, you don't notice the ambience in the second room, as you are accustomed to it. But if you leave a safe room and enter a dangerous place, you will notice the sudden change in ambience immediately. We are naturally sensitive to sudden, large changes in ambience, but rarely ever to small ones.

When you remote view, you move your mind from one environment to another. If there is a very large change in ambience, you will notice it. Not surprisingly, dangerous sites are the easiest kind of target for most psychics to view. It is one reason psychics often see only visions of doom and gloom while sitting in their very safe and comfortable studies. You won't always be tasked with dramatic, exciting, dangerous, romantic, ecstasy-inducing targets. You will often be asked to describe an ordinary person's ordinary location and/or ordinary activities. That person might be sitting at a desk writing something on paper. You will be sitting at a desk to view him/her, also writing on your paper. If you have not developed an acute sensitivity to ambience, you will notice nothing about the target person. You will think that you are not getting the target. In fact, you may be receiving impressions just fine, but they are so much like what you have in your own surroundings that you can't notice them.

So this exercise is designed to sensitize you to ever smaller changes in the ambience surrounding you. It will strengthen and heighten your ambience awareness. It will wake up a sense that you have used very rarely in your lifetime. It opens up your sixth sense. As you practice this exercise, you will become aware of things that have always been around you, but that you never noticed before.

Here is the exercise. Beginning immediately, notice every doorway you go through. Before you do, stop and see if you can get a feel for the ambience in the room you are leaving. Then step through the door and see if you can feel the *change* in ambience. Although it would be nice if you could describe the change exactly, at this point, you are only concerned with sensitizing yourself to finer and finer amounts of change in ambience.

This exercise should be done with *every* doorway you go through from now until you die. That means doors between rooms, entrance and exit doors in buildings, the bathroom door, the bedroom door, the car door, etc. *Every* doorway. At some point, it will become second nature to you, and you will have added an entirely new dimension to your awareness, and therefore to your life. You will be as the sighted are in the land of the blind.

I estimate that probably 90 percent of the events and actions that pass for "psychic" are nothing more than ambience. You know you are doing this exercise correctly when people around you start asking, "What are you? Psychic or something?"

THE VOCABULARY EXERCISE

It is a proven fact that you will tend not to make any permanent mental record of anything for which you do not have a word to describe it. It is therefore very important to expand your vocabulary. Since reporting your findings is a major part of all parapsychological work, you need the vocabulary with which to recognize and report what is at the site. If you cannot do that with something right in front of you, then you will not be able to send your mind halfway around the world and perceive and report what is going on there.

Do this exercise about once a week. If you have children whom you could involve in the "game" of it, please do so. The spin-off of this exercise is that it will make anyone practicing it better writers, reporters, public speakers, and conversationalists.

Exercise 3: Vocabulary

Scientific studies of the mind and how people think show that the way you think determines the words you use, and the words you use determine how you think. This second finding is the subject of this exercise, for not only do your words determine *how* you think, but they even determine what you *can* (and cannot) think. If you don't have a word for something, you tend not to objectify it—that is, even if you can sense it on a subconscious level, it never reaches the conscious level of thought, so you don't become aware of it. In effect, if you don't have a word for a thing, feeling, situation, or even desire, you can't think about it. You may feel "something vague and nameless," but you can't mentally or logically work your way through it. If it is a problem, you can't solve it, and if it is what you want to do with your life, and you don't have a word for it, you'll spend your life not getting it done. Once you have a word for something, you tend to also become aware of (and can think about) those things that are similar, even if you don't have a word for them. You form what are called "cognotrons" around the first word.

In CRV work, this means that if you get a subconscious perception and do not have a word for objectifying it, then it will generally never make it to your conscious mind, and you won't know you perceived it. But let's say that you grasp at straws and come up with the wrong word for the perception. The word you come up with will have its own set of cognotrons, and the rest of your descriptors will tend to match that first (incorrect) word—and so will the rest of your perceptions. Herein lies one of the greatest pollution problems the CRVer will face. The problem, however, is not the result of insufficient ability to view, but simply of insufficient vocabulary.

The average American has a vocabulary of almost two hundred thousand words—that is, an inactive or passive vocabulary. They know that many words, but don't ever use them. The average businessperson has an active vocabulary of only about two thousand words—that is, words he/she uses on a daily basis. When we refer to "active" vocabulary, we are not only talking about the number of words a person uses every day, but also about the range of thought that person is capable of thinking, and the range of perceptions that person has, as well. If something happens outside their normal range, it is generally not noticed, noticed but then ignored, or quickly forgotten.

If you can't notice, describe, or even perceive the things in the real world around you, because of the size of your active vocabulary, how can you expect to perceive and describe the things at a far distant site? The answer is that you can't.

This is different from any "vocabulary exercise" you've ever done before. This is not a "learn a new word every day" type of exercise. It takes for granted that you already have the vocabulary, but that it is passive. If someone says a word, you'll recognize it at least well enough to get a meaning out of that person's sentence. The object of this exercise is to transfer those words into your active vocabulary. You will be pleasantly surprised to find that you open up new thought patterns in the process. Because it is designed for CRV work, the exercise first enhances sensories and dimensionals. The exercise goes like this:

1. Get a group of two or more people together to do the exercise. Sit around a table, with a pen and paper in front of each person. It is important for each person to write each word down as someone says it, simply to get that person's body involved in the process of activating the vocabulary. The body's interaction with the mind is paramount in all phases of CRV.

2. Select *one* of the sensory groups at random (sounds, colors, smells, tastes, textures, temperatures, luminances, etc.) or one of the dimensional groups (sizes, shapes, directions, orientations, etc.). Write the group selected at the top of the paper.

3. In either columns down or lines across, each person writes a vocabulary word as someone calls it out. If you can add a word, call it out, too.

That's it. It is a very simple exercise on the surface, but in practice, it becomes very hard. Here is an example:

When someone in the group says a word that you don't know, ask them to describe it. In this way, you not only bring words from the passive vocabulary to the active, but

---

COLORS

red, yellow, blue, brown, green, gray . . .
(pretty soon you come up with words like . . .)
hazel, auburn, mauve, magenta . . .
(and then get desperate and move to colors that use nouns as descriptors. . .) **brick red, fire-engine red, ruby red, blood red, sky blue, baby blue, etc.**

you also expand your vocabulary in the process. The end result of this exercise is that it gets people to think about things they haven't thought about in years, to increase their ability to describe things in more minute detail, and thereby to expand their ability to perceive things.

This exercise should be practiced at least once a week If you have the chance to include school-aged children in the practice, the benefits for their education are enormous.

THE SENSORY ENHANCEMENT EXERCISE

This exercise is designed to develop your five physical senses. Practicing this exercise will hone your sensory awareness to heights presently unimaginable. You will find, if you practice the "Go Hug a Couple of Trees" exercise properly, that almost every physical sensation you now take for granted will become more experiential in nature.

The theory behind this exercise is that, if you can/cannot perceive the things in the physical world around you, then you can/cannot experience them in the mental world of a target halfway around the world. The side benefit is that it can enhance your life and your awareness to degrees you never thought possible before.

Exercise 4: "Go Hug a Couple of Trees"

We are more sensitive to changes in the environment than we are to factors that make up the environment itself. Constant weather or temperature is not noticed after the first few moments. A sudden change, however, and we become aware of it immediately. We can study in a quiet library as long as there are no sudden noises. We can also study in the noisiest cafeteria or train station, because the noise is constant. But a change in the noise we will notice immediately.

Not only is change what we notice most, but we notice it as a relative change, not an absolute. Junior high school science teachers have their students do experiments in which you place one hand in hot water and another in cold water until you get each hand used to the temperature. Then you take both hands and place them in room-temperature water. The hand that was in the hot water feels the room-temperature water as cold, while the hand that was in the cold water feels the room-temperature water as hot.

This is a useful demonstration for CRVers. The impressions that come to us early on in the session come as sensory input. The body is doing its job translating the most primitive impressions, in order to get us into closer contact with the target. We can help it do that by simply realizing that it is most sensitive to change; the more sudden the better. If we dwell on each sensory input, the process is slowed down. The "body translator" has less of a chance to sense sudden changes in color, texture, temperature, sounds, etc. It becomes important then to work quickly. This not only allows your translator to notice more, but also keeps it from getting used to one impression and then interpreting another as a relative. For example, if you remain focused on a hot part of the site for too long a time, you might tend to describe the rest of the site as cold, in spite of its being room temperature, or maybe even just very warm.

By the same token, it is important to have a sufficiently active vocabulary to name the impressions quickly so the translator can bounce toward more impressions. Hence, the importance of the vocabulary exercise.

But there are some impressions for which there just aren't words. There are also times when two impressions will be so alike that our translator won't be able to feel a change. As you "wink about the site," getting impressions, you may, for example, get "smooth," followed immediately by "smooth." A quick thought goes through the mind about why the impression repeated; it is usually dismissed by the novice CRVer. The trained CRVer knows that if you get an impression twice, you write it twice. The very similar impressions come so quickly that the viewer doesn't realize that two parts of the site have been visited and found to be smooth.

This exercise is designed to help sensitize you to those impression differences for which there just aren't any words and those that are so close together that you would normally tend not to notice them. The exercise is simple:

1. When at a store, swap meet, yard sale, or even just around your own home or yard, touch something and try to give it a one-word descriptor. For example, let's say that as you sit here reading this, you touch the paper and say, "smooth."

2. But then, you must immediately look around and find something else that would also be described as smooth. Let's say it is the desk or table on which the paper is sitting. Touch it and again say, "smooth."

3. You know that there is a difference, but would probably be very hard put to adequately describe the difference between the two "smooths." That doesn't matter. You have shown your body's sensory mechanisms that there are small differences, and that it should be aware of them, even though you don't have a word for the difference. In effect, you are teaching your body to become more sensitive.

This exercise should be done with each of the five physical senses. For example, look at some specific point on the wall and note its color. Now, look at the wall at a point three feet away from the first point and see if you can see the difference in color. There is almost always a difference. While you can't usually name the difference, you have just helped your eyes become sensitive to it. That is the important point to this exercise. Try the same with the sounds around you. Try the same with textures, temperatures, tastes, smells, etc.

This exercise, practiced correctly and regularly, will heighten your awareness of the physical world.

THE DETAIL RECOGNITION EXERCISE

You will find this exercise surprising. Most people do not see what is directly in front of them. Police know that an eyewitness sees everything through filters of biases, fears, desires, upbringing, social mores, and so forth. An eyewitness to a crime is probably the least reliable source for information about it.

The slight embarrassment caused by this exercise is enough to make you become aware of more and more details whenever you look at anything, either in the world around you or at some remote viewing site.

There are two major spin-offs to this exercise. First, you will begin to see implications and ramifications in things with which you work each day. In business meetings, you will become the person who is capable of seeing the "big picture" and its benefits and potential problems before others can.

A second and stranger benefit comes from this exercise. In confusing situations, you can zero in on the heart of the problem.

Exercise 5: "Phase II It"

 When we compare our list of descriptors from a remote viewing session to the feedback, we see what an incomplete list we have made. What if we had perfect knowledge of the target so that we could get *all* the descriptors? Wouldn't that be great? Then the list we created would only be limited by our attention to details and our ability to notice what's right in front of us. The purpose of this exercise is to do just that: to increase our attention.

PART I

1. Get out a target picture and a blank sheet of paper.
2. At the top of the blank sheet, write "Phase 2."
3. Turn the target picture so you can see it.
4. Make your list of descriptors, all the while having the picture there to look at. Remember to get descriptors for supposed temperatures, textures, smells, tastes, etc.

PART 2

1. When your list of descriptors is as complete as you can make it, find someone who will look at the list and the picture to check out what you have written.
2. Ask them to point out to you anything you missed.

This exercise reveals things that you were looking straight at and missed. Because of this, it causes you to be more attentive next time. Don't worry—the next time, you will miss something else and, then, having had it pointed out to you, will become even more aware. As many times as you practice this exercise, you will probably never get so attentive that you will see everything. But you will become more attentive. The good thing is that this exercise isn't only for CRV, but improves your attention span for the other aspects of your life as well.

THE EFFICIENT REPORTING EXERCISE

This exercise will not improve your viewing the target, but it will help you become more proficient at reporting what was found at a target site.

I would urge every manager in every company to try this exercise with their salesmen, their managers, and everyone in their company who has to interact with another person in any way. It will teach each participant that their communication skills are not nearly as honed as they believe; that they are not as clear to others as they are to themselves; that the spoken and written word can (and usually does) have many ways of being interpreted; and that given even the slightest chance, the receiver of the spoken or written word will usually perceive it incorrectly.

This exercise, when practiced on a regular basis, can teach people how to become clear and concise in their speaking, writing, and communicating. It can also teach them how to think from a listener's viewpoint, rather than from their own viewpoint.

Exercise 6: "Do You See What I See?"

Let's say that you have just been given all the knowledge in the universe, but that there is a time limit on how long you will be able to retain it. During that time, you will naturally want to write as much of it down as possible so you can relearn it later. In your haste to write down as much as possible, you try to make each statement as succinct as possible. When your time limit is up, you forget all that knowledge. No problem. You have it all written down. You then take up your notes and read, "The crow's flight is as butter." What? You think back and try to remember what you meant by that. You know that just moments ago, it had a deep and significant meaning, that it had something to do with the basic tenets of subatomic theories as yet undiscovered. Something about the very nature of matter. Maybe the next sentences will clear it up: "Three corners are needed for e to equal mc^2 when traveling sideways through time," and "Without gravity there is no fire."

The point here is that when you get into session, you begin to access knowledge about a far distant site. It is knowledge that other people do not possess—and won't if you can't communicate it to them. "No problem!" you say. "I can explain what I get in session."

Can you, though? This exercise not only tests your ability to explain what you are seeing but it trains you for the job of simply reporting what you can see and others can't. The exercise:

Select a target picture at random. Do not show it to anyone else. Then, have other people draw the picture as you describe it to them. Remember that this is a CRV exercise, so you will be required to *describe, not identify.* That is, you must keep the use of nouns to the absolute barest minimum.

The exercise is performed in two stages: In the first stage, which should last from three to five minutes, people cannot ask questions. In the second stage, they can.

Another form of this exercise is to give your description in written form and hand it to someone who is then to redraw the original picture from your verbal description. Scoring and feedback come when you compare the original picture to the one that was drawn using your descriptions as a guide.

While it may seem that this exercise is somewhat useless to remote viewing, the fact is that a remote viewer, no matter how talented and well trained, is useless if he/she can't report accurately what was perceived.

APPENDIX 5

METHODS FOR SCORING
REMOTE VIEWING SESSIONS

CAVEAT AND A WORD OF ADVICE

Computers are a tremendous tool for statistically proving the existence of PSI, and actually scoring its capabilities overall, and the proficiency of any one viewer or psychic. Before the computer, the method for showing a person's success was limited to telling stories of how "I did this once" and "One time, I . . ." This kind of anecdotal evidence is not real evidence at all.

The computer has become a necessary part of the field of parapsychology. Almost every computer sold these days comes with a simple database program that can be used for scoring and scientifically maintaining data on the work of any other psychic or remote viewer.

Scoring a remote viewing session, or the results of any psychic session, for that matter, must start with the question "What am I trying to find out?" Because there are many answers to that question, it should not surprise the reader that there are many ways of scoring.

Method 1: Success/Failure

This is the simplest scoring method of all, but also the least accurate. It is simple because you simply ask the question at the end of the session, "Did I give the customer what he needed?" If the answer is yes, then you had a successful session. If the answer is no, then you failed to do the required job.

Note that this method does not take into account anything other than meeting the customer's needs. Even if all your perceptions were 100 percent correct, if you did not provide the one bit of information required to meet the customer's need, you failed.

To score in this manner, you only need to set up a database with the following fields:

The project name	(text field)
The viewer's name	(text field)
The customer's question	(memo field)
The viewer's answer	(memo field)
Successful?	(yes/no field)

A record in this database might look something like this:

Project #:	991012
Viewer:	John Koslowski
Question:	What was the color of the getaway car?
Answer:	Red
Successful?	————

Note that you cannot fill in the "Successful?" field until the customer has returned information to let you know whether the viewer's summary information helped them or not.

Although the above fields are the only ones you really need, you might want to add some other fields for date of session, time of session, type of target, and so on. Such information will then let you go back later and look at all the sessions in the database to determine, for example, what time of day or day of the week the viewer does his best work. It will also let you analyze what type of target the viewer works best. Some viewers cannot work "blood and guts" types of sessions with any success, but can work such things as descriptions of the locations, persons involved, manmade objects, and other target aspects that do not deal with the more emotionally charged target aspects.

This is the least accurate type of scoring simply because the customer will almost always waffle for the viewer, saying, for example, "Well, it helped some, but it didn't give us exactly what we needed." How would you score feedback like that? Even when a viewer has been no help at all, the customer will tend to find a way to avoid coming right out and saying so.

Method 2: Applicability

Closely related to the success/failure method, this method requires much more evaluation, but also provides much greater information on a viewer's true ability to "go to the heart of the matter" and get pertinent information, instead of just randomly viewing anything to do with a target site.

In this method, you must keep track of every perception the viewer makes and judge it for its applicability to the customer's stated needs and/or question(s). The steps for handling this type of scoring are time consuming, but very simple in practice.

Let us say that the customer asked, "What was the color of the getaway car?" and the viewer returns the following summary:

> The site is parklike and quiet. There are swings nearby and a small red car, which is used by the criminal for escape. There are no other people nearby.

Step 1: Rewrite the essay-type summary with only one perception per line:

Perception
The site is parklike
The site is quiet
The site has swings
    Which are nearby*
The site has a car
    Which is small

---

*Note that "nearby" describes where the swings are, not the parklike area. Therefore, it is placed indented under the perception "swings," and not out at the margin with the other descriptors of the area.

And red
And is used for escape
By the criminal
The site has no other people
Who are nearby

Step 2: Place a line to the right of each perception and score it for applicability toward the customer's question.

Perception	Applicable?
The site is parklike	_____
The site is quiet	_____
The site has swings	_____
Which are nearby	_____
The site has a car	_____
Which is small	_____
And red	_____
And is used for escape	_____
By the criminal	_____
The site has no other people	_____
Who are nearby	_____

Step 3: After the customer gives you feedback, score the perceptions with a *Y* for yes, an *N* for no, or a *?* for "can't feedback." Note that you wait until the customer returns feedback, because information that might not be apparent by simply comparing the customer's question with the viewer's answer might have wound up being of extreme importance to the customer, in spite of all logical appearances. The final summary, then, would look like:

Perception	Applicable?
The site is parklike	N
The site is quiet	?
The site has swings	N
Which are nearby	N

The site has a car	Y
Which is small	Y
And red	Y
And is used for escape	Y
By the criminal	Y
The site has no other people	Y
Who are nearby	Y

Much to the surprise of the scorer, the last two perceptions may have been of extreme importance to the customer, who is very anxious to find eyewitnesses who could identify the car. Therefore, even though these perceptions do not appear to be pertinent to the question asked, they are applicable to what the customer needs to know about the car. The perception that the site is quiet may or may not be of importance to the customer, since there is some confusion in the evidence about when the crime was committed. Therefore, the presence or absence of traffic noise in the area may or may not be important.

Step 4: Get the total number of perceptions. In the above example, the total is 11.

Step 5: Subtract the ?s. The remainder is the total number of scorable perceptions. You cannot accurately count ?s as either appropriate to the target or not appropriate. They cannot, therefore, be considered in the score.

Step 6: Divide the total number of scorable perceptions into the total number of Y perceptions and multiply the answer by 100. This will give you the percentage of perceptions that the viewer had that were pertinent to the customer's needs. In the above example, the formula would look like this:

$$\text{Total perceptions} - \text{?s} = \text{Total scorable}$$
$$11 - 1 = 10$$
$$(\text{Total correct} / \text{Total scorable}) \times 100 = \text{Applicability}$$
$$(7 / 10) = .7$$
$$.7 \times 100 = 70\%$$

The applicability score for this session was 70 percent, or to put it another way, 70 percent of the scorable perceptions were pertinent to the customer's needs.

This method does not take into consideration whether the viewer was right or wrong in his perceptions. It only judges how well a viewer can stick to the topic at hand and how much the viewer tends to wander around the site, picking up useless information. It is possible to add a second column of blanks to the right of each perception, for also scoring whether the viewer's perception was correct or not, thus giving a rating of accuracy, as well as applicability.

Method 3: Viewer Track Records

This method establishes a track record or dependability rating for the individual viewer. In addition to an overall track record, it also establishes a score for judging how well the viewer will perform when tasked against different types of targets and different perception categories. It reveals the viewer's strengths and weaknesses. The first step is much like the applicability method, but goes one step further, adding a second set of lines for perception categories. The first column of blanks in this example is for scoring whether or not the perception was correct (not whether it was applicable to the customer's question).

Perception	Correct?	Category
The site is parklike	Y	Ambience
The site is quiet	?	Sounds
The site has swings	Y	Objects
Which are nearby	N	Relationships
The site has a car	Y	Objects
Which is small	Y	Sizes
And red	Y	Colors
And is used for escape	Y	Purposes
By the criminal	Y	Persons
The site has no other people	?	Persons
Who are nearby	?	Relationships

Scoring is relatively the same. Question marks are removed before scoring and the remainder of scorable perceptions are divided into the number of Y, or correct perceptions, with the answer multiplied by 100. So, in the above example, the viewer's score is:

$$\text{Overall score: } 11-3 = 8 \text{ (scorable perceptions)}$$
$$7 / 8 = .875$$
$$875 \times 100 = 87.5\% \text{ correct}$$

That is, 87.5 percent of everything the viewer said about the target (that we could score) was correct. But there is even more information to be gained from this:

The viewer was: 100% correct on all scorable ambience perceptions.
0% correct on all scorable relationships.
100% correct on all scorable object perceptions.
100% correct on all scorable color perceptions.
100% correct on all scorable size perceptions.
100% correct on all scorable purpose perceptions.
100% correct on all scorable human-related perceptions.
50% of all human perceptions could not be scored.
100% of all sound perceptions could not be scored.
50% of all relationship perceptions could not be scored.

The viewer gets an average (so far) of 11 perceptions when given a task.

Overall, 27.27 percent of this viewer's perceptions will not be scorable.

Other analyses can be derived from the data, as well.

Obviously, such conclusions cannot be drawn on the basis of a single session. Over time, as more sessions are performed, the viewer's scores will move away from the 0 percent, 100 percent, and 50 percent levels to a much more realistic profile of the viewer's capabilities, strengths, and weaknesses.

A third column can be added to score the applicability of a viewer's ability. Still another column can be added for "Target type" (criminal, scientific, "blood and guts," R&D, and any other target types for which a viewer will be used), providing a profile of the viewer in each category for each target type.

This type of scoring takes a tremendous amount of work, but also provides a tremendous amount of information about a viewer's capabilities. In the practical world, it is most important to say to a customer, "That viewer has proven to be 89.73 percent reliable in getting the type of information you want a viewer to find." Computers have, we hope, put an end to the days of anecdotal, unscorable, unprovable evidence presented in the place of proof.

Method 4: Laboratory Proof

For those who only want to prove that PSI functioning exists, there is a much simpler method. This method takes all of the overall aspects of the viewing process and melds them into a single score, without taking into consideration how well a viewer performs on any certain aspect of viewing, how well he can write his final report, or how competent the customer is at reading that report. It does not consider the scores of individual viewers or their individual strengths and weaknesses.

Step 1: Give the viewer a target which has feedback readily available.

Step 2: Get the viewer's summary of findings

Step 3: Either have the viewer compare the summary to five different targets (only one of which was the actual tasked target), or have an impartial set of judges perform the comparison. As they compare the summary to the separate targets, they rank them according to which they think is:

1. most likely the target
2. second most likely
3. possibly the target
4. probably not the target
5. least likely to be the target

Step 4: See which one is actually the target. The sum of the rankings is the viewer's score. For example, let us say that the five target pictures have been pulled out of a pile at random. They are:

Picture A	A barn on a farm
Picture B	A Swiss chalet on a mountainside (the actual target)
Picture C	Niagara Falls
Picture D	An opera being performed
Picture E	A box of corn flakes with a slightly open top

The viewer performs his session and reports that there is a big, tall, rectangular thing, which has sharp corners and a slanting top. There is an Oooooooo sound. There is something cold and white around it.

Usually with this type of scoring, five people are grabbed out of the hallway, and asked to be judges for this experiment. They are asked to rank the targets according to how probable they think the summary describes them. They are not told which picture is the actual target. Let's say they rank the targets as follows:

	Most likely	2nd most likely	Possible	Probably not	Least likely
	5 points	4 points	3 points	2 points	1 point
Judge 1	Picture A	Picture D	Picture B	Picture E	Picture C
Judge 2	Picture B	Picture E	Picture D	Picture A	Picture C
Judge 3	Picture E	Picture A	Picture D	Picture B	Picture C
Judge 4	Picture B	Picture A	Picture E	Picture D	Picture C
Judge 5	Picture D	Picture E	Picture A	Picture B	Picture C

All the judges agree that Picture C, Niagara Falls, is not the target. Why the differences in the other judging? If we ask them, they might reply as follows.

Judge 1:
Because the barn is a rectangular thing with a slanting top.

When asked about the fact that there is nothing cold and white around it, Judge 1 was surprised. After reading the first sentence, he had made up his mind, and had not paid any attention to the rest of the summary.

Judge 2:
Well, a couple of the things were rectangular with a slanting top, but this was the only one that had the wind whistling around it, making an Ooooooo sound. And a lot of snow and ice.

Judge 2's NAG had jumped in to identify what each descriptor meant. Luckily, he had done this correctly.

Judge 3:
It was obviously the box of cereal, which is rectangular with sharp edges and the partly open top is slanted like the viewer said. Although it doesn't show in the picture, there is bound to be a bowl of cold, white milk somewhere associated with it. Since it is a corn flakes ad, it implies a kid saying "Oooo" about getting his corn flakes.

Judge 3's NAG was also at work, but not as correctly as Judge 2's.

Judge 4:
I don't know. I picked B because it is a really attractive place and fits all the descriptions. I liked that picture best and thought that's one they would give to a viewer. These others aren't interesting.

Judge 4 decided that he would analyze the process and figure out how he would do it. Judging the summary against the pictures was not a factor in his decision.

Judge 5:
The picture of the opera shows a dark theater with a brightly lit rectangle. The ceiling of the room is slanted back over the audience's head for better sound. It looks like the Vikings, so there had to be cold and ice. I hate opera, but the woman singing is wearing a horned helmet and looks a lot like a cow to me. With

that brass bra, she has to be cold, so she must be hollering, "Oooooooo!"

Judge 5 was busy when dragged in from the hallway and did not really want to take part in the judging. Both consciously and subconsciously, he wanted to make light of the whole test. The NAG is very capable of cynicism, as well as humor in creating its pollution.

Obviously, the phenomenon of "the analyst's CAT" is in full play here. In spite of what the viewer perceived and wrote, the judges all placed their own perceptive overlays on the written text and interpreted it differently.

So, in this experiment, the correct target got scores of 3, 5, 2, 5, and 2 points. That is a total of 17 out of an ideal score of 25. The viewer is said to have been 17/25, or 68 percent correct. The fact that everything the viewer perceived and wrote about the target was correct plays no part in this scoring technique.

This scoring method does not take into account that the specific viewer may not be able to write a coherent summary, or that the judges ranking the summary have cognitive skills or attention spans capable of giving an impartial evaluation. If the viewer is not trained and experienced and is the one doing the judging, the problem of "temporal attractors" will almost certainly be a large factor in the selection process, further contaminating both the scoring and the viewer's session.

This method of scoring is saturated with problems and inaccuracies, but is the one traditionally and stubbornly held by the researchers in this field, and is therefore widespread. It is designed only to prove the overall process of psychic functioning. For that purpose, it has done a very good job.

A SAMPLE REMOTE VIEWING SESSION

The following session was a demonstration for an advanced CRV class. The target was selected at random from a pool of targets. The purpose of the demo was to show the students how to progress through the stages and give them a rough idea of how to work in each stage.

When people look at this, they should not think, "This is what is always done," but "This is what can be done on a good day." They should also look at it critically. Note that the session was quicker than most—it only took eighteen minutes. I was hurrying through it so I wouldn't take up valuable student-session time. Also, it had a lot of perceptions in it that were "probable" and many of them were "very probable" and "almost certain," but since there was no hard-and-fast feedback on them, they couldn't be scored with anything except a question mark. That happens very often when the viewer describes the actual target site instead of the feedback picture. The viewer experiences feelings, etc., for which the picture can't provide feedback information.

When I did this session, I wasn't very impressed with it, but my monitor was, so I accepted his critique that it was a good session. If I had had longer than eighteen minutes, it would have contained a lot more information with much greater detail, maybe a few sketches, etc. Only forty-seven perceptions made it into the summary.

Since my handwriting turns to something akin to Swahili on pot when I'm in session, I have provided a typed transcript of my original handwritten pages.

In evaluating the session, I also noticed that the Phase 3 sketch appears to be right/left reversed. This is a common situation in remote viewing. The problem was solved in Phase 6.

I'm not ashamed of this session, but would like to have had more time to get more information and greater details.

The actual target, a biker warming himself by a fire.

    Because people send me targets that are simply clipped out of magazines or newspapers, they often do not have proper captions on them or documented sources. I do not know the source of the original photo, so I could not get permission to reprint it. This is therefore a replication of the original.

A Typed Version of the Session

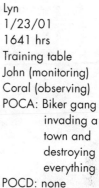

Lyn
1/23/01
1641 hrs
Training table
John (monitoring)
Coral (observing)
POCA: Biker gang
       invading a
       town and
       destroying
       everything
POCD: none
SA: biker gang

Frontloading:
The target is a location. Describe the location

012301
018011

A: across
   hard
   rough
B: Land

012301
018011

A1: across
    hard
    rough
B1: land
A2: across
    angle
    down
    hard
B2: Manmade
SC: Motorcycle

012301
018011

A1: over
    down
    across

                                                    hard
                                                    rough
                                            B1: Land
                                            A2: up
                                                    Solid
                                            B2: organic
                                            SC: Biker gang
                                            EA: surprise:
                                                    New idea.
                                            A3: rising
                                                    Curving
                                                    Faster
                                            B3: Energy
                                            A4: up
                                                    Down
                                                    Across
                                                    Hard
                                            B4: Manmade

(Monitor: "Describe the land")
P2: (Land)
    Dark
    Red
    Side lit
    Dark
    Powdery
    Flat
    Open
    Outdoors
    Dark
    Semi-dark
    Locally lit
                                                    SC: Lantern

    Dirty
    Loose
                                                    SC: hat

    Black
    Clothy

                                            NOTE: I think I've jumped
                                                    Target from "land" to
                                                    some other part. Feels
                                                    like I'm describing
                                                    the organic.

Jeansy

SC: jeans
SC: Does that mean
it's "common"?

(Monitor: "Describe the organic")
P2: (organic)
Common
    Ordinary
    Young
    In dark
    Resting
    "time-outting"
    black

NOTE: I think I've jumped
target to the manmade.

(Monitor: "Describe the manmade")
P2: (Manmade)

AI: flat land in
    Front of me.
    I feel envy
Confusion break:
    Why envy?

P3: Sketch:

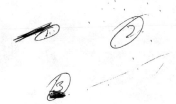

(1) Manmade
    Black
    Thin
    Balanced
    Mechanical
    Metallic

P7: "Hog"

    Balanced
    Leaning

Stopped
Resting
Not working
In dark
Dark
(2) open
dark
(3) organic
young
male

NOTE: Not "male" as in gender
But "male" as in ambience:
"Macho."

Down
Kneeling
Squatting

AI: sore legs
Sore butt

P4:
P2:   D: AI: SI: T: C: SC: CS:
                                        (Describe the organic)

tall
male
human
alone
tired
resting
thirsty
cool/warm
red

NOTE: jumped target

P5:
"biker gang"
prior emanations?

"hog"
black
metallic
noisy
bike shape impression

P6:

SC: Must be on
targett: I can't
even spell "see"
right or "target"
either.

(Note: The numbers in parentheses indicate the place on the map where the perceptions were found.)

P2:   D: AI: SI: T: C: SC: CS:
(1)   (Me. This is where I am at the site)
(2)
dark
cool
cold
dark

Feeling of danger from behind me

Like the
feeling
you get
from
being in
the dark.

(3)
sage smell
(4)
sandy feel
(5)
sage smell

(6) Organic
("describe the organic")

black
male
caucasian
short haired
clothed

(7) created
        dependent

NOTE: as though the person has
created something here and is
now dependent on it.
(8) Energy
    ("describe the energy")

hot
red

fire

Caveman
Campers
Yellowstone
Natl. Park

.   Monitor called Session end: 1704 hrs

SUMMARY:
The target has land, manmade, energy, and organic elements.
The target is outdoors.

The land is flat, dark (but locally lit), open, powdery, and has a sage smell to it
and a sandy feel.

The manmade is black, thin, metallic, mechanical and balanced. Right now, it is
stopped, leaning, at rest, and located in the dark.

The energy is red and hot. It is some kind of fire. It is located in one central
place and is providing some light to the darkness. The further away from it, the
darker it gets. When I stood facing it, I felt a feeling of danger from behind, like
that feeling I always get of what might be in the darkness when out camping.

The organic is a young, "macho" type male Caucasian who is squatting or kneeling down. He is tall, alone, and tired, with sore legs and a sore butt. He has short hair and may be wearing jeans. He is thirsty. He feels warm, but has that cool-on-the-skin feeling of the outdoors in the darkness.

I got the impression that he had built or created something on which he is now dependent (I think it is the fire).

REMOTE VIEWING DATA WORKSHEET

Problems>Solutions>Innovations
37 Camino Ranchitos
Alamogordo, NM 88310
(505) 437-8285 e-mail: rviewer@netmdc.com

Viewer ID: ___LYN___
Target #: ___011___
Location: ___TRNG TBL___

Date: _1_/_23_/_01_
Start: ___1641___
End: ___1704___

Actual site is: _BIKER CAMPING OUT_____

Category	PERCEPTIONS Y	N	?	Category	PERCEPTIONS Y	N	?
Alignment		—	—	Objects	lll	—	l
Ambience	llll	—	—	Patterns		—	—
Biologicals		—	—	Positions	lll	—	—
Colors	ll	—	—	Purposes	l	—	—
Composition	llll	—	—	Relationships	l	—	—
Conceptuals		—	—	Shapes	ll	—	—
Density		—	—	Sizes	l	—	l
Directions		—	—	Smells		—	l
Emotions		—	Ⲏtt	Sounds		—	—
Luminance	Ⲏtt	—	—	Structure		—	—
Meanings		—	—	Taste		—	—
Measures		—	—	Temps	l	—	ll
Motions	ll	—	—	Textures	ll	—	—
Numbers	l	—	—	Weight		—	—
				Other	Ⲏtt	—	—

Scoring	Perceptions
1. Enter the total number of perceptions (Y + N + ?)	_47_
2. What is the total number of unknowns? (?)	_10_
3. Subtract Line 2 from Line 1. This is the total scorable.	_37_
4. What is the total number correct? (Y)	_37_
5. Divide Line 4 by Line 3 (Y/total scorable)	_1_
6. Multiply Line 5 by 100. This is your overall score.	_100%_

Viewer's Summary / Notes   SKETCH IN P2 WAS R/L REVERSED.
LOTS OF "PROBABLES," HAD TO COUNT THEM AS ?.

APPENDIX 7

OTHER REMOTE VIEWING METHODS

If you can't be with the one you love,
Love the one you're with.

—Stephen Stills
"Love the One You're With"

The work required of the U.S. military's viewers varied widely over a range of target types. Each type had its own difficulties and problems, and Controlled Remote Viewing was not always sufficient to provide the answer we needed.

Numbers, for example, are probably CRV's biggest drawback. It is virtually useless when trying to find, say, house numbers, street numbers, exact dates, and other numerical data. There are other forms of remote viewing, but the most commonly used within the military unit were Associative Remote Viewing (ARV) and Extended Remote Viewing (ERV).

ASSOCIATIVE REMOTE VIEWING (ARV)

Associative Remote Viewing is a simple application of remote viewing. Its main purpose is to view those tasks that have a limited set of outcomes, all of which are known. For example, it is the best method for determining, through remote viewing, the answers to questions such as:

Which number will appear on the first ball of the Pick-3 lottery?
Will the value of stock X rise, fall, or remain the same in tomorrow's market?
Which of five possible options should our company choose in order to make the most profit down the road?

Probably the best way to explain how ARV works is to show it in action. Let us use the Pick-3 lottery drawing which takes place in most states every evening at about 7:30 P.M. We will try to predict the number of the first ball chosen. We will need at least two people to work this example. Let us say that you are the monitor and Generic John will be the viewer.

We now create a set of activities and consider the entire set as one, single event. The set of activities we call "the event" will be as follows:

The Event

1. The ball will be chosen at 7:30 P.M.
2. The number on the ball will be made to relate to something easy to view, like a basic sensory impression—let us say, taste. We will make a list of all the possible numbers (0–9) and relate a taste to each one.
3. At 8 P.M. we will have Generic John taste whatever relates to the number that was on the ball.

Item number 2 says that we will create a list of tastes that we can associate with each possible outcome. An example list might look like:

If the ball shows a 0, we will have him taste vanilla.
If the ball shows a 1, we will have him taste vinegar.
If the ball shows a 2, we will have him taste mint.
If the ball shows a 3, we will have him taste coffee.
If the ball shows a 4, we will have him taste a lemon.

If the ball shows a 5, we will have him taste some Tabasco sauce.
If the ball shows a 6, we will have him taste some cooked oatmeal.
If the ball shows a 7, we will have him taste some salt.
If the ball shows an 8, we will have him taste some chocolate milk.
If the ball shows a 9, we will have him taste some wine.

So, if the first ball has a 4 on it, we will get John to his assigned place at 8 P.M. and have him stick a piece of lemon into his mouth. That will happen no matter what else comes up. If all-out war between the planets begins before that, we will still have John sitting there at 8 P.M. doing his assigned task and tasting whatever is associated with the number drawn at 7:30. *Whether he predicted correctly or not, we will still have him taste the flavor that is associated with the number on the ball actually drawn.* We have set up a totally nonnegotiable event in time.

I cannot stress enough that, in order for ARV to work, you *must* make this future event happen. So, if we were to draw a timeline of this event, starting, say, at noon, the timeline would look like this:

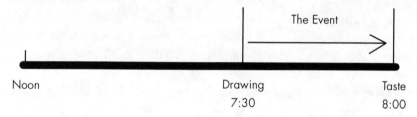

Now, we no longer have to view the number on the ball. Numbers, remember, are very hard to view correctly. But tastes and other sensory impressions are very easy to view. All we have to do now is to associate the result of the event with, say, a taste. Then, instead of asking Generic John to view a number, we will simply ask him to view the taste he will get at 8 P.M. The timeline now looks like this:

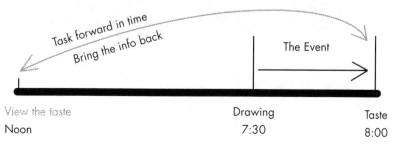

Once we know what John will taste, we know what the number on the first ball will have been. If we repeat the process for all three balls, we can go out and buy a winning ticket. The timeline now looks like this:

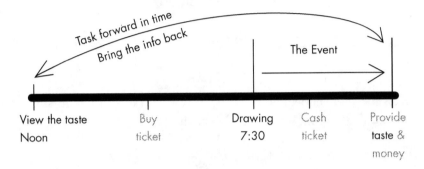

In other words, we have created a future event composed of certain actions, which we can predict (that a ball will be chosen), and a single result which we cannot (what the ball's number will be). We have also created, as an integral part of this future event, a resultant action, which is both unpredictable (because the number on the ball will determine the taste) and predictable (we *will* have John taste it). We have made the result something that is easy to view (the taste) and let that stand for the thing that is hard to view (the number). That, in its most simple form, is Associative Remote Viewing.

I have watched as the public has received the idea of ARV, and have seen that, almost without exception, the first thing they want to do is to "complexify" it. The more complex it is, the more scientific it seems to them. For example, instead of simple sensory impressions, most people decide to use, say, ten different very complex remote viewing target sites and have the viewer describe the one he will receive as feedback at 8 P.M.

Another favorite complexification is to have a viewer perform maybe a hundred sessions, and see which target or sensory impression he comes up with the most times, and then bet on that one. This is actually an attempt to bypass the training period and allow the computer to weed out any error sessions the inexperienced viewer might have. In reality, it trains the viewer to distrust his subconscious and the viewing process, and the viewer's training basically halts without further progress or growth.

Almost without exception, these complex methods take years longer to bring to proficiency and rarely work as well.

There are other ways of doing ARV sessions, and it is always the simpler ones that work the best. One of the researchers at Stanford Research Institute would have a neighbor place an object on the living room coffee table at a certain time every morning. The researcher and his wife would then go into separate rooms without seeing the object and begin to view it. When they finished, they would both score their sessions against the real target. If his wife was more accurate that day, they would buy stock. If he was more accurate, they would sell, and if their scores were within so many points of each other, they would do nothing. Working in this way, they made a sizable amount of money— simply by letting his or her session's result associate to the stock market's activity for that day.

Basically, no matter how you do it, simply associating an easy-to-view target with a hard-to-view target qualifies as a form of ARV.

BINARY REMOTE VIEWING (BRV)

All types of remote viewing have difficulty making specific choices, particularly when the choices are limited to a small number of options. The most difficult of all is when there are only two choices, such as yes and no. Binary Remote Viewing (BRV) takes care of that problem, but it is almost solely dependent on such aids as ideograms, which require much practice and considerable expertise. Many people, seeing the heavy requirements for BRV, turn to ARV and simply limit their choices.

There are some special techniques one must learn for keeping the conscious mind out of the process when using BRV. BRV is always worked with three choices: "yes," "no," and "I cannot decide right now." Again, an example best demonstrates the method.

Take a deck of cards and remove all the jokers, advertising, and anything else that is not a number or face card. For this example, we will not try to determine the suit (which would require ARV), but simply the color of the suit, thereby limiting our choices to two. Hearts and diamonds are red, spades and clubs are black.

Using the ideogram exercise, spend about a month developing and thoroughly mastering an ideogram for red and another for black.

Now, shuffle the deck of cards and turn them face down. Right before you turn a card over, make an ideogram. The ideogram will either be your ideogram for red, black, or some other ideogram that is for neither. In this case, the other ideogram (they usually pop up at random) simply stands for "I can't decide right now." If your ideogram was correctly red or black, put the card into a "Got it right" stack. If your ideogram was red or black and was incorrect, put the card into a "Missed it" stack. If the ideogram indicated that your mind did not want to decide right now, simply move the card to the bottom of the stack and continue. It will come up again, later.

Once you have called all the cards, count the ones in the "Got it right" stack. Simply by blind chance, you should have had twenty-six cards in each stack. If the number of cards in the "Got it right" stack is greater than twenty-six, then you performed above chance. If the number of cards in your "Missed it" stack is greater than twenty-six, then your work was below chance. Record your actual score (not just whether you were above or below) and keep it in a safe place.

Over the period of the next few months, perform this task again and again, about a hundred more times. Keep your score each time. Once you have done a hundred sessions, look at the overall trends in the scores to see whether you are improving, getting worse, or simply maintaining your level of proficiency. If you are like most people, your score will begin around chance, then grow to a respectable amount above chance, and then level off at your first "proficiency plateau." From here on, it is simply plateau learning. That is, you will try and try and try to raise your score and it will not happen until one day, it jumps another five or ten points to reach another plateau. You continue working through plateau after plateau until one day you are working at a proficiency level which you find satisfactory.

So, the three choices in BRV are: Option 1, Option 2, and "pass," or "I can't decide right now—ask again later." Obviously, the first two options can be such things as live or die, up or down, right or left, sell or don't sell, buy or don't buy, move to a new home or don't, and so forth, for the many potential applications of this difficult but very useful form of remote viewing.

By the way, I was in Las Vegas once and stood watching two roulette wheels, predicting whether the ball would land in a red or black slot. I called it correctly thirty-three times in a row, and once, even felt some frustration and said to myself, "Hell! I don't care. It'll land on green." Sure enough, that ball landed on one of the two green slots on the roulette wheel. I did not know before that there were green slots on a roulette wheel.

Another potential use of this skill in the gambling arena is for the game baccarat. Most people in the U.S. do not know anything about this game, but it is the one game in the casino with which the gambler has the best chance of not losing, on a normal basis. With BRV added, it can be profitable. Once you learn to perform BRV, learn to play baccarat. You'll be glad you did.

EXTENDED REMOTE VIEWING (ERV)

Another kind of highly structured remote viewing is called Extended Remote Viewing (ERV). ERV is normally thought of as CRV's sexier sister. When performing CRV, you sit in a chair, fill out papers, draw sketches, answer questions, and keep to a rigid structure. With ERV, you lie back on a bed, close your eyes, and more or less do "free flow" visualization. ERV is highly experiential, often highly sensual, gives a feeling of flying through the air to reach the target, and in general, has all of those things that everyone imagines when they think of "doing something psychic."

If you read David Morehouse's book, *Psychic Warrior: Inside the CIA's Stargate Program,* you will recognize his descriptions of his sessions as ERV sessions, not CRV. Dave was very good at both, but preferred ERV to CRV because of its experiential nature.

The problem is that, for all general purposes, ERV does not exist anymore. ERV is really a kind of highly advanced form of guided visualization, but in fact, is so far advanced over it that the two are drastically different. Guided visualization is really not a remote viewing method because it is neither standardized nor scientific. It is not structured, scientifically tested or accepted, or proven in any way, even after centuries of use by many psychics.

Guided visualization involves giving the psychic a task, after which the psychic, usually with eyes closed, goes into a trance or to sleep, and begins visualizing the answer to the tasking. Guided visualization is so heavily prone to contamination by the psychic's predetermined conclusions that a clean result is extremely rare. Add to that the psychic's social, personal, and political mindset, and almost every perception that does make it through the maze of biases gets lost or rejected because it does not fit the "castle" the psychic almost invariably builds.

Much better is a second form of guided visualization that uses a monitor to ask the tasked questions once the psychic gets into his/her altered or relaxed state. This method achieves greater accuracy, and sometimes succeeds, though its results are still heavily polluted. Yet talented natural psychics can quite often come up with amazingly good information, even if heavily biased. The average person, though, usually comes up with meaningless and useless results using even this enhanced method.

In ERV, the monitor is required to have a thorough and complete knowledge of the ERV process, as well as a full, working education in the states of consciousness through which a viewer will be taken during the session. Most people believe that there is simply a hypnogogic state between the awake state and the sleep state. In fact, there are many separate levels of hypnogogia, and each is useful for viewing different kinds of information. Although viewer training helps, the viewer does not need to be well trained in order to make the ERV process work. But in ERV, the monitor absolutely must be a trained and experienced ERV monitor. Without that, you have guided visualization.

As the ERV session begins, the monitor must watch the viewer's state of consciousness. At the exact and appropriate stage of hypnogogia for cueing, the monitor gives the first cue. The monitor, then, almost like a trained hypnotist, talks the viewer up or down to the specific level of hypnogogia that is best for answering that question. The monitor must have complete and total control—and hold the viewer in the hypnogogic state for long periods of time, hours if need be—to allow the viewer to receive tasking questions and procure the target information that will answer those questions.

During that time, the monitor must ask questions of the viewer in such a way as to push the questions through to the viewer's subconscious mind, hopefully without the viewer's conscious mind even being aware that a question has been asked. As the ERV monitor receives answers back from the viewer, he must be able to discern whether or not the answer came from the viewer's conscious or subconscious mind, and evaluate it accordingly. Since different types of questions and information flow at different levels of the hypnogogic state, the monitor must also be fully educated to the various levels of the hypnogogic state, and what kinds of information can be retrieved from them. He must be able to quickly evaluate which level the next question requires and move the viewer to that level without the viewer either waking up or going to sleep, or even being consciously aware that a change in level has been made. All of this takes considerable training and experience, and cannot in any way be accomplished by an untrained and inexperienced amateur.

Many people are presently selling courses in "ERV" to the public and raking in some very good money in the process. There are also hundreds of people who will tell you that they work targets using ERV. When you ask them who their monitor is, they will either say that they work alone, or will say that it is a neighbor, friend, or fellow ERVer. When you ask for the monitor's specific ERV qualifications, you find that they have none. These people do not know, and usually do not care that they are performing guided visualization, not ERV. They are either uneducated about the actual definitions, or have been instructed incorrectly by someone who either did not know the differences himself, or did know and misrepresented his product to get their money. More than likely, they have been trained to ask themselves a question before lying down to sleep. They then try to hang onto the hypnogogic state for a minute or two when they pass through it into sleep. Sometimes they can, but never for very long. The viewer will feel that he was in that state for a long period of time, but in reality, an unmonitored person can remain there for only a few seconds or so, at the most. Since any activity in this state can lead to dreaming, the viewer will mix dreams with perceptions, and the result is usually less than intelligence-gathering quality, to say the least.

All of this is not to imply that guided visualization is useless for information gathering. In fact, several very notable psychics have used this method to gain extremely valuable information of very high quality and dependability. The two most notable that come to mind first are Edgar Cayce (who always used a monitor) and Joe McMoneagle (who does not). The only problem is that, in order to be really good at it, you have to be a natural psychic on the level of Cayce or McMoneagle. Good luck.

OTHER TYPES OF REMOTE VIEWING

There are, of course, other valid formalized types of remote viewing, but most have highly specialized uses, and are not heard of by the public.

Other forms of RV that the public does hear about, though, are quite a different matter. Some trainers talk about such things as TRV (Technical Remote Viewing), SRV (Scientific Remote Viewing), and so on. While these may be derived from formalized methods, they are not, in and of themselves, formalized at the time of this writing. There are a few things missing which they have to complete first before becoming formalized. Those things are:

1. Forming and keeping a database of results. The results must be on real-world operations that have exacting feedback. Without that, accurate judging and scoring are impossible, no matter how the originators try to rationalize them.
2. A written and formal manual telling what methods, practices, and protocols do and do not make up the RV methodology. Because of the need for such a manual, in order to train students, most of the not-yet-accepted methods have managed to perform this step. This manual should also include sections on the theory behind the practices.
3. Impartial oversight and analysis of results. This includes the willingness to consider and heed suggestions for change and improvement.
4. A successful track record, which takes into account all the bad sessions as well as the good ones. It also includes the performance track records of the methodology in terms of its various applications. All methods have their strengths and weaknesses, just as individual viewers do.

BIBLIOGRAPHY

REMOTE VIEWING

Buchanan, Lyn, and Joseph McMoneagle. "Remote Viewing: The Viewpoints of Two Professional Remote Viewers" (video tape). Charlotte, N.C.: Vision Alliance Network, 1999.

McMoneagle, Joseph. *Mind Trek: Exploring Consciousness, Time, and Space through Remote Viewing.* Charlottesville, Va.: Hampton Roads, 1997.

———. *Remote Viewing Secrets: A Handbook.* Charlottesville, Va.: Hampton Roads, 2000.

Morehouse, David. *Psychic Warrior.* New York: St. Martin's Press, 1996.

———. Psychic Warrior (audio tape series). Los Angeles: Dove Audio.

Smith, Angela Thompson. *Remote Perceptions.* Charlottesville, Va.; Hampton Roads, 1998.

Swann, Ingo. *Your Nostradamus Factor: Accessing Your Innate Ability to See into the Future.* New York: Fireside, 1993.

MILITARY AND GOVERNMENTAL USES OF PSI ABILITIES

Dong, Paul, and Thomas Raffill. *China's Super Psychics.* New York: Marlowe & Co., 1997.

Ebon, Martin. *Psychic Warfare: Threat or Illusion?* New York: McGraw-Hill, 1983.

Gris, Henry, and William Dick. *The New Soviet Psychic Discoveries.* New Jersey; Prentice Hall, 1978.

Gruber, Elmar. *Psychic Wars—Parapsychology in Espionage—and Beyond.* London: Blandford, 1999.

————. *Die PSI-Protokolle.* Munich: Herbig Verlagbuchhandlung, 1997.

Lyons, Arthur, and Marcello Truzzi. *The Blue Sense: Psychic Detectives and Crime.* New York: Mysterious Press, 1991.

Ostrander, Sheila, and Lynn Schroeder. *Psychic Discoveries.* New York: Marlowe & Co., 1970, 1997.

Schmicker, Michael. *Best Evidence.* Shanghai: Writers Club Press, 2000.

SENSES AND PERCEPTION

Byles, Monica. *Experiment with Senses.* Minneapolis, Minn.: Lerner Publication Co., 1993.

Classen, Constance. *The Color of Angels: Cosmology, Gender, and the Aesthetic Imagination.* New York: Routledge, 1998.

Cytowic, Richard E. *The Man Who Tasted Shapes.* Cambridge, Mass.: MIT Press, 2000.

————. *Synesthesia: A Union of the Senses.* (Springer Series in Neuropsychology.) Cambridge, Mass.: MIT Press, 2002.

Daniells, Trenna. "Exploring and Developing Your Natural Senses" (audio cassette). Trenna Productions, Ltd., 1986.

Dann, Kevin T. *Bright Colors Falsely Seen: Synaesthesia and the Search for Transcendental Knowledge.* New Haven, Conn.: Yale University Press, 1998.

Friedman, Morton (editor). *Cognitive Ecology: Handbook of Perception and Cognition* (2nd ed.). Academic Press, 1996.

Harrison, John. *Synaesthia: The Strangest Thing.* Oxford, U.K.: Oxford University Press, 2001.

Harrison, John E. (editor). *Synaesthesia: Classic and Contemporary Readings.* Blackwell Publishers, ISBN: 0631197648 1996.

Luria, A. R. *The Mind of a Mnemonist: A Little Book about a Vast Memory.* Trans. Lynn Solotaroff. Reprint 4th ed. Cambridge, Mass.: Harvard University Press, 1988.

Werner, Lynne A., and Edwin W. Rubel (editors). *Developmental Psychoacoustics.* (APA Science Volumes.) Washington, D.C.: American Psychological Association, 1992.

Wilmes, Liz, et al. *2's Experience: Sensory Play.* (2's Experience Series.) Building Blocks, 1997.

Woodhouse, Mark. *Paradigm Wars: World Views for a New Age.* Berkeley: Frog Ltd., 1996.

TIME

Davies, Paul. *About Time: Einstein's Unfinished Revolution.* New York: Simon & Schuster, 1995.

McMoneagle, Joseph. *The Ultimate Time Machine: A Remote Viewer's Perception of Time, and Predictions for the New Millennium.* Charlottesville, Va.: Hampton Roads, 1998.

SCIENTIFIC STUDIES OF PSI

Abell, George, and Barry Singer. *Science and the Paranormal.* New York: Charles Scribner's Sons, 1981.

Nash, Carroll. *Science of PSI, ESP, and PK.* Springfield, Ill: Charles C. Thomas, 1978.

Targ, Russell, and Keith Harary. *The Mind Race: Understanding and Using Psychic Abilities.* New York: Ballantine Books, 1984.

RELIGION AND PSI

Pike, Bishop James A. *The Other Side: An Account of My Experiences with Psychic Phenomena.* Garden City, N.Y.: Doubleday & Co., 1968.